North Rd, Poole — Tel: 01202 205803

Learning Resources Centre

CONSTITUTION HILL
LRC
Tel: Parkstone

This item must be returned to the LRC by the last date stamped, or fines will be charged. If not in demand it may be renewed by telephone or personal call. Maximum loan 6 weeks. For telephone renewals, please be ready to quote your borrower number.

*For Sasha, Siofra, Grainne
and Cara, with all my love.*

The Full Room
An A-Z of Contemporary Playwriting

DOMINIC DROMGOOLE

Methuen

Published by Methuen 2002

10 9 8 7 6 5 4 3 2 1

First published in Great Britain in 2000 by
Methuen Publishing Limited,
215 Vauxhall Bridge Road,
London SW1V 1EJ

Methuen Publishing Limited Reg. No. 3543167

A CIP catalogue record is available from the British Library

ISBN 0 413 771342

Typeset by Deltatype Limited, Birkenhead, Merseyside
Printed and bound in Great Britain by
Cox and Wyman Ltd, Reading, Berkshire

Contents

Introduction   vii

Sam Adamson   1   Kate Dean   66
John Arden   3   April De Angelis   68
David Ashton   5   David Edgar   71
Alan Ayckbourn   8   Helen Edmunson   77
Biyi Bandele   11   David Eldridge   79
Howard Barker   13   Ben Elton   81
Sebastian Barry   16   Kevin Elyot   83
Alan Bennett   20   Peter Flannery   85
Simon Bent   22   Brad Fraser   87
Steven Berkoff   25   Michael Frayn   88
Simon Block   28   Brian Friel   91
Edward Bond   30   Christopher Fry   92
Howard Brenton   34   Athol Fugard   94
Lesley Bruce   39   William Ganimara   96
Jez Butterworth   41   Lucy Gannon   97
Richard Cameron   44   Pam Gems   99
Marina Carr   48   Peter Gill   101
Jim Cartwright   49   John Godber   104
Caryl Churchill   52   Murray Gold   106
Jane Coles   55   Simon Gray   110
Ray Cooney   57   Trevor Griffiths   113
Lucinda Coxon   58   Nick Grosso   117
Martin Crimp   61   John Guare   119
Mike Cullen   64   Lee Hall   121

Christopher Hampton	123	Tamsin Oglesby	218
Chris Hannan	125	John Osborne	219
David Hare	128	Joe Penhall	221
Tony Harrison	134	Winsome Pinnock	223
David Harrower	136	Harold Pinter	225
Jonathan Harvey	140	Stephen Poliakoff	229
Robert Holman	145	David Rabe	231
Declan Hughes	148	Mark Ravenhill	235
Catherine Johnson	151	Yasmina Reza	239
Judith Johnson	154	Philip Ridley	240
Terry Johnson	155	Billy Roche	242
Charlotte Jones	159	Peter Shaffer	246
Sarah Kane	161	Sam Shepard	248
Charlotte Keatley	166	Jack Shepherd	251
Barrie Keefe	168	Shelagh Stephenson	252
Franz Xavier Kroetz	170	James Stock	254
Tony Kushner	173	Tom Stoppard	257
Tracy Letts	175	David Storey	262
Doug Lucie	178	Judith Thompson	269
Roy MacGregor	180	Naomi Wallace	270
Frank MacGuinness	184	Nick Ward	273
Conor McPherson	186	Keith Waterhouse	276
David Mamet	190	Irvine Welsh	277
Patrick Marber	193	Arnold Wesker	281
Martin McDonagh	197	Peter Whelan	284
Arthur Miller	201	August Wilson	286
Adrian Mitchell	204	Snoo Wilson	288
Gary Mitchell	206	Charles Wood	291
John Mortimer	208	Nick Wright	295
Gregory Motton	209	Richard Zajdlic	298
Jimmy Murphy	211		
Tom Murphy	212	Afterword	
Phyllis Nagy	214	to the 2002 edition	300
Anthony Neilson	215		

INTRODUCTION

In Celebration

Never before in the history of humans wandering, waving, shouting and scrawling their way across the face of the earth, have so many of them been engaged in the peculiar business of writing plays. This book's main purpose is to celebrate that fact. Like it or lump it, we are living in the middle of a carnival, a free revel, a fete, a flower show, a harvest home, a steam fair, a rock festival, a grand glorious tender wild burst of new plays.

It's a time of bloom. It's not the first. Fourth-century Athens threw up an extraordinary rate of playwrights per capita (and an even more extraordinary density of genius). In Elizabethan/Jacobean London, the world's twin pathologies, blood and science, found their voice in a touched brotherhood. Boundlessly vigorous stories gulped in air in Renaissance Spain. Classical form found a new streamlined solidity in seventeenth-century Paris. In Restoration London, fatuity and fun returned to the culture courtesy of a gaggle of playwrights. There have been times, and times. Yet at no point before have so many men, women and children been engaged, and practised, in the art of writing plays.

Nor, crucially, from such a broad range. The luxuries of education and leisure have historically proved the preserve of the few. The aspirant lower middle class has thrown up its fair share of genius, including heaven's captain, Shakespeare, and his able lieutenant, Chekhov. But we live in an age of greater enfranchisement than any previous. It's not universal, it's not perfect, but it's considerably more inclusive than anything that's gone before. Many of today's boldest and brightest talents would not even have developed an appetite for drama in previous ages, let alone the confidence to create. This breadth of authorship has led inevitably and happily to an enormous broadening of content. Ideas, rhythms, worlds and concerns have reached the stage that would not have been mentioned in the drawing room just fifty years ago. Or even the toilet. Democracy flowers into represented life faster on the stage than in any other medium.

Our culture is so determined by denigration and complaint that we spend too little time celebrating anything, let alone that simple fact. By dint of sheer number, this is a unique age. Small people can climb on a box and act tall by sneering about quality. There's no shortage of thin pedantic voices airily sneering, 'Well, there may be many, but where are the few? Where are the great plays?' The pretension to an understanding of true greatness is the first resort of the bereft, whether it's in the pub or at the awards ceremony. The truth is none of them know. None of us know. History will choose and select, driven by the passion of audiences to see work and actors to act it. What will rise and what will fall is way beyond our knowledge. What is beyond denial is that there is no more fertile soil for greatness than an enthusiasm for the task, and there has been no more enthusiastic time than the one just past.

I set out, with a missionary gleam, to present an authoritative overview of contemporary playwriting. I haven't got close. The more writers I covered, the more I realised were beyond me. The casual conversations that follow certainly walk the waterfront but they don't cover it. I have been counselled not to include a list of those who are omitted, so as not to offend those who are omitted from the list of those who are omitted. But suffice it to say there are a hundred other writers I feel passionate enthusiasm for who I have been unable to include. Such is the breadth and range of what's on offer.

It's also a happy platitude to admit that this book will be out of date by the time it's published. New voices, new perspectives, new attacks, pop up with an alarming, an unnerving frequency. Each month produces a talent from nowhere. Each new talent is nervily dubbed 'promising', since no one can deal with the unpalatable truth that these new plays are often just as good and sometimes better than what's come before. We like the fiction that artists progress from apprentice to master. It's less than true. If they're good, they're good from start to finish. Do we think of *Romeo and Juliet* as promising?

Do we live in a Golden Age? It's a foolish question. Over tea with Stephen Daldry, before he took over the Royal Court, we discussed what was out there. 'We're living in a Golden Age,' I said. 'Are we?' he asked sceptically. 'Fuck knows,' I replied, 'but if we start saying it often enough, people should join in.' We did, Stephen with his genius for PR most persuasively, and they did. Is it a Golden Age? Well, of course.

This is Not a Book of Criticism

This is not a book of criticism. This is not a book of criticism. I am not right. Nothing I say is right. There is no right. I don't know how often I can say this. My greatest nightmare is that I give the impression I'm sitting in judgement. I'm sure I will, since I'm saturated in the language and attitudes of judgement. But it's as far from the intentions of this book as an in depth discussion of trade relations with the Sudan. I do not want to judge, nor am I qualified to. You are as likely to be right about a play as you are to be right about a human being. You can have impressions, thoughts, insights, ideas, opinions, attitudes, whatever – you should have – but you should never judge, nor ever think you're right.

Criticism is a farce. For some unknown reason we've all given our consent to the act of maintaining its credibility. It's a nonsense based on what someone had for lunch, when they last shagged, where they went to school, when they were last bereaved, the school play they failed in, their athlete's foot. The idea that there is some independent zone of pure judgement where a critic can float above all these contingencies is in a realm of madness beyond the pathological.

The book is a revelation of my present prejudices, and as such will hopefully provoke thought, and ignite a few fires of enthusiasm. The prejudices are those of a white, Oxbridge, bohemian/Victorian, middle-class, socialist, Anglo-Irish child of the Cold War. I try to defeat those prejudices constantly, to extend my palate and develop new appetites. But I doubt I'll ever be able to disguise the point of origin. Yet these are not the prejudices of my youth, and I very much hope they won't prove the prejudices of my age. One of the joys of theatre is being wrong and rediscovering one's own stupidity. Theatre's trump card is its occasional reminder of the world's infinite capacity to surprise.

I would never criticize a play, since I've some idea of how difficult they are to create. I wrote a play once. It was a clumsy blend of the awful, and the not quite awful. It was what we used to call at the Bush a 'therapy' play – a writer expelling anguish away from life into a dramatic vessel. That is fairly precisely what I had done. Having been in a fairly dark place, the creation of the play was a path to some sort of light. The result was articulate, spasmodically wise and dramatically completely inert. What it lacked was gift, the gift that's at the heart of all true playwriting, the ability to write dialogue and imagine separate worlds. Lacking that gift myself, I have nothing but undying love, respect and envy for those that have it.

This is not a book of criticism (the man doth protest too much, perhaps): I'm just trying to keep the conversation lively.

The Cathedral of Fire

This was almost the title of this book. Phew. I tried it out with trembling enthusiasm on a host of friends, colleagues and publishers. Eventually the sheer weight of embarrassed silences, grimaces and stifled sniggers convinced even a mule like me that it might not be a winner.

Two important tranches of this book were written in Kraków – a town uniquely adapted for thought and alcohol. The market square is an elegant, open repository of the ambitions, aesthetics, tragedies and triumphs of many centuries. In its corner, one endless steeple towering over it, is St Mary's Church. I spent a fair amount of time here, contemplating the panelled altar, the naves, the icons, the roofs, the chapels, the Christs, the neo-pagan gargoyles, the stations, the paintings, the Black Madonnas. It's an enormous edifice, bursting with bits and pieces of beauty. It took 140 years to complete, well beyond the dreams of its first architects. It's a great holy mess. I could happily wish away a week of my life sitting there. I could happily return to it every Sunday for a lifetime. It would surprise and sustain.

Its principal surprise is its internal chaos. Though the whole is symphonically orchestrated with a telling grace, each corner, each nook, each cranny is a riot of individualism. The hand that carved this bit of stone bears no relation to the hand that painted that icon or shaped this bit of wood or decorated that wall. Each creator would have lived in different places at different times, with completely different takes on religion and life. In its own way the church is as gaudy a market place as the cloth halls in the centre of the square. It may trade in the spirit and the heart, but it is as diverse and as self-advertising as any souk. We tend to associate churches with a monolithic sameness, a crushing uniformity. This one magnificently contradicts that.

This gathering of individual voices within a spiritual whole made me think of the new writing of our age in a completely different light. Rather than seeing each play as wholly separate, why not, as in the church, see a collective of disparate visions? All around you in St Mary's are stories, images, questions, terrors, comforts on display. They contradict each other, they enhance each other, they promote each other. Each delivers a huge reward in isolation. Each is worthy of its own shrine. But together, together is something else. Breathe the lot in to your mind, or as much as you can cram in, and what joys are there. Rather than seeking everything in each tiny corner, why not look to the whole and enjoy the comprehensive splendour of the all. Rather than hoping for each new play to be a cathedral in itself, why not view it as an altar, a candle, whatever.

It was then I saw how fatuous is our quest for greatness in individual playwrights. How dumb the parallels with Shakespeare and Aeschyllus. It doesn't matter what any individual is building, it is what they are all making together that is so remarkable. They are not all building in stone, they are not all pursuing a common purpose (far from it) but together they are constructing a unique record, a unique indictment and a unique celebration of the modern human spirit. Over a matter of many years, from many different ears, eyes and imaginations, from Sarah Kane to Arthur Miller, from Harold Pinter to Martin Crimp, from David Storey to Richard Cameron, from Brian Friel to Billy Roche, they have created this unique and extraordinary cathedral.

It's an edifice built from the most insubstantial material – words. And, to add a further degree of insubstantiality, words that do not even exist until they are incarnated by actors. Yet in this age of insubstantiality, of cyber messages, of voices hanging in the air waiting to be picked up on mobile phones, words are probably the most suitable form of brick.

How We Live

This is another title that bit the dust. Double phew. But it would be hard to imagine a better record of the way we live now than could be drawn from the plays of the last forty-five years. Not necessarily a documentary record. Newspapers and television can give a far better account in that mode. But if somebody wanted a sense of the surfaces and the depths, you'd look to the drama. If you wanted to know the range of feeling in Northern Europe in the mid-fifties, what better seismograph than *Waiting for Godot, Look Back in Anger, The Bald Prima Donna* and *Separate Tables*. If that was when the great effusion began, by the early nineties each year could turn up twenty or thirty plays that would give you a sense of life lived.

Not that the record is necessarily truthful. Some plays are misleading, some wrong, some downright dishonest, but the majority reflect an honourable attempt to describe the way we live. The honesty is forced on each by the nature of theatre, and the pressure of the audience. A new play has to come to life in the space between the stage and the spectator. That life depends wholly on shared experience, shared signifiers, shared understandings. The nature of the life will, of course, depend on the level at which you're dealing. A bum joke will provoke a certain response. A journalistic reference another. An act of violence yet another. A moment of tragedy yet another, and so on. But whatever the level, it has to come to life. And every writer in this book, and many more, has made that happen. It is a formidable achievement.

This immediate communal test is unique to the theatre. The novelist never has to face it. He never has to test every word in front of a hungry thousand. Novelists who are so quick to sneer at the theatre should remember that. They can be picked up, put down, packed, taken on holiday, forgotten, returned to, revisited. Easy. A playwright has to grab – not one critical intelligence but many – and hold them. Playwrights write prose to relax. Also novels are by nature particular, personalized, they lack the tribal connection that is necessary in drama. And that connection is only reinforced by touching on tribal concerns, directly or subliminally. By touching on how we live. That is how theatre is able to matter, to be important in a way that the novel can't manage.

And film, whose potential trumps all other media, is so lost between being an entertainment on the one side and an art on the other, that it has little time left to remember to reflect the world. Its energies are so consumed in proving itself profitable or beautiful, that there's little left over for the world outside.

No, for the sense of how we live now, and by extension how we have always lived and always will, collect the plays by the writers herein. It is the task that theatre is made for, and the one that these writers have achieved.

Sam Adamson

As the audience was shuffling out of the Bush theatre one
night, after a performance of Sam Adamson's *Clocks &
Whistles*, I fell in behind Michael Codron, the venerated
and venerable West End producer. He turned to his friend:
'I liked that very much,' he said. Then, after a pause, he
whispered, 'Was it any good?' 'Yes. Yes, it was . . . very
good,' his friend replied. Michael looked happy, 'Was it?
Oh good, I am glad.' I was delighted, not by the approval,
nor by the insecurity, but by the suggestion that no one
knew the rules any more.

If there is one gift without which it is impossible to write
plays, it is the gift for dialogue. You can steal plots, you can
borrow characters, you can learn themes, you can invent
worlds, but if you can't write dialogue, you're stuffed. My
own paltry attempts at writing drama have always tripped
on the dialogue hurdle and ended up face down on the
asphalt.

Sam Adamson writes the best dialogue I've ever read, or
had the pleasure to direct. It's metropolitan, quick-witted,
alive with internal tensions, graceful, lightweight and
profound. Listening to sharp musical dialogue done right in
the theatre is one of its greatest pleasures, like listening to
the sharpest jazz. Listening to clumpy, angular, pointed
writing is one of theatre's greatest tortures, like listening to
the treble recorder section of the primary school orchestra.

Adamson's chosen milieu (so far) is the metropolitan

young in all their glorious wannabe absurdity. With a delicate touch he catches their uncertain identities, their casual savagery and the quiet voice of their inner despair. His first play, *Clocks & Whistles*, was fast, funny and sexy. It was praised to the sky and became a big hit. His second play, *Grace Note*, was serene, contemplative and sad. It was comprehensively shat on and limped a bit. They were, needless to say, equally strong dramatic experiences.

The dazzling dialogue, the psychological acuity and the unsentimental wit combine to form Adamson's other great strength – he provides great turns for actors. His first play was fired up by a dazzling turn from Kate Beckinsale, his second by a class act from Geraldine MacEwan, and both benefited from the brazen chutzpah of Neil Stuke.

He's only two plays down the road, and will spread his wings over wider territory, but if he can continue to look after actors as he has done so far, they should look after him.

John Arden

What sort of world is it, where the man who wrote *Sergeant Musgrave's Dance* sits languishing in obscurity on the west coast of Ireland, his plays unperformed, while *Naked Flame*, a new comedy about firemen who can't keep their clothes on, tours England breaking all known box office records? Or where the author of *Armstrong's Last Goodnight* can hardly get a production, while the world awaits with baited breath the latest slice of glib urban chic from some Patrick Marber lookalike? The world we live in, sadly.

Admittedly John Arden hasn't helped his own cause by picketing some of his own productions. Waving placards and shouting scab at your audience is unlikely to attract the coach party audience. Nor is interrogating your potential directors about their politics going to make that tricky relationship any easier. But there should be ways round a little intransigence.

Arden wrote on an epic scale that few have attained since, but also with a consistency of poetic richness that few have approached. His plays tumble with action, and with vivid human response. There is little of the introspection and self-examination which has slowed down so much post-war theatre. It's almost as if he was writing from a pre-Freudian age. The subtext in his work is moral, political and historical choice, rather than the individual neuroses that reduce so much modern work.

Arden was and is a giant of modern playwriting. He

aimed high and he got there. He deserves a little more respect.

David Ashton

Many talents coalesce to form the trunk of the tree. They sit – heavy, strong and taut – in the middle of the culture, feeding and securing the rest. Some talents head off together to create branches large and small. Their mutual tensions keep the line jagged and twisting, as first one energy, then another comes to the fore. These are the schools of this or that, groups of writers who grow away from the trunk, but can't lose their connection to it. Some angry mavericks wrench themselves away from their previous schools, and form individual twigs of resistance.

And (to pursue an analogy a bit too far) some talents sit at the end of the twigs, cradling the buds in their leaves. They seem disconnected from the rest of the tree, as if from a different world. Small blazes of colour and texture, their brightness and insubstantiality are a rebuke to the surrounding solidity. Wrapped up in their very difference is their fragility, and the knowledge that their first life may be brief.

Many of the greatest talents around at the moment suit this role. These are the Büchners of their age; the wild ones, the fantasists, the mavericks, the dark imaginers. Most prominent among these to my mind are Philip Ridley, Snoo Wilson, James Stock and David Ashton. It's their ill fortune that the present is too prosaic to appreciate them as well as they deserve, and they will have to wait for the future.

Ashton wrote three almost perfect lyric miniatures, tied together under the title *Passing By*, which I was lucky to direct at the Old Red Lion in 1990. Utterly strange, and utterly individual, the first, *Stations*, sees an old man take refuge in a church from a posse that believes him a paedophile. The play takes him through the Stations of the Cross as he remembers the execution of a deserter in the First World War. The second, *The Eagle*, follows the ramblings of a baglady as she waits on a roof for an eagle to come and abduct her. Without shame she reviews her prolific sexual past, hymning the 'sections' of the men and women who have passed her by. The final play, *Me . . . Dancing*, a dialogue, charts the impossible romance of two down-and-outs, an old man and a young woman, through summer, autumn and winter. The woman believes that the Angel Gabriel has impregnated her, endures an entire phantom pregnancy, and eventually, after giving birth to a non-existent baby, teaches the man the virtues of the imagination.

Incomparably odd and incomparably strong, these plays received little exposure, but had a profound effect. The small numbers of cognoscenti who turned up could see the signs of something new stirring underneath these plays. Weary of political lectures, journalism and dry debate, audiences and artists were starting to hunger for something more. And Ashton was exploring new territory. He was addressing the forgotten muses – spirit and imagination.

He followed up this triptych, with three wonderful full-length plays for the Bush. When we first commissioned him, he asked what sort of play we wanted. We told him to write whatever he wanted, and to write as ambitiously as he could. So true to order, he put God in his first play, the Devil in his second, and eternity in his third. In each of the three, *A Bright Light Shining*, *The Chinese Wolf* and *Buried Treasure*, he takes a well made play situation, and fills it with outlandish incident, gothic imagination, terror and delight. He doesn't just break the rules; he makes them laugh at themselves. And all the time, the spirit, an undernourished animal in the early nineties, dances to his tune.

The plays did very well, although they fell foul of one critic's squat literalism. David would probably have liked a louder huzzah. But like the leaf, his work drew the light and fed the tree, and like the bud, it has an outside chance of being the trunk of the future.

Alan Ayckbourn

For a long time Ayckbourn was a great shibboleth for the young. All was right that was not Ayckbourn. At a job interview, if you asked any woolly hatted youth what sort of theatre they wanted to work in, you often knew what you would get. After some incomprehensible burble about Jacques Lecoq, video screens and their problems with their mother, they'd snort and say, 'Well . . . y'know . . . not Alan Ayckbourn!', as if that was the final word on the matter. It was the equivalent of being sent to some sort of theatrical Coventry.

It's one sign of our temporary maturing, and our greater inclusiveness as a culture that you meet such idiotic wank much less frequently now. Thankfully the bogus values that were always held up as virtue in opposition to Ayckbourn – plain meaning, fake suffering and self-admiring passion – are now far less prevalent than they were. So now we're able to see Ayckbourn for what he is – a genius of the suburbs.

Probably no one – bar Pinter – is now more respected by the younger generation of playwrights than Alan Ayckbourn. Partly this is because he is a dedicated and generous patron. At Scarborough he has always found time, money and resources to spend on the young and untested. And partly it's because he has found a way to play the game according to his own rules.

As Clint Eastwood operates within and without Hollywood, so Ayckbourn (our smaller, balder Man With No Name in the wilderness of the sitting room) operates within and without British Theatre. He is beholden to no one. He has, of course, flourished mightily in the subsidized sector, and in the West End. But the construction of Fortress Scarborough means that he is one of the only barons who doesn't bow his head to any king but the audience.

Principally he is respected as a radical re-inventor of form. For some unknown reason he has acquired a reputation as an arch purveyor of the well-made play. Nothing could be less true. In play after play he deconstructs the conventions of dramatic structure, then recreates them as he wishes. Occasionally this search for new forms becomes a bit boffinish and adolescent (e.g., the toss of the coin to determine the course of the evening) and content is obscured by the allure of the gimmick. You suspect while watching that he dreamt up the trick before he decided what to do with it. But where he finds the right form to match his theme, it's an exhilarating ride.

What I've always most admired about him is the astonishing deftness of his stroke as a draughtsman. With a couple of half-finished sentences, he can take you right into the heart of a rotting marriage, a dysfunctional family or a half-lived life. The stroke is as light and quick as a cartoonist's pencil, but there is always a surprising three-dimensional life beyond it. His ear for the collapsed cadence of middle-class life is unparalleled.

He also proved during his purple patch for the National during the mid-eighties that he could write a cool state of the nation play. He genuinely understood most people's bewilderment in the face of the opportunities and the necessary moral loss that came with Thatcherism. His pulse-taking was far more compelling and honest than the clumsy preaching and journalism of some contemporaries.

Finally, his output is staggering. Anyone who knows how difficult it is to write a play isn't going to sneer at a man who can write upwards of forty and counting. Never mind the details just take a look at the fucking size. All in all, what with the prolific quantity, the formal innovation, the brilliant brushwork and the strong moral centre, he has every right to a peculiar title – naturalism's Lope de Vega.

Biyi Bandele

Biyi, a piratical Nigerian, has an engaging 'I can do that' response to most twentieth-century culture. He's an enthusiastic playgoer, something rarely true of many of his contemporaries. When he likes something, he seems to return home and dash off his 'I can do that' version.

Death Catches the Hunter, a delightful, funny piece of distorted anecdotage for three voices, is alarmingly similar to Brian Friel's *Faith Healer*. When we mentioned this rather obvious fact to Biyi, there was a teeny pause, followed with huge aplomb by, 'It is, of course, a homage to Brian Friel.' His play *Two Horsemen*, which played at the Bush, is a delirious and wild hybrid of Pinter's *Dumb Waiter* and much of Beckett. It's clear he follows the good principle that if you're going to rob, you might as well rob a rich man's house. He has also adapted novels successfully, working on Chinua Achebe's *Things Fall Apart*, and providing an exuberant version of Aphra Behn's seventeenth-century novella *Oroonoko*.

If all he did were imitate he would of course have been hounded out of town long ago. But the imprimatur of his own style is so strong and so unique, he genuinely transforms the material he feeds on. He brings piquant humour, a surrealism, a strong sense of imminent violence and an extravagance in the pomposity of his characters that defies further imitation.

Soon we can only hope, he will put homages, transcriptions and adaptations behind him, and find in the world or in his imagination an entirely original story that can release and cohere his entirely original style.

Howard Barker

'The audience is sick,' said Howard Barker, and a delicious chill of disapproval lightly froze the room. He sat there, smooth and well groomed, in his dapper suit, having arrived in a cashmere coat, and said the unsayable. 'The audience is sick.' After the chill, there was a fair amount of coughing and spluttering, some choked rage, then a few muted denunciations. He refused to elaborate, or get lost in justifications. He just wanted to leave the thought hanging there. 'The audience is sick.'

The occasion was one of David Edgar's monthly conferences on this or that, and an impressive line-up of speakers were comprehensively silenced by Barker's well-timed little grenade. It's the thought that worries theatre practitioners more than any other. If we love good work, rigorous work, demanding work, provocative work, pure work, then why does it always empty the houses? And why do audiences love *Murder at the Vicarage*? If audiences are upset by moments of truth and honesty, and love charm and manipulation, what does that say about them? If they prefer last year's tricks to genuine imagination, conservative comfort to hard questions, or unambitious achievement to wild ambition, then how should we respond?

If audiences are the final arbiters, which they are, since they either attend or they don't, and without them theatre is invalid, then what should we do? Follow them, and give them what they want, which is the craven course of many, or stand against them and stand alone? Are they right or wrong, or is the artist? Who is the judge of the work? Somewhere between those two poles, between endlessly succouring the audience and endlessly satisfying the self, any artist has to find out where they stand. But for a theatre artist it is a more acute problem than for any other. That is why Barker's statement was so bold, and so bracing. He was setting out where he wanted to stand. Alone and disdainful. Many others would like to go there, but lack the courage.

No writer has a more sharpened sense of this problem than Barker. He is a great artist, and has written some of the most extraordinary works of the last thirty years; *Victory, The Castle, The Love of a Good Man* and *Scenes from an Execution*, to name but a few. He is a poet with a rich and pungent imagination. He creates situations that demand actors to let their restrictions go, and surrender themselves. He writes words, lines and images like Giacometti sculptures that actors and audiences can endlessly walk round, as different lights reveal fresh contexts and meanings. He possesses an entirely unique understanding of the world.

His later work has defied the sympathy of even the most faithful. Whereas previously his firework displays of spirit and sensuality were presented with a modesty, humble before the overall sensibility of the piece, some of that humility has now been lost. This can mean you just get a firework display, a lot of banging relentlessly in front of you, but it's still quite a show. He has also written one of the most valuable books about contemporary theatre that exists, *Arguments for the Theatre*.

His plays have continued to invigorate and refresh for several decades. But he can't find an audience. Even with a company, The Wrestling School, devoted solely to his work, presenting it with selfless dedication all over the country, he still cannot find an audience. Why? Because they are sick? Who knows?

Sebastian Barry

Sebastian is, for me, the foremost innovator writing today. And the foremost radical. He has attempted the impossible, and brought it off. In that achievement, he has rewritten the rulebook for what a play is, and what drama can be. Put quite simply, he has attempted to abolish conflict.

Conflict is and has been a staple way of understanding drama forever. It is a central plank of the blah blah blah of platitudes that school teachers, theatre critics and script editors trot out when describing how drama works. It's probably the first one they jump to. Before they move on to a similar barrage of platitudes about journeys (or transformational arcs as they are now described in film circles). But conflict always comes first. At school it's 'What is the basis of drama, Dromgoole?' 'Conflict, sir.' In the papers, you get, 'The middle sagged due to the lack of that inalienable fundament of all drama, conflict.' And in script meetings, you get, 'Can't you beef up the third act? Put a fight in or something? I mean, drama is about conflict, isn't it?'

Well no. Not necessarily. Drama is whatever the audience, the actors and the writers choose it to be. And few have explored the possibilities of what it can be further than Sebastian. His project is apparently simple and modest – a cycle of plays dealing with the long distance story of his family. He records or imagines moments from the Barry past that have left a mark, an emotional electro-magnetic stain on the world, moments that have warped his own

DNA with love or pain or joy. These incidents are the ones that chimed for him, and by recording them with sufficient investment, he makes them chime for everyone.

The ambition is substantial and complex. The surface is the tapestry of his own genetic history, but through the weave, we see a larger tapestry beyond, depicting the history of his country, Ireland. And through the mesh of that weave, we see yet another cloth beyond, on which is traced the history of us all.

His primary tool is an extraordinary gift for rich poetic prose. His language is rich with allusion, sensuality and a wild humour. A humour that walks close to madness. It has all the specific density and resonance of Toni Morrison or Cormac McCarthy. He also has an incredible gift with anecdote. He has many of the storyteller's tricks buried within him. Somehow he can make a tale a character is telling as important to you as the first story you heard from your father. There's a capacity for innocence and wonder, even given knowledge, which seems endlessly renewable. And he knows about the kindness of people – his world depends on it – and he portrays it without condescension. This is how his plays contradict the norm. There are no baddies, no neurotics, no aggro. In Sebastian's world it is not necessary.

We were aware at the Bush of *Boss Grady's Boys*, and *Prayers Of Sherkin*, his two plays for the Abbey, when we decided to commission a play from him. *Sherkin* was clearly the work of a master, the tale of the break-up of a small community on one of the Western Isles of Ireland, when their youngest daughter chooses to follow love to the mainland. It is a tragedy of good spirits. Everybody means well, everybody wants the best, everybody wants to help each other. They are simply trapped by the gates of history, and there is no escape for them. The play laps to a gentle close as the woman is gently rowed from the lights of her family to the lights of the port town Baltimore, and her new love. There is no sense of progress, just a sense of what has to be, and its effect on people.

The play we received, *White Woman Street* remains one of my all-time favourites. The pleasure taken in reading it the first time was enough to make all my work in new writing worthwhile. It's the story of an ageing gang of cowboys on their last ride through Ohio in 1916. They are heading to rob a gold train, and they have to stop off in a small town called White Woman Street, named after a famous whore who lived and died there. They ride, they shoot a boar, they cook, they sleep, they wake, they ride into town, they go to church, they visit the whorehouse, they drink and sing, they confess, they sleep, they go after the gold train.

All the time they tend to each others needs, listen to each other's stories and release each other's pain. Old men with little left but their love for each other, they know their time is past, but need to find out where they stand before they die. Its effect was extraordinary. Many didn't get it, and wondered why Sebastian hadn't beefed it up with a bit of conflict. But for many others, they simply sat there and wept. All the way through. It was magic.

Sebastian went on to have a huge hit with *The Steward Of Christendom*, and *Our Lady Of Sligo*, blessed by the benediction of perfect performances from Donal McCann in the first and Sinead Cusack in the second. He also found the ideal director in Max Stafford-Clark, whose sublime literalism is the perfect complement to Sebastian's rich poetics.

The central rip, tear or 'conflict' in Sebastian's work, the one that will invigorate the spirit and oxidize the soul, is this. That he and all his characters know what it is like to wake up in love with the world, breathtakingly in love with all its innocence and generosity and promise, and know what it is like to spend each moment of each day being steadily more and more heartbroken and disappointed and battered and abused by the tawdriness and the shallowness and the endless violence of what the world has turned into. That journey in each day and each moment from hope in love to grief in loss.

And yet. And yet they still believe in what they saw in the morning. And they still try and hold the faith the next morning. And the next. It is that courage in holding on, in awaiting the sunrise without cynicism, despite the evidence, that makes many weep.

Alan Bennett

It's a long way from Aeschylus' Agamemnon to Alan
Bennett's Susan, the vicar's wife. It's hard to trace the
lineage from a king returning from an epicly pointless war,
a concubine in tow, to be murdered by his adulterous wife,
to a genteel but sexually frustrated lady finding her joy in
the back of a grocer's shop lying on a bed of lentils. Three
thousand years ago a handful of myths and legends
wrapped up enough meaning to keep everybody happy.
Now we feel the need for three hundred thousand little
stories – snacks, nibbles and crackers under the settee – to
try to contain all the strangeness that confronts us. Then
we made patterns from the large shapes carved out by
giants, now we make some sense from the human figures in
the box in the corner.

No one writes on the small scale of the modern better
than Alan Bennett, and that is where I always think he is
happiest. The *Talking Heads* scripts, both on television and
on stage, were his apogee. His one big attempt at an opera,
The Madness of George III, is a better attempt than most
could bring off, but its non-stop, full-on bravura never
seems to be quite at ease with itself. It's as if it's running
away from itself. Similarly, *Habeas Corpus* is a rather
effortful farce, *Getting On* is a rather effortful West End
play, *Forty Years On* a bit of effortful elegiac state of the
nation play, and so on. As I say, what you get from such
effort is rather marvellous, and worth the money for

attendance, but it's not the glorious, reassuring spectacle of a writer at ease with himself.

When Bennett constructs a play it's one thing, but when he just takes a character or a situation and simply lets it be, then it's quite another. Either in the monologues, or in the wonderful dialogic confrontations – the Queen and Anthony Blunt in *A Question of Attribution*, Guy Burgess and Coral Browne in *An Englishman Abroad*, or Bennett himself and his quasi-lodger in *The Lady in the Van* – he chisels out of these small moments something perfectly formed, deeply humorous, and mysteriously instructive. Few people would have the courage to make the Queen a small character, but Bennett with his wonderfully democratic, benevolent cruelty, turns her into as suburban and small a character as any others.

In Bennett's world everyone is small. There are no great displays of courage, or spirit, or vigour, nor is there any outsize cruelty, or savagery or plans for world domination. But whereas elsewhere in this book and in art, I loudly bemoan such smallness, with Bennett it's never a problem. This must be because under the gaze of his microscope, everything looms large. Within his miniature focus, the smallest act of kindness becomes a major charity, the briefest silence can be the cruellest blow. In the dolls' house of small lives he controls so fastidiously, we see ourselves. The pattern can be large or small; its proportionate truth is what matters.

Simon Bent

Simon, true to his few drops of Welsh blood, is a master of the late-night, or early-morning, rant. One of his favourites is the malevolent effect of George Bernard Shaw on British theatre. 'All big schoolboy plots, big schoolboy messages; all that fucking blah blah blah; all journalism and debate . . . all that aaahhhrgument . . . all that big childish meaning . . . no life . . . where's the life? . . . and everybody thinks he's God al-bloody-mighty and he's bollocksed it all up for the rest of us.'

The mix of temper and immovable insistence that Simon can summon means few challenge him, and he soon moves on from late-night angry to late-night maudlin. 'I mean what about Chekhov . . . it's just not fair . . . I mean read it . . . it's just gold dust . . . gold . . . dust . . . why don't we study that at school, eh? . . . why aren't we told to write like that? . . . *people*, you know, *life*, actions, little moments . . . that's *it*, isn't it . . . I mean, that's it . . . just not fair.'

The meaning is often blurred, but the sentiment is just. Trained in the Peter Gill school at the National Theatre Studio, Simon was nurtured on a reverence for life. Without being slavishly realistic, the mystery he searches for is the mystery of life, rather than of thought. He abhors the English twentieth-century tradition of argument, politics and journalism, preferring the longer reach of Chekhov and Strindberg, Beckett and Brecht. It is funny how we have been steered away from such figures, with the innate poetry of their stage action, towards the plonkier prose of figures such as Shaw.

Success these days depends more on the commentary than the work. All is spin. And commentary is much easier if a play is resoundingly *about* something. Before a play of his opens now, David Hare will appear in two or three interviews and announce what the play is *about*. The play then appears like a solid Sunday newspaper article, filled with its own aboutness. Everyone knows what they're getting. Everyone gets it. Everyone is happy.

It is far easier to spin a play about abortion, about concentration camps, about the church, about the Labour Party, than it is a play featuring a collection of losers in a council house in Shepherds Bush (*Goldhawk Road*), or a gang of sexually frustrated teenagers in Scarborough (*Bad Company*), or the occupants of a sinister boarding house in the same place (*Sugar Sugar*). Simon has never fallen into the trap of colour supplement drama, nor would he ever want to.

But to say he is just a purveyor of realism is to underestimate his achievement. Technically he is a very skilled craftsman. He's one of the few people who can still write group dialogue. He can keep afloat a quick, light and twisting conversation between five or six people more dextrously than anyone at the moment. He is a master of the funny and mysterious non-sequitur. He has a magpie's instinct for thieving the more extraordinary and batty moments from the *Daily Mirror* and the *Sun*, which reveal the lurid surrealism of modern life. And the work is often hysterically funny.

But his main achievement is to bring the spirit of Chekhov so vividly back to life in our own age. His indirect quotation of the Russian is his least great achievement. What is extraordinary is his ability to recapture the stuck monomania of Chekhov's characters, and to uncover the yawning and terrifying chasm of nothingness which lurks underneath an unboiled egg or a milk carton that won't open. The sudden holes that appear in everyday life are his milieu. He captures the essence of Chekhov – that there is no essence, just a tremendous amount of furious, beautiful and inconsequential activity around a hollow. Meaning, point and definition are the territory of lesser dramatists; that hollow is the territory of the true ones.

Steven Berkoff

The work of Steven Berkoff always reminds me of a wonderful 1950s Stan Freberg skit on the recording of 'Day-O'. Every time the wildly enthusiastic calypso singer launches into his full-lunged cry of 'Day-O', the bongo drummer, the epitome of stoned chill, stops playing. 'Too loud man,' he tells him, 'would you mind standing a little further away.' The singer tries again. 'No, no, too loud man. Too loud.' They argue. Eventually the singer is persuaded to leave the room. He sings 'Day-O' from behind a closed door. After a few wild dashes in and out, finally the singer finds himself locked out. The bongo drummer is pleased, 'Far out man.' There is a pause, and then the sound of breaking glass. 'I came through the window,' says the singer before launching into a last triumphant yell.

It would be as impossible to silence the roaring lion that is Berkoff. For three decades he's ranted and raged and snarled. Through *Decadence* and *East* and *Greek* and *Kvetch* and *Metamorphosis* and a whole tranche of monologues, his energy has spewed forth. Sometimes it's hard to tell exactly what is under attack. Sometimes the 'them' who have so greatly to be despised seem a bit inchoate. It could be the ruling classes, it could be the lethargic, it could be the inauthentic, it could be the quiet, it could be all four, or more. It seems to be a state of being that is under attack, a spiritual torpor that has to be sloughed off.

Rather like that other spiritual *ubermensch*, Bono, he is frequently asking us 'Do you believe?' without specifying exactly what we're supposed to believe in. Tinkerbell? Karl Marx? David Icke? Though the real question is closer to 'Are you alive?', a challenge which betokens a magnificent arrogance in both men. The presumptions behind the question are preposterous, but I for one am more than happy that there is someone out there asking the question. The fact that there is little intellectual cohesion behind the work matters not a jot, there is a vivacity that works like cocaine in the system.

The rampant insecurity which lurks not too far beneath all the energy, noise and bluster, makes it very hard to attack Berkoff, but also reduces it slightly. You don't feel you're getting the delivery of the whole of a person. Works that are fuelled by rage, in a frenzy, are some of my all-time favourites – *Troilus and Cressida*, *The Bacchae* or *Prometheus Bound* are magnificent – but you never feel that the writers are writing from their centre. They're writing at force, a different sort of art altogether. It delivers the most thrills, but the least completion. It is gloriously irresponsible to itself. Berkoff is in that company.

The least remarked upon achievement of Berkoff is his influence. His one-off splendid isolation tends to make him appear to be an island shut off from the rest of culture. Far from it. In terms of what has followed his example (although many wouldn't credit it), he is a waterfall. Much of physical theatre stems from his inspiration and his experiments in the seventies. The whole cockney geezer linguistic richness you find in Jez Butterworth et al., was learnt from the freedom and range Berkoff found in the vernacular in his early work. Verse drama took a new lease of life from his boldness. Storytelling is a more ancient tradition than any one writer, but the joy and drama Berkoff put back in it will have helped such later innovators as Conor MacPherson. Throughout the 1980s he ran counter to the prevailing political dreariness, and was scorned for his innocence and naivety, but he midwifed a lot of the richer drama that was to follow.

He will continue proving an inspiration, as long as he continues talking to his most receptive constituency, students. There can be no more performed author on campuses up and down the country. Ranks of long-haired youth in non-descript greatcoats and boots, aping a heaviness of life, that they can only imagine, will continue to worship at his altar. And though they may later scorn the passions of their youth, the influence of Berkoff will still stain them a slightly brighter colour. Long may he continue to be too loud.

Simon Block

Simon Block is one of the most able young writers around. He has written three coruscating comedies: *Not a Game for Boys*, a tale of three men in an amateur ping-pong team; *Chimps*, a real-time comic thriller, during which two salesmen break the fragile bonds between a man and his wife; and *A Place at the Table*, a satirical comedy about the uses and abuses of authenticity in theatre and television. He writes wonderful edgy dialogue; he has a great understanding of the insane rituals of male bottom sniffing, and women's despair at the sight of it, and he has a strong sense of the hidden unease that lurks underneath banter.

He could go on writing such plays till the cows come home. Theatres will produce them. Critics will come and applaud them, saying they're tight and well honed. The view of the world, of territoriality, aggression and power games, is a commonplace that's not going to challenge anyone, nor are they going to argue with it. Audiences will come and have entertaining evenings out. All will be well. In a world that worships achievement, why should we ask anything further of a playwright than that they achieve. No matter how wide the bull's-eye, nor how short the distance from it.

In a healthier culture, artists are less frightened of aspiration and failure. In ours, they loom like two of the four horsemen of the apocalypse, the other two being life and truth. Mix with those four and your career gets fragile fast. You're much better hanging out with achievement and success and cynicism and artifice, our present foundation stones. But on such plinths are erected only the smallest sculptures. If we don't encourage our talents to aspire, we do nothing for them.

It sounds dreadfully pretentious to encourage an artist to *stretch* himself or herself. It always sounds like an unholy mix of a smalltime ceramics tutor and the teacher in the *Karate Kid*. But it remains a truth. Simon Block has written three excellent plays. He knows actors, he knows theatres, he knows audiences. Now he should have a go.

Edward Bond

Traditionally any response to Edward Bond has always been a hugely complex divergence between the work and the man. The plays have never deserved anything but massive respect. The man has occasionally had entire theatre companies jumping out of third-storey windows at the mention that he might be dropping in.

Now I've never met him myself, and hearsay is a devil anywhere, but particularly in the theatre. There is not a director, writer or actor anywhere, however saintly or beneficent or wise, who is not regularly carved up by his colleagues or her peers. It's a slagging profession. By and large the more successful the target, the sharper and swifter the darts. But Edward Bond has often provoked a special kind of non-malicious awestruck disapproval. He terrifies people. From the box office to the actors to the artistic directors, Edward Bond knows how to do each job better and will let them know. His scorn is Olympian and merciless.

Now that might seem a justifiable attitude for a great artist, but theatre is only ever great art if everyone is joining in, and you have to bring the people with you. Collaboration and compromise are at the heart of what we do. Dictation isn't. A theatre after working with Edward Bond can be a very wounded and demoralized place; one young actor friend of mine was crucified by Bond over a rehearsal process, and took months to recover. To be schoolmarmish for a second, there's simply no call for that sort of behaviour.

It seems even more justifiable for such a great moralist. Bond, in his plays and in his writings, has spotlighted the theatre as a moral space, a space where actions matter and carry consequence. The morally sloppy, careerist, success-worshipping theatre of the present must justifiably appal him. The whole recent infantile 'theatre-must-be-theatrical' movement is dealt with analogously, in his 1974 comments on science; '*Science for science's sake is as misleading, as unobtainable as art for art's sake. When scientists talk of pure science, or knowledge for its own sake, they're asking to be allowed to act like apes. Apes make H-bombs. Being human is a matter of choosing to be human.*' It's not surprising that a theatre culture whose apogee was *The Blue Room* makes him feel a little queasy.

Happily the signs are that he is mellowing. He has recently collaborated generously, judiciously and gracefully on a revival of one of his plays. He has given advice, support and good hard questions, unravelling some Gordian knots and adding some mysteries. God alone knows how hard it must be for a writer to watch some of their soul's vomit being turned over by strangers thirty years after it was up-chucked, but Edward Bond seems to have found the right way of dealing with it. We can only hope so, since there are few plays that so regularly and so urgently demand revival.

The work, particularly the early work, is peerless. In one early burst of activity he produced a tranche of work that no other post-war writer has bettered. Just as David Storey, and later Billy Roche, have taken the Chekhov legacy and extended it into new classes, new worlds, and a new age, so has Edward Bond with Brecht. This is not a matter of imitation, it is re-invention. With the cool modernist naturalism of *Saved* and *Early Morning*, with the epic myth of *Lear*, with the wild exuberant invention of *Bingo* and *The Pope's Wedding*, and with the mystical subversion of *The Sea*, Bond took Brecht's model of hard rational thought, big imagination and crystalline clarity, and brought it into a new world. The originality, the aspiration and the achievement are all Olympian, so why does he rant and rage?

Because he still wants the world to be bettered, and its injustice still hurts. Because he is gobsmacked at much of the theatre that is celebrated, and rightly so. Besides a work like *The Sea*, many of this year's models do look shallow, trite, manipulative and self-approving. Because his own well may have dried up a little. His more recent work has tended to favour the intellect a little too heavily. His earlier great gift of an exuberant, specific and plastic imagination is less in evidence. But principally because, his own work is afforded so little attention.

I remember seeing Bond leave a world première of one of his plays in a student theatre, while I was at university. There were four people in the audience including him and his wife. We, the heaving crowd in the theatre bar, all stared in amazement as he shuffled out. The disjunction between by day writing essays on a great man of literature and at night seeing him walk away from a deserted première embarrassed us. We sniggered, of course, as students do.

Later, when I understood better the acute pain of empty houses, I felt sorry for him. Now I just feel rage that we leave our greats so unsupported. No wonder that small or large clouds of anger and bitterness cross their brows – the Ardens, the Weskers, the Bonds, the Osbornes – when they are left so cheerlessly out in the cold, by the world that once fêted them. The Irish have a marvellous self-selecting club called Aosdana, which invites great artists into its embrace at any age, then gives them a stipend for the rest of their lives. It secures them in money and respect, two of the principal arteries into the heart of a writer. Edward Bond deserved, and could have done with, an awful lot more of that.

Howard Brenton

Richard Eyre, the ex-director of the National Theatre, recently came up with the most extraordinary idea. He expanded on it in a speech and later in print. Amongst a collection of accurate and articulate gripes about the present state of theatre and society, he proposed a bold solution. That there should be a sort of theatre tsar, an arbiter elegentiae, a play potentate, who would attribute funding according to whether it matched his or her own standards of good work. Well, every ex-Artistic Director has their own private Elba moment, but few are quite so naked about their dreams of returning.

As well as revealing much about his own present feelings of dispossession, it also retrospectively reveals a little about his own reign at the National. A glittering time in terms of box office and critical success, at the centre of which was much beautiful and unheralded work by Eyre himself, it also marked the beginning of a sort of Stalinist middle-class hegemony of good taste. Nothing was allowed that was not well mannered. Shocks were permissible, to a degree, but just enough to make it saucy, not so many as to make it unpleasant. Professional niceness was the order of the day. And so the audiences built, but their range got thinner and thinner, until you ended up with a ruling, white, aged upper-middle class.

Peter Hall's National, although never so consistently praised, was a different story. Peter has an abiding affection for, and a genius at dealing with, hooligans. His National was an anarchic place, at war with itself. Peter Gill was in one corner preaching jeremiads of dissent about every- thing, and producing beautiful work; Bill Bryden's com- pany was writing new legends in the ability to combine conviviality and performance, and working together better than any other company since the war, bar Joan Little- wood's; Ken Campbell opened the Cottesloe with his *Illuminatus*; the good, the bad and the ugly were all invited in, given a company, a few slots and left alone. The result was often a mess, but a mess that reflected the world; and when it was beautiful it was stunning, and created theatre events that became necessary to the nation – *The Oresteia, The Mysteries, Glengarry Glen Ross, Pravda, Antony and Cleopatra.*

There was considerably less mess in Richard Eyre's time, there was infinitely better organization, and a terrifyingly well-run PR machine, but also less real glory. The David Hare trilogy was supposed to speak to the nation, but only seemed to address a large metropolitan salon. Where *The Oresteia* spoke to every inch of you within and without, the Hare trilogy picked and picked off a smaller target. Complicité, *Inspector Calls, Guys and Dolls*, Patrick Marber – theatrical, stunningly well achieved, sophisticated, vivid, but dangerous? Really dangerous? Not so sure . . .

The other terrifying misconception behind the idea of a theatre tsar is how on earth could anyone define standards? There's no rulebook, no guidelines. This year's disaster is next year's prophetic masterpiece; this year's Broadway triumph is next year's collective amnesia. One of the enduring joys of theatre is how frequently one learns how wrong one was in the past. Perceptions, personal and public, shift constantly. How can we say with any authority that we're in the right today, when we hope to be surprised tomorrow. The present funding system is loose, mad, messy, anarchic, but it has to be, to reflect the world around it. Richard Eyre's idea of what is right could be antithetical to someone else's, so who should assume the authority? Better the mess we know, than the order we don't.

There is no more revealing case of this argument than Howard Brenton's play *Romans in Britain*. A ton of nonsense fell on the head of this play, and then settled around it. So the poor play has hardly ever been seen for what it is. It became a *cause célèbre* for all the wrong reasons. It drove headlong into the last vestiges of Victorian English prudery, and the collision became more important than what caused it. Mary Whitehouse hated the play on sight, or rather on smell, since like all moral watchdogs she refused to witness what she wished to condemn. There was a court case, which ended in anti-climax; there was a plethora of think-pieces, and way in the background there was a play. Even in my childhood, it assumed significance. 'Let's play *Romans in Britain*,' my older brother would darkly chuckle from a corner of the room, and I'd run screaming from the house.

The critics and the cognoscenti played their normal trick when confronted by something genuinely new. They discreetly let you know it was actually quite dull, 'poorly constructed', 'hard to know what all the fuss is about', and turned their eyes away. This is classic English second-wave conservatism. The shock troops go in first, and beat the new on the head with truncheons. The liberals turn up a little later, and politely tell the new it's not worth the attention. The second wave is often more crushing than the first.

Romans in Britain is actually a magnificent play, by a magnificent writer. It is formally inventive, tripping backwards and forwards between time schemes, with a symmetry and asymmetry that manage to run parallel and divergent lines at the same time. The madness of empire building is exhibited in a variety of modes. It vividly creates a sense of pre-Roman Britain, post-Roman Britain and modern Britain, texturing each with beautifully adept brushstrokes, and a linguistic richness that is astonishing. You can smell the earth, the panic of people lost in history, and yet get a genuine sense of what it is to be Celtic, a sense I've never seen so well achieved elsewhere.

But what would a theatre tsar have made of it. Who could have been strong enough to have resisted the assault of the illiberals and the deadly indifference of the liberals? Well, Peter Hall could, but such combinations of childish mischief and moral strength don't fall off trees. Plays like *Romans in Britain*, plays that live on the edge, and extend the boundaries, can only be thrown up by, and survive in, a mess. We don't want a municipal gardener trimming our garden, and telling us how it should be arranged. We need it to grow.

Brenton is a great lover of chaotic mess, of an anarchic theatre. His work veers joyously from strip cartoon to Brechtian parable to dirty joke to high lyricism. Occasionally he veers too far off his own road onto a side-track, and his work becomes too easily categorizable. But when he stays true to his own particular voice – sexed-up, wildly romantic, egalitarian, and full of adventure, he produces extraordinary work.

The Genius, although marginally dated by its cold war context, is a beautiful piece, marrying science, pure thought and the theatre in a way that's rarely been surpassed. It interrogates progress acutely, asks evergreen questions about actions and responsibilities, and throws in the air a beautiful love story of the mind. The romantic strain, which pulses through all Brenton's work, is nowhere more evident than in *Bloody Poetry*, his 'at home' with the romantics, Byron, Mary and Percy, and Claire Claremont.

This is a painfully accurate and unforgiving picture of utopians, the fervour of their dreams, and the dreadful mess that they leave behind them.

If you put beside those plays, the early short sharp shocks (*Christie in Love, Lay By*); the exuberant carnivals like *Epsom Downs*; the adaptations, *Galileo* and *Danton's Death*; the epic combos with David Hare, *Brassneck* and *Pravda*; the best television series of the 1980s, *Dead Head*, and if you turn a blind eye to the more recent work with Tariq Ali, then you have one of our most consistent, surprising and rich dramatists.

Brenton is the sort of socialist playwright we can do with more of. His voice is not thin, doctrinaire or argumentative. It is mucky, bloody and explosive. His subject is the one true journey, the journey towards the light. He once tried unsuccessfully to adapt William Morris's masterpiece, *News From Nowhere*. The light from that sun, and from others' (Shelley's, Byron's, Brecht's, Büchner's, Bob Marley's) has poured through his work all his life.

Lesley Bruce

Any actor who is worth his or her salt has, in trade parlance, 'a secret'. It's impossible to define, but you can always sense its presence. The moment you meet them or see them walk on stage, you feel something extra is there. Something in reserve, something they're not giving away – and it's that something that keeps your eye on them.

You can't fake it. Lots of actors haven't got it, and try energetically to work it up. When you see a lot of aimless brooding and smouldering, or hear half-finished sentences and self-important silences, it's often an attempt to fake a secret. But that's not it. It has nothing to do with quietness. Many a chatterbox can still have a secret. It's not even a secret, in the sense of 'I committed adultery' or 'I spent time in jail', not a hidden fact. It's more of a hidden reservoir of energy, born of emotion, either despair or joy, and nurtured over time. It's a reservoir, which can be drawn on by the bearer, and by nobody else.

The best writing (the best of any art) often has the same quality. Lesley Bruce wrote two wonderfully tidy plays that seemed innocuous at first, but in performance bore a huge punch. *In Broad Daylight* was about a man kidnapped in the Middle East, and the efforts of his girlfriend in the face of a mulish Whitehall bureaucracy to agitate for his release. *Keyboard Skills* was about the hapless gyrations of a junior cabinet minister trying to wriggle free from a succession of lies, as he talks to his wife through one long dark night.

Both subjects seem on the surface journalistic, and that contributed to their excitement. Both subjects seem political, and that too added weight, although the attack was more on the corruption of power than on a particular party.

But the real strength of both plays is that lurking behind the thriller/entertainment façade of each is an enormous swell of anger, and loneliness, and need. It is never referred to. It is never revealed. There is no big third act emotional speech, or phoney breakdown. It is a gentle pulse heard behind the play, a distant echo. Lesley Bruce writes beautifully, because she writes with a secret.

Jez Butterworth

Late in 1994, in the lull between Christmas and the New Year, I went for a drink with Stephen Daldry. It was to be a retrospective on the year past and a look forward to the year ahead. Stephen was cagey about his future programme; I was pleased with myself, and my line-up for the Bush. Foolishly so. I had *Killer Joe*, *The Present* by Nick Ward, *Trainspotting*, *True Lines* (John Crowley's devised piece), *Boom Bang-a-Bang*, the new Jonathan Harvey, and a funny, stylish and delightful first play by someone called Jez Butterworth. Or I thought I had.

The play, commissioned and then passed on by the West End producer Andre Ptaszynski, was a clever post-modern piece of ersatz gangster myth-making set in 1950s Soho. His agent had sent it to me on an exclusive basis. A completely exclusive basis. Six months later *Mojo* was on at the Royal Court. This was my fault rather than Stephen's. I would have done the same. The two rules to be learnt were first, never trust an agent, and second, until all parties have applied monikers to a document crammed with heretofores and wheretofores, keep your trap shut.

The play remained funny, stylish and deeply clever. Its greatest virtue was always its jokes, some of the best heard on a London stage for decades. These were proper jokes, triple layered, jokes that a Woody Allen or a Larry Gelbart would be proud of. They were delicately constructed but very strong. You'd get their first meaning straight off, then another shade shortly after, then a final nuance ten seconds later. By which time another couple of jokes would have lined themselves up. The opening rapid-fire stichomythia between Sweets and Potts is the highlight of the play. It is pure circus, exhilarating showing off, joke tripping on joke spilling on joke. This is the talent. The emotionality elsewhere is less convincing.

Was the play worthy of all the brouhaha around it? No. It falls short of the achievement of many plays before and since within the same renaissance. So why the fuss? Partly because it is close enough to a well-made play to delight all the critical devotees at that shrine. Partly because there is an interesting story hiding in there about the emergence of a psychopath, and the slow striptease of his inhibitions.

Accidently, because he struck on one of the most potent metaphors for a particular nineties condition – the way that everyone tries to fuck talent up the ass. The moment anyone appeared that had a new voice, a new look, a new thought, a new rhythm, a new anything, within twenty minutes they would be surrounded by a gallery of ghouls. These bloodless, incisored, Paul Smith suited figures would try first to exploit the new for profit, second to drink it for youth, and third to destroy it from envy. Jez's metaphor defined that Transylvanian action perfectly.

But *Mojo* took off principally because it was *cool*, cool with a little smattering of dark. It walked the walk. It talked the talk. At last theatre's defenders could swagger a bit. Rather than promote or proselytize something subtle or humane or heart-rending or insightful or mysterious, they could finally back something with a little bit of attitude. Theatre nerds could don Raybans and murmur, 'Hey. You seen *Mojo*?'

Thus the action of the play was curiously mirrored in life. In the play, a number of seedy saddoes encircle a young rock star. They try to control his talent, they try to bed him and they live a vicarious life through his 'connection with the kids'. Much the same thing happened with Jez. Ageing male theatre directors, television controllers and film producers fell on him, chucking money and gifts, as if he was the elixir of youth. There are few more miserable or more perennial sights than old media bods trying to shed years. But there is one huge difference from the play. Silver Johnny is a victim. Which is one thing Jez is never going to be. He is sharp as a knife.

I hope he goes on to write many plays. He has a unique gift. Beyond the jokes, there is an extraordinary flair for texture and atmosphere. There's a Byronic dash in the way he maintains a mock-heroic high style over almost epic distances. And I hope for his sake, his plays are judged as plays, not as lifestyle accessories.

Richard Cameron

Just as Billy Roche has his Wexford, Simon Gray his Hampstead, Chekhov his boho *fin de siècle* Russian intelligentsia, so Richard Cameron has his Doncaster. For each of them, a place both minutely real, drawn from observed facts, and entirely imaginary, a stew-pot bubbling with personal concerns. For each of them, the specific provides the route-finder for the universal.

There's no great distance here from the Greeks plundering their shared myth-pool for stories that corresponded to the patterns in their heads. For them, the Trojan war was at once real – a historic event – and imaginary, a projection of their shared stories. There remains in much cultural discourse a snobbery that maintains there is something superior in a story involving Agamemnon to one involving Arthur Middleton. That such work reaches further, that its patterns have a wider ripple. This is patently bollocks, yet the prejudice endures. Any play, whether by Aeschylus or Cameron, has to balance the concrete and the exemplary. The writers who realize that and create these imaginary zones for themselves, are often the ones with the widest reach.

Richard Cameron's Doncaster is twinned with various other exotic locales, most particularly the deep south of Tennessee Williams and William Faulkner. His South Yorkshire is a place of prickly heat, low-level sensuality, strong but vulnerable women and confused violent men. It is this ever-present sensibility that makes his work stand out. There is a sticky atmosphere, a lyricism that works against all the presumptions about plays in working-class environments. The English tradition has always tended to point up the grimness and greyness of working-class life. It has presented worlds bled of life, and shorn of wit. Or if there is any wit, it's of the hard, loveless variety; the sullen type that erupts into middle-class worlds and spoils their fun.

In modern times, Pinter has caught the idiom best, but he has chosen to dwell on its inherent violence, anger and fear. Gray and Stoppard simply haven't bothered, choosing sensibly not to bat on such a clearly sticky wicket. Ayckbourn hovers in the class just above, a wonderfully hermetically sealed zone where patricians and plebeians rarely wander. Hare makes the occasional patronizing foray, rather like a bishop visiting a homeless centre, and always comes badly unstuck (his police-room scenes in *Murmuring Judges* wouldn't pass muster on *The Bill*). Wesker, Arden and Storey were of course comfortable and magnificent poets of dialect, but their stories usually set that gift in a context where the world created was a weapon, rather than an end in itself.

You have to look to the Irish (or occasionally the American tradition), to see how it is properly done. From O'Casey down through Synge, J.B. Keane and Tom Murphy to Billy Roche, they have happily inhabited working-class areas, and given them a comprehensive humanity with warmth, wit and a rich sensibility. They have worked from within rather than without. They have presented a world, both in ease and in difficulty, rather than force that world to make a point or mean something. Richard Cameron is closer to this way of working, so he sits slightly oddly with his English contemporaries.

In a collection of plays, *Can't Stand Up for Falling Down*,

Pond Life, Not Fade Away, Mortal Ash and *All of You Mine*, Richard has created his own landscape. It's a post-industrial world, where the fall-out from the end of the mining industry still reverberates but does not dominate. Enterprise schemes and garden centres stand with a certain fragility on sites where men once blackened their lungs. And in backyards on hot days children play, women manage and men try to work out their new identities. It's a world of tadpoles, Gameboys, washing lines, tea and gossip.

Besides a wonderful ease with subtly charged naturalistic dialogue, Richard has a startling capacity with lyricism. As the old remember their past or the young speculate on their future, he can imbue their words with an almost Wordsworthian richness, without ever seeming fey or stepping out of context. Just as with Faulkner or Tennessee Williams, he can summon up mystery and fragility, and their concomitant beauty, in a world of urban decay.

Yet Richard doesn't only borrow sensibility from literature, he also steals structure. He does it so deftly that no one notices. *Mortal Ash* was a beautifully crafty amalgam of Miller's *All My Sons* and Ibsen's *Enemy of the People* (adapted by Miller). When we produced it at the Bush, I was dying for someone to spot the structural references, but no one did. The bodies were too well buried.

Too few writers steal other people's plots. I'm never sure why they don't. It's been going on for centuries. The Greeks copied and called it tradition, only daring at their peril to deviate from the stories of their forefathers. The Jacobeans copied and called it competition, nervously aping each other with the same hit-hunger that Hollywood shows today. Genres would all appear in bizarre clumps – revenge plays then, space operas now. Shakespeare copied Marlowe, until his great rival died. Melodramas were as derivative as soaps. It is only recently, since arts and ethics have got all jumbled up, that narrative thievery has come to be frowned upon. Copying plots is thought to be immoral – as if playwriting, an occupation that combines art and commerce, could ever be moral. If you can get away with it, steal. The only rule is, don't get caught out, unless you're ostensibly better than your predecessor.

The other tie that binds Richard's work is a cloud of semi-distant violence. In *Can't Stand Up* an abusive man has been terrorizing three young women; in *Pond Life*, a half-remembered rape still traumatizes a community of teenagers; in *Not Fade Away*, a woman exorcizes the cruelty she suffered at the hands of a monstrous grandfather; in *Mortal Ash* an industrial accident pollutes a family, and in *All of You Mine*, a savage off-stage beating has to be accommodated. Cameron doesn't revel in the violence, nor does he indulge the victims. He simply shows how violence fractures communities or individuals, and how surviving it helps them to cohere and advance. It's a tough lesson, since there's never any sense that violence will go away, but it's a good one.

Marina Carr

Marina Carr has been nurtured by the Abbey, the National Theatre of Ireland. This is a singularly perilous position to be in. Since its glorious inception, the Abbey has a distinctly wobbly record when it comes to fostering new work. This is why such a disgracefully large number of Irish plays and writers have had to forge a reputation elsewhere in Ireland or often abroad in London or New York. Anywhere but in their own national theatre. The Abbey has inculcated a certain style – high, literary, sorrowful, washed by water and weeping women, that still lies under the cloud of Yeats. Unfortunately for the Abbey, but fortunately for the rest of us, few of the recent greats want to follow the style. And thus the diaspora of talent.

Carr fits the Abbey bill to a certain extent. *The Mai* and *Portia Coughlan* are not without their quota of water and weeping women. They share an unbruised preciousness, which can get a trifle wearing. But there is a dark humour, and a suppressed sexuality which enlivens it. One can only hope that she escapes the long arm of the Abbey, and lets her devils out to play a little more often.

Jim Cartwright

The king of the wordsmiths. Nothing in my theatre-going
life has beaten the raw excitement of *Road*. I saw it four
times downstairs at the Court. Together with a few other
connoisseurs, I worked out the best positions from which to
see each scene in the promenade production. I ate the
chips that were handed out, danced to the music, snogged
my girlfriend during the smoochy bits, laughed like a child
at the funny bits, and wept like a baby at the end. It was,
and remains, around the top of the list.

It was a beacon forcing its way through a dark age.
Cartwright dived down into the underclass and found
together with an unspeakable pain, a richness, a vitality, a
toughness, an imagination and a romance that took the
breath away. These were not the mewling underclass
victims of the hackneyed middle-class paternalism, they
were themselves, with their own self-destruction and their
own dignity.

Above all, and epitomized by the character Scullery
(especially as manifested by the gravelly warmth of Ian
Dury), what marked the play out was its generosity of
spirit. This is subtly different in kind from dramatic
compassion, the quality which has marked out a line of
writers from Chekhov to Billy Roche. Compassion allows
characters wisdom, an awareness of their own merry
insignificance in the movements of the world. Generosity

like Cartwright's allows his characters to see their insignificance, but also through a crucible of rage and love and hurt to redeem it. Stuck in their piss and vinegar, screaming under the stars, like amateur Buddhists, they connect.

His two great later plays, *To* and *The Rise and Fall of Little Voice*, are quieter but equally strong achievements. These are marginally more respectable worlds. Their characters live lives on fragile stilts, hovering shakily above the underclass they are terrified of falling back into. *To* is an ensemble achievement equal to *Road*, but the beads are more tightly strung together by the thread of the old man–woman thing. It is a wonderfully varied picture of the terrors and the consolations of how relationships become patterns. *Little Voice* is a beautiful distillation of all Cartwright's energy and invention into a thoroughly modern fairytale.

The plays ramble, but that is part of their purpose. Structure would undermine their energy and their originality. The rhetoric frequently borders on excess, but that is the indulgence we allow romantics. We don't let the way Shelley or Keats over-egg their puddings detract from our respect, nor should we with Cartwright.

Possibly his greatest achievement is as a dramatic poet. No one throws more into the furnace to make the right words. Some writers throw in a bit of politics and a bit of character; some a bit of pain seasoned with wit: Cartwright shovels the lot in – anger, mind, history, hurt and heart, rounded off with a big helping of soul. From that furnace he draws words, phrases and lines that satisfy with the same completeness that was involved in his creation. He gives everything, and we take it.

Cartwright is patted on the head as a maverick, while drearier and smaller talents dominate the arena. A class system as painful and obtuse as much else in England keeps him away from the centre. But he's probably happier there anyway.

Caryl Churchill

The queen of all she surveys. From am-dram halls to student lecture theatres to avant-garde studios to big subsidized houses to the West End, she is the most loved one. And she deserves every ounce of love thrown in her direction.

Like David Bowie at his peak, but with a lot more class, her greatest talent has been staying well ahead of her fans. She has never ceased to experiment, nor to re-invent herself. Just when her legion of followers might suspect that she would settle into a pattern, she pulls the rug from under their feet.

It would be comfortable to say that she has worked in genres, but it would be underestimating her achievement. Each play is a category smasher, interweaving different genres, different styles and different forms to create entirely new dramatic possibilities. Her particular courage is that every time she starts, she seems to wipe her own slate well and truly clean. Most good writers are able to ignore what others are writing or have written, but very few are strong enough to ignore the allure of their own previous work.

Yet the playfulness of her imagination always manages to steer clear of self-indulgence. It is reined in by her respect for content. Her plays must have a centre of gravity. They must have heart and human content. That provides the ballast, which keeps the balloon of her imagination from disappearing into space. Yet what is most radical about her work, and what makes her a supreme artist, is that she is alert to the new content of human life, and creates structures suitable to that.

Contemporary human sexuality is such an exploded bomb that no traditional story structure could contain it. *Cloud Nine* is the most dazzling construct within which to hold such peculiar energies. The linear, driven, accelerating plot of the first half proves the ideal vehicle with which to parody the rigidity of our inherited Victorian sexuality. Artificially straight lines, for artificially straight lives. The still, episodic, Chinese construction of the second half – brief stories woven together in a park – is a beautifully relaxed exemplar of a less motivated, more meditative age. Each half complements the other, in a yin-yang way, as well as providing a perfectly apt demonstration of its subject.

Top Girls also famously divides, into three sections. Taking on a subject as mountainous as women in history, it covers a huge expanse of terrain, while remaining elegantly concise. The first section, the dinner party of famous historical and fictional women, is a dazzling intellectual fantasia, a technically brilliant circus act, which flings around heavyweight intellectual content as if it was as light as air. The second section sketches a vivid picture of the modern world, its snakes and ladders for women trying to find a way. The third section is a big, old-fashioned, stichomythic fistfight, a ball of love and rage, a classic scrap where two political philosophies and two sisters rehearse how much they loathe, and how much they need each other. The play is a journey from high style to high naturalistic emotion, changing gears imperceptibly, and laughing at the notion that any one part is more valuable than any other.

The rest of the work is too rich a feast to outline in detail here, but its variety should be respected; from the rampant narrative and broad satire of *Serious Money*, to the delicate absurdity, raucous hilarity and emotionality of *Blue Heart*; from the fantastical primitivism of *The Skriker* to the anecdotal reportage of *Mad Forest*; from the cool modernity of *Ice Cream* to the historical passion of *Light Shining in Buckinghamshire*. Always bold, always new, always ahead of the game.

She has been lucky in her most regular collaborator, Max Stafford Clark. His literal-minded quest for clarity has been the ideal foil, and probably the ideal spur, to the wildness of her imagination. You can imagine her handing in each new play, madder than the last and saying, 'Go on then, action *that*.' Although Max is certainly the ideal midwife of Caryl's work, it is interesting to see other takes on it. Tom Cairns did a full-on operatic production of *Cloud Nine* at the Old Vic, which brought out an emotional and sensuous resonance in the writing that proved a genuine surprise.

Caryl herself has an extraordinary presence, rather like Jocelyn Herbert, one of the great theatre designers of this century. Both have a profoundly civilizing effect on their surroundings. Without any hauteur or arrogance, I've seen both walk into the Bush at its roughest, and I've watched the wildest people, junkies and drunk coppers and all, start to behave imperceptibly better in the atmosphere they create. Although both can be naughty and humourful, a completely un-faked goodness radiates gently from them both, and calms the air around them. It's a natural, liberal aristocracy of the spirit, and the sign of a great artist. She is the queen of all she surveys.

Jane Coles

Jane Coles is a marvellous picker of situations. Some people need a good plot to get them going, some need an image, some need a relationship: Jane always goes for a strong situation. She places it in her mind, like one of those crystals we grew as children, and slowly lets themes, images and people accrue.

Her first play for the Bush, *Backstroke in a Crowded Pool*, revolved around a municipal swimming pool. Throughout we watch the efforts of two female bodyguards to keep order, in a chaos of screaming infants, and drowning geriatrics. It spins outwards into the rest of their lives, consuming animal rights, halal butchery, racist violence and terrorism along the way. The tone of writing is lyrical and lush, but it's always pulled back from indulgence by an uncanny integrity to the shape and symmetry of the crystal.

Crossing the Equator, her second for the Bush, picked equally fertile ground – a post-war liner carrying disaffected Brits out to Australia. This was part of the Assisted Passage scheme, which was a sub-section of the grander Keep Australia White policy. That subject in the hands of others, or of anyone ten years before, would have led to a load of thin preachy rant about racism and empire. But Jane managed to incorporate those themes into a piece with a much wider reach. The post-war and post-empire insecurity resonated into the character's sexual insecurity, and the trip across the equator and into the unknown became a metaphor for their search for sexual confidence. There were no endings or conclusions, but as an analysis of the British at sea, it was painfully exact.

Her writing is rich and literary, and for some, who like their naturalism straight and cynically downbeat, it's a bit too rich. But the theatre would be much duller without such exotic crystals.

Ray Cooney

The only really genuine, cast-iron farceur left in the business. Ray Cooney is an honourable torchbearer for a tradition as old as . . . well as old as the oldest profession. From Aristophanes through Plautus down, they've been raising laughs from making fools out of the pompous, driven wild by sexual lust. The only philosophical dictum at play is the simple one – 'A stiff prick hath no conscience'. There's no great linguistic distinction in his work, no enormous wit – jokes like 'Ahoy in front and a vast behind' won't shorten Tom Stoppard's fingernails. There's no big idea or sharp satire. Keeping a plot moving is what counts most.

But he's a great technical innovator, and has a very sure theatrical sense. He creates insane situations, the taxi driver with two wives, the found briefcase with £5 million, and drives them as far as a theatre will stretch to take them. Occasionally the wildness and exuberance of the inventions takes you into an area of innovation that outdoes the avant-gardists of the physical theatre world, and with a thousandth of their pomposity. He's only ever going to be as fashionable as Lionel Blair. But just as I'd rather watch Lionel Blair tapdancing, than see some self-appointed genius waving his willy round while talking about stone-age caves to disguise his mid-life crisis, so I can think of worse evenings to be had than watching a Ray Cooney play.

Lucinda Coxon

That there's been a new writing renaissance over the last ten years is now, we should all hope, beyond question. There's been a variety of work, a quality of excitement about it and a quantity of output that has never been matched before. What will survive, whether any of it will survive, we won't know for thirty, sixty or a hundred years, once time has sorted the wheat from the chaff.

But where did the renaissance begin? Where did it first emerge? If you wanted to be comprehensively wrong, though not alone, you'd say the Royal Court. The Court proliferated the renaissance, spun it giddily into new arena, and made the loudest noise about it. But most of the time they were copying ideas, cannibalizing talent and stealing energies that had first happened elsewhere. Magnifying the effect is not the same as originating the idea.

If you wanted to be less wrong, and still in good company, you'd say the Bush, which between 1990 and 1993 stood its ground on behalf of new writing within a culture that had begun to cherish heritage, expressionism and chicken impressions above anything that breathed. The Bush also showed a range, type and vivacity of work that had not been thought possible (or tasteful), and that opened a huge number of doors. But still you'd not be right. The Bush was lucky enough to harness and legitimize an explosion of talent that had been brewing on the further reaches of the fringe for two or three years before.

If there were two organizations that could genuinely claim to be among the prime movers, they'd be the Old Red Lion and Loose Exchange. You probably won't have heard of them, but that is probably also some sort of guarantee that they are the real thing. If you can rely on one thing in modern life, it's that the man bearing the new idea is almost definitely not the man who had it. The poor soul who came up with it is most probably upended in some squalid side-street a few blocks back, his face streaked with blood and tears. While Captain Shiny, surrounded first by lawyers and then by bootboys, proclaims his wonderful new thing.

The Old Red Lion is a pub theatre that's been run for almost fifteen years with terrific taste, ease and style by Ken McClymont. He has an eye for talent, a relaxation with big risks and an openness to innovation that few can match. If there was a single progenitor of what happened in theatre in the 1990s, it would be the Old Red Lion's *annus mirabilis* of 1989/90. New plays, new directors, new producers were pouring out of the place, desperate to take over the theatre establishment, and by and large they did. Heat was steaming off the place.

It was also coming from Loose Exchange, an affiliation of writers, directors and actors, loosely led by a benevolent genius called Nigel Halon. They popped up here and there and wherever – the Finborough, the Man in the Moon, the Old Red Lion and the old Soho Poly – doing plays, devised pieces and shorts. Sarah Kane, in her rather humourless Native American phase, was a very young devotee, and learnt her passion from this group. The writers included Lucinda Coxon, Vince O'Connell and Peter Lloyd. It would be hard to say why they were so influential but there was some mixture of unfettered freedom, intellectual rigour, warmth and soul that unlocked many a door, and inspired many who came into contact with them.

Not many of the group went on to stellar success – Vince and Peter have had successful careers in TV and film, Sarah shone all too briefly, and Lucinda has done better than well in theatre and film. Nigel Halon, the quasi-leader, has moved away from the theatre. It's sadly the case that prophets, original thinkers, people who can initiate new energies are destined to go unnoticed. Those who ride the wave, looking good on a board, are far more noticeable than those who started it, far out at sea and now sinking. But I hope that those who worked at the Old Red and with Loose Exchange can look on all that followed with some form of grandparent's pride.

Lucinda has written two unique, original and beautiful plays since that time – *Waiting at the Water's Edge* and *Wishbones* – both of which were produced at the Bush. Hers is a defiantly female voice. By that I don't mean every character wears dungarees and talks about their vagina: I mean that she foregrounds women's stories, and writes with a lightness of touch that Jane Austen would be proud of; a febrile, sensitized poetry that recalls Virginia Woolf and a sense of magic that reminds you of Isabel Allende. Her first mature piece of work – *Water's Edge* – weaves together an Edwardian domestic home, a sea journey, Thatcherite politics and an undying female friendship. It is exquisite. Lucinda achieves her fineness – 'like gold to aery thin-ness beat' – through slow and careful work. She doesn't bash her plays out. But they are worth the wait.

Martin Crimp

Rather as when you walk the medina of Tangiers you are hailed with a litany of English associations – 'English, hey English . . . Bobby Charlton . . . Marks and Spencers . . . Kevin Keegan' – so when you do the rounds of European theatres, you will often be familiarised by an earnest stare, and the words, 'The work of Martin Crimp, especially his *Play With Repeats*, is extremely beautiful.' This is always supposed to make you feel that you are at home.

I usually have a slight flush of the Little Englanders when it comes to European new writing. Or for that matter English work that goes well in Europe. It's a *Daily Mail* anti-intellectual prejudice that lurks close to the beating heart of every badly educated Englishman, and it's nothing to be proud of. It's also based on a large amount of painful personal experience.

Intellect and image rule the theatre in Europe. Various poisonous tributaries create this river. The baleful influence still exerted by the Theatre of the Absurd (as silly and long a cultural cul-de-sac as history has ever walked down) is an enormous contributory factor. There's another idiotic movement called inter-textuality, which results in hideous dramatic confections with titles like *The Three Sisters Of Madame Bovary*, or *Queen Lear – The Ghost Of Electra?* And there's all the other angry, affected and disaffected grand-children of modernism which blast the landscape. Little grows in this bleak environment.

Happily we seem to have managed, in our cautiously inclusive way, to have slowly consumed the virtues from each intellectual movement without succumbing to its further excesses. Attention to truth has remained foremost. Each intellectual fad has proved a useful new tool for cultivating the garden of life.

There's also always a suspicion with work that is translated into a hundred languages that the language that flourishes best in translation is frequently the language that has least flavour at home. Translatable work lacks the zing of untranslatable. This is a silly and wrong prejudice, but it pertains.

Martin Crimp is a truly European writer and, happily to subvert all my little Englander prejudices, a rather wonderful one. His work drips with a cool formal sense of theatrical possibility. Perspective is as significant in his work as content. Incidents occur and are then reflected in different mirrors, refracted through different lenses. With *No-one Sees the Video, Dealing With Claire, Attempts on Her Life* and *The Treatment*, Crimp has carved out his own theatrical territory, Crimpland, full of hollow folk, all with offstage lives of loneliness and mystery, suddenly trapped together in a mutual obsession. The incidents within the plays, often revolving around violence to women, are only as significant as the manner in which they are interpreted, understood and represented. This all sounds pretentious, and it is, properly pretentious, as much theatre must be.

But the pretention is contained within his astonishing skills of draughtsmanship. He is an avid student of speech, its trips, stumbles, losses of way, and occasional scary definiteness. The accuracy with which he catches the insecurities of modern speech, its need for affirmation and terror of exposure (the 'isn't it?', 'doesn't it?', 'don't we?', that lurk after every phrase are never spoken here, but always felt), that accuracy becomes strangely transfixing, and beautiful. Together with the linguistic skill is an almost unparalleled deftness at summoning up atmospheres. Be they hotel rooms, New York cabs, offices or whatever, within a few phrases, Crimp will have you there. These are the primary building bricks of any writing, dialogue and texture. No one has more facility with them than Crimp. Whatever he builds with them is a bonus.

In *Dealing With Claire*, a delicate, sensitive and insightful fictional recreation of the Suzy Lamplugh incident, Crimp takes a commonplace negotiation over the selling of a house, and turns it into a terrifying disquisition on the emptiness of modern living. In *The Treatment*, with a lightly held scimitar of irony, Crimp savages the modern world's cannibalization of experience, and how the entertainment industry eats reality. The second play is also hysterically funny, revealing a capacity for exposing the mutual incomprehension of a group that would be the pride of a master of farce. Such verbal high spirits were released even further in his wild updating of Molière's *The Misanthrope* to a flash contemporary London.

The virtues that ground Crimp's work are the solid ones, his precision, his life, his wit, his truth. The formal European experiments float him off the ground. He maintains a terrific balance between the two.

Mike Cullen

It always pays to have friends in. During the first preview of *The Cut*, the play's wit and passion gripped the audience while the dialect confused them and the red-blooded plot made them suspicious. They looked as if they were being mugged, but enjoying it. Accustomed to pale and bloodless affairs, they were all at sea, lost in a classic London confusion. They had enjoyed it, but didn't know if they were allowed to like it.

There was strong but equivocal applause, then a millisecond of silence settled on the room once it had died down. It could have swung either way. Then the director's brother turned to him, and filled the silence with a loud Scottish brogue: 'Fuck me, Martin, that was fuckin brilliant.' The audience laughed, nodded their heads, and all was well.

A Scottish ex-miner turned poet, Mike Cullen came to playwriting late. *The Cut* was written with a thick Scottish dialect and a density of four-letter words that would make a Mamet blush. The combination of the two created a thick wall of black sound, studded with moments of lyrical memory, scabrous wit and ancient rage. It wasn't easy to digest, but the company rightly played it according to their own rules and not the audience's.

All set in the claustrophobic depths of a mine, the rapacious plot shows how four miners manoeuvre for position warily around each other, aiming both to settle old scores and to gain future position. There is absolutely no sentimentality, no noble cause, no stirring emotionalism. It showed, without preaching, how far the pressure to survive had eroded the values of these men. The miners' strike had left nothing but old scars in the heart, which had to be avenged.

Some Hammersmith socialists took me on one side after a performance. They were enraged. How could the writer show such a bleak picture, how could he ignore all the positive qualities that came out of the strike, the solidarity, the creativity, the new sense of justice. Well, he was there and they weren't.

Cullen proved he was far from a one-hit wonder with two composed and original chamber plays for the Traverse. *The Collection* echoed the greed and cut-throat power plays of *The Cut* in the salesman's world. *Anna Weiss* took off in a new direction, exploring the horribly blurred lines of abuse and false memory syndrome. Again the set-up was tight, the construction concise, the acceleration relentless.

There's a rare capacity here for short, sharp body blows. Behind each punch there's a blend of pain and rage, an emotional force that is contained, controlled and directed to where it can have the maximum effect. There's every possibility that he will be eaten alive by television, which would be a shame, since not to avoid an obvious analogy, he probably still has a rich seam to mine.

Kate Dean

It's quite hard to retain a balanced attitude to a young writer who announces in the Writer's Guild Christmas magazine that her ambition for the next year is to have your babies. Nor is it easy to judge her work when having travelled to Birmingham to see a play of hers performed, she bites your neck. But Kate Dean is not someone for a bit of old-fashioned schmoozing. She favours the full-on approach.

Kate wrote a series of striking plays about a community of young people living on the margins of normal society in Worcestershire – *Rough, New England, Down Red Lane*. A variable bunch, her characters are addicted to their own outsider status and to whatever gives them their own rush, be it cider, smack, doing 120 on a bike down a country lane or a decent dawn. What matters most to them is that they stay real, alive and authentic. The plays are written in a beautifully studied naturalism that recalls David Storey in its modesty and precision. They smell, sound, look, feel right, and offer an object lesson in how to create a dramatic world.

What they lacked was objectivity. Kate was always so passionately involved in her characters and their world that she would often forget to step back and take a look at them. Everything they did – falling in love, raging, shooting up, slagging each other off – was so deeply fascinating to her that she forgot to worry about the broader spread of its popularity. Now, that enthusiasm is a major bonus, and a play can't be started without it, but a play needs more food than just, 'Look at these people. They exist!' But there can be no more solid foundation than life achieved, and Kate's enormous skill at that should promise great things in time.

April De Angelis

'Let's all shag the writer', one actor toasted at the end of a long and enhanced party. We were celebrating the end of *Playhouse Creatures* at the Old Vic. April was getting ready to go, and a queue was forming to say love you, love your play, blah, blah, when this fizzy grenade was thrown in. Like all cheap attempts to *epater les feministes*, it got a big laugh. Well, from me, anyway. I vividly remember the look or looks that spasmed across April's face – surprise, anger, tension, flattery, hurt. She quickly and graciously let it go and left.

Anyway, this confusion and this mess, this oscillation between empowerment and debilitation, is a subject that April herself treats dazzlingly and wittily in her work. She hasn't become shy of gender politics, although we are all supposed to have moved on from such issues. (Though what exactly we've moved on to remains an occasional mystery.) April has kept the debate alive, most clearly in *The Positive Hour*. She draws no obvious conclusions. In fact the confusion that crossed her face at that remark characterizes the honest confusion that courses through her play, as a woman finds herself lost between dependence and independence, sexual authority and sexual need.

But April is far from a single-issue politician. Sexual politics remains as a pulse underneath, but she has also explored medieval life and language in *Iron Mistress*, the state of England in the very splendid *Hush*, and the

Restoration Theatre in *Playhouse Creatures*. Her imagination can encompass and reproduce worlds very distant from her own, and she has an ease with non-naturalistic dialogue that carries the audience with her. Even when attempting a language far removed from her own, as in *Crux* or *Playhouse Creatures*, there is a central coarseness, a vitality, a rudeness that keeps it fresh and alive. This is rare. Usually non-naturalistic language is a sort of elegant, elitist affront, a frightened sort of affectation. With April you've got the constant sense that there's someone lurking behind it, saying 'knickers'.

At one point at the Bush, we had a string of writers who came in to meet us, who all told us in confidential tones that they liked to use 'heightened language', as if it was a sort of mystic ketchup that you poured over a play. You see this ketchup effect quite often in bad plays – a purple patch, where the lights go coloured and the actors put on that glazed 'help' expression. You also see plays where the reverse is the case – streams of heightened language are suddenly leavened by cheap modern colloquialisms; 'Yeah, right' or 'Fuck this'. Cue very cheap laugh. They beg. Or the third sort of play which heroically tries to take us back to poetic drama, where Amazons and Danubes of dry, pompous, inorganic, affected prettiness assault your ears for a couple of hours.

Everything in every play of quality should be poetic. Breaking up the lines doesn't make a pipfart of difference. The language, whatever it is, has to come from an organic source within the writer and the world of the play, and has to remain consistent to itself and its own internal contradictions throughout. It has to be true. Shakespeare most brilliantly brought off the marriage of poetry and prose, but the wellspring of Pandarus and Troilus, of Falstaff and the King, are the same. It is the wellspring of life.

April can pull off both as well, largely because of a

magnaminity and vigour in her own writing. *Playhouse
Creatures* is a wonderfully robust noise about theatre and
the Restoration period and how women made a life then,
and make one now. We produced it at the Old Vic
alongside Vanbrugh's *The Provoked Wife*, a work which is
rehearsed in April's play. The Vanbrugh was, of course, a
classic, and was accorded the appropriate courteous
respect. But the audiences knew which was the event.

David Edgar

There is a thrilling moment towards the end of David Edgar's late cold war epic, *Maydays*. Pavel Lermontov, a Russian defector much prized by his conservative hosts, looks around a room he is addressing. He has been invited to lecture on freedom, but as he surveys the fat and settled faces around, he sees that he has been tricked, and that his new liberators are much the same as his old captors. That authority is a constant wherever you go. That authority always ends up in the hands of those who most want it. And that those who most want it are almost always the last people it should be given to. He cannot finish his speech.

By a strange parallel irony, I was often reminded of that moment on my travels through the old Soviet Union and the Eastern Bloc countries. During the earliest and most impoverished days, any visitor from the West was treated as a possession to be protected assiduously from rival groups. Whoever first met you would spend the following week or month or whatever beating off anybody else who wanted to say hello. In Georgia we were given a guard, though whether it was to save us from kidnapping by gangsters or rival theatre groups was always uncertain.

But at some moment we would always have to meet the local Theatre Writers' Union. Housed in some grand old aristocrat's house, out they would shuffle, the social realist apparatchiks of the old regime. Detested by the young for their association with the old regime, seared with bitterness

at the grand cheat of history, their early charm would soon
dissolve into softly spoken jeremiads against all that was
new. They wore grey and dark suits, lapels covered in
badges; they were filling out slightly and their faces were
gently purpling. The ghosts of their fiery youth hovered
around them asking awkward questions. The similiarities
were breathtaking. There they were – David Edgar,
Howard Brenton, David Hare, Harold Pinter. The East/
West mirror has never seemed so true.

My discovery of David Edgar's work coincided with my
discovery of politics and the relationship was passionate.
His grand state of England epic, *Destiny*, about the dangers
of neo-fascism plotted around a West Midlands by-elec-
tion, and his even grander state of the world epic, *Maydays*,
turned me on to the potential of political theatre. Both had
a sweep that had eluded playwrights since Tamburlaine,
they had a message and they had this overwhelming
sincerity. The passion was so reasoned, so wonderfully dull.
As a pale student, one could stand in front of a mirror like a
child with a cowboy hat on, and mouth such dream-
crushing speeches as,

> In the end what they are doing, what we are all trying to do,
> in our many different ways, can only be accounted for by
> something in the nature of our species which resents, rejects
> and ultimately will resist a world that is demonstrably and
> in this case dramatically wrong and mad and unjust and
> unfair.

Oh, the joyless beauty, the magnificent Protestant plainness
of it all. It's that complete lack of flourish, of glamour, of
mystery, that could seduce so completely any young person
who lived in fear of their own colourlessness. No more
worries. In a new grey dawn, the whole world shall be made
colourless. And all shall be well.

But like one of the many ex-communists who pop up in

Edgar's work, noisily eschewing the passions of their youth, I've walked in another direction since. Not politically – if anything, I think my politics have hardened – but aesthetically. And any reasonably developed aesthetic, in some form of contact with reality, just can't accept an exchange like this one from *Destiny*.

> PAUL: All history's the struggle of the classes.
> TONY: No. All history's the struggle of the races.
> *Pause.*
> PAUL: The workers of all races must unite.
> TONY: The workers of all classes must unite.
> *Pause.*
> PAUL: Come down to it, the choice is socialism or barbarity.
> TONY: Come down to it, it's Zionism, One-World tyranny or us.

The shame is that these are two well-developed, well-drawn characters, who suddenly become possessed by historical forces and lose all their life. This is not truth, this is intellectual construct. It is true to an idea, an idea of George Steiner's, of how 'the emotional authority of the historical . . . surpasses the claims, the intensity of the self', but it is not remotely true to the world we live in.

Who essentially is that sort of nonsense written for? It's hard to tell, if it's not for some pale, woolly hatted souls who are grateful for the underpinning of their delusion that there is no such thing as personality, since ten of them couldn't raise a personality even with a steering committee. Nothing scares them as deeply as personality.

Praise God, we are now living in an age where we no longer kid ourselves that there is no such thing as personality, and that personalities do not affect history. When Rupert Murdoch divorced his wife and remarried, millions around the world were affected directly or indirectly. When Bill Gates launches a new software range, the world quakes. When Zinedine Zidane knocked in two easy headers against Brazil, he woke France up to a new multicultural future. When Slobodan Milosevic decided one afternoon in Kosovo to leave the light behind and let the darkness pour through the door, Europe was changed irreparably. These individuals, and every single other, change and shift the tide of history just as the climate or economics or culture does.

Nor are we living in an age of the little person, Chaplin's tramp, the everyman, the stock old working-class nothing, facelessly washed up and away by bigger forces. In our culture, as in our lives, everybody has a right to themselves, to their own individuality, their own choices, their own mystery, their own unpredictability. It simply won't do to subjugate them to some imagined historical force any longer. David Edgar's characters, with their entirely honorable resignation before historical forces, just don't wash. His one attempt at an Ibsenite character-driven play, *That Summer*, set during the miners' strike, has some wonderful moments, but eventually buckles under the weight of history, ideology and symbol.

I blotted my copybook with David Edgar early on, at one of his many conferences arranged to discuss the Death of something (Theatre, Language, Politics, Socialism – they were all fairly interchangeable, and whatever it was would have been heralded by The Future Of . . . conference six months before). I made a short, nervous and red-faced contribution suggesting that the way to revive new writing in the theatre possibly wasn't to spend a weekend moaning about it, and that if some of the energy the practitioners spent on complaining was spent on producing, there might be a revival. It was rather as if I'd pulled a Christmas cracker at a funeral, and then donned a party hat. From there on David Edgar always treated the Bush as a sewer, until I moved on and a fellow beard took over. What we were about – metaphor, imagination, relationships, truth, wit, life *and* politics, seemed like too rich a stew for him.

Edgar always felt safer at the Court. They continued to put on enough plays *about* things to keep him happy. The zeitgeist play, the bits of extended journalism into heavily indulged shocking malaises, kept him and his acolytes reassured that theatre was doing the right job.

It seems grossly unfair to be unkind about David Edgar since he is so palpably sincere about his mode of work. Still more so since he has tried so hard to propagate that method by running one of the best known writing courses in the country. He makes a serious investment in young talent. It would be grudging not to celebrate that. Even if, as I do, you think that the whole idea of teaching playwriting is daft. There are only two ways to learn about the creation of plays. One is to work in the theatre, preferably as an actor. The other is to live. Watching a show assemble, being in it, whoring a bit, drinking a lot, eating some curries and waking up at five in the morning with a twisted tummy are better paths to theatrical life, than preparing for a scheduled discussion on narrative structure.

It's also unfair since much of the work is so strong. His early work abounds with a sense of *jeu d'esprit*, of wit and fun. There is a long play in verse, *Dick Deterred*, which exuberantly lampoons Richard III, at the same time as dealing with Watergate; there's a collection of delightful sketches, *Ball Sports*, casting a political and absurdist eye over sport; there's the incomparable adventure of *Nicholas Nickleby*, which was such a defining event for theatre generally. And to re-read *Maydays* and *Destiny* is an enormous help in regaining insight into those fog-bound days. They also still thrill. Though I'm not sure why. Maybe because of the sweep, and the sense of history, and the powerful intellect behind them, they provide some of the same awesome excitement as watching armies on the move. Maybe old socialists get the same thrill from these as old soldiers do from studying the theory of Clausewitz or the manoeuvres of Napoleon.

Theatre would have been greatly the less for David Edgar having not been around. The ambition, the sincerity and the intellect all serve as an interesting addition to the overall scenario. But he is more healthily viewed as a particular playwright than as an important influence.

As I grow older, the older forms of socialism appeal more and more, and nothing is more attractive than the dreamy utopianism, joyous anarchy and Christian generosity of the Victorian socialists, of William Morris and Oscar Wilde. It's a form that includes wine, cakes, whisky, blow jobs, ghosts, grief, pain and envy, that includes all the world, and all our sharing in it. It's a form that isn't all about minds in smoky rooms carving up power. That's still what worries me about David Edgar – the suspicion that behind it all lies a desire for authority.

Helen Edmundson

No single instance of press stupidity has infuriated me as much as the reception for Helen Edmundson's play, *The Clearing*. Here was an enormous, muscular, rich, political, poetical, historical, personal play. For every dreary question that had been asked ad infinitum; 'Where are the big plays?', 'Where are the plays that combine the personal and political?', 'Where is the historical landscape?', 'What happened to dramatic language?'; for every one of these miserable questions, and many more, here was the answer. 'Here it is, you dumb wazzocks, over here', we all felt like shouting, '*HERE*!'

But they couldn't see it. The response to a mighty production of a landmark play was, with a few honourable exceptions, lukewarm. A couple of glib paragraphs in the *Guardian* were squeezed into a page overwhelmingly dominated by Michael Billington's ravings about a piece of Strindberg senilia at the Gate. What we do, what audiences enjoy, what moves the world forward and what critics write about, very often occur on completely separate planets.

The public ate it up. They came and they adored it, and perception changed sufficiently quickly that it ended up garlanded with awards. Subsequent productions cropped up here and all over Europe. It now looks as if it will be a huge movie. The strength in the play was too great not to survive, but the fact that it wasn't celebrated for what it was the instant it appeared is all of our loss.

Helen has made a name for herself adapting epic books

for Shared Experience – *Anna Karenina*, *Mill on the Floss* and *War and Peace*. She gleaned many virtues from the novels for her own play – a broad narrative sweep, philosophical rigour, grand romance and an austere tragic vision. She applied these to *The Clearing*, and took the audience on the most extraordinary journey.

The play is set in 1650s Ireland, shortly after Cromwell has swept through the country, inventing modern genocide and incubating his own form of early fascism. Set against this grand backdrop, the play follows the collapse of a marriage between an Englishman and an Irishwoman, and the almost inevitable death of their child. The language is strong, rooted, pungent and resonant of the period without being twee or archaic. The relationships are passionate, operatic even, without losing the fabric of everyday life. It is an extraordinary achievement.

Unlike *The Crucible*, with its modern parallels, Helen felt no need to draw simple contemporary lessons. Her play stood up as an imaginative achievement in its own right, with a life of its own, and hence, an infinite number of tangential references to individual lives and societies. An allegory immediately imprisons itself. It can only be about what it is about. A work of art such as *The Clearing*, has a much wider reach.

Putting on naturalistic single-set plays at the Bush or any other small studio is wonderful, but not a surprise. There is a body of opinion that that is all the Bush, or any other studio space, should do. Helen, and many others, exploded all that.

David Eldridge

The writer as bloke. David often has the air of someone who's doing it for a bet. No more loveable, big-hearted person exists in the catty world of theatre. But you sometimes suspect that he sneaks back to Romford, joins his mates and laughs himself silly, positively pisses himself, over the silliness of la-la land. 'I've just been to a conference on political theatre', 'What you, David? Fuck off', 'No, I have. I was the keynote speaker', etc.

David exploded on to the scene with his first play, *Serving It Up*, a blunt, spirited and lacerating portrait of contemporary East End life. He pulled no punches, laying bare the racism and sexism that coursed through his characters' veins. He handled a difficult story about a cross-generational affair with skill, eloquently showed the sadness and self-loathing that underpins most violence, and created a genuine modern monster in the skinhead Sonny. It was a thrilling debut, and brought an electric edge of contemporaneity back to a theatre that was getting a bit anaemic at the time.

His second and third plays, *A Week With Tony* and *Summer Begins*, were less assured, but revealed the same skill at deceptive banality, and the same cool look at modern life.

Behind the blokish façade, David is a keen student of the theatre, and has a broader knowledge of modern playwrights than almost anyone else. His questions are often more interesting than most people's answers. What seems raw is often thought through, what seems careless is often deliberate. His love for his chosen medium is genuine. I hope it's rewarded.

Ben Elton

If it works, who can argue with it, and Ben Elton's plays work. They deliver. They bring in crowds to enormous theatres in London and around the country; they generate big laughs; they provoke thought, and their fantastic plots provide extreme situations that serve as instructive patterns, *reductiones ad absurda*, to show the demented directions the world is going in.

It's a good soup that Elton has put together – sex, in the old-fashioned whoops-missus sense; political dialectics of a fairly blunt or broad sort, and most importantly jokes. The jokes are not delicate, sophisticated or subtle, but they are big. It's hard to write jokes that fit a large hall. Jokes for a studio theatre are one thing, for television another, for film something different, but those that can reach out, clutch and tickle a thousand people at a time are something different. It's a rare skill, and Elton has it.

There's a Jacobean vigour and energy to much of the writing, which is genuinely refreshing. The characters are Jonsonian; mad obsessives stuck in their grooves. They seem incapable of change, they are only capable of inflating or deflating like painted balloons, according to the relative merit of their *idée fixe* at that particular moment. There's also a Jacobean flavour to the language; mad hyperbole, wild ranting and long lists. Lists are the key similarity. It's a technique from both Jacobean and Restoration comedy;

character is defined by an accumulation of things, and the humour comes in the repetition, and the slow exaggeration.

Elton hasn't got the shifts and changes of mood, the sudden swallow dives into lyricism or the shafts of emotional seriousness, that distinguish the great seventeenth-century writers, nor the same robust breadth of life lived. But his plays do have the same refreshing frankness about their own two dimensionality.

Ben Elton let himself down recently by writing an angry piece in the *Sunday Times* about the need for middle-brow theatre. He was certainly right about that – we do need a middle-brow theatre, and one enlivened by his zest. But he went on to ally himself in a historical line with Rattigan and Coward. Well, he's not them. The delicacy of the human heart, the subtle music of dialogue and light perfection of form, this is all beyond him. So far.

If there is one thing that militates against the plays being as good as they want to be, it is their neediness. They keep needing our attention, and that reduces their authority. 'Look at me, Mum,' they keep shouting, 'I'm being funny, I'm being political, I'm being paradoxical.' 'Yes dear, very good.' 'You're not looking.' The staples of playwriting – people, relationships and texture – require a calmer voice. But those probably aren't the relevant criteria, here. Ben Elton puts the ball in the back of the net.

Kevin Elyot

Long volumes have been and will be written on the impact of AIDS on contemporary culture. How it struck too many too young, how it came out of nowhere, how it concentrated on one community, how it had a particular effect on those in the arts (the past tense in all these verbs may be a little optimistic). All these factors combined to maximize its effect on the culture. It was the shock above all. We all write potential scripts for our lives from an early age. We imagine certain patterns based on what we've observed. For most of the post-National Service generation, the long goodbye to loved ones and friends was discreetly programmed in for fifty on. We had not expected to be holding so many cold hands by hospital beds before we were thirty. The effect was shattering.

Life was rendered more fragile, friendship more important. Politics, of the theoretical variety, paled. Morality of the personal kind came into sharper focus. Sensuality bloomed in the shadow. And our eyes woke up to the world around us – dizzying in its excitements, deceitful in its promises and deeply delightful.

Whatever is written about that culture, at the centre of it will be Kevin Elyot's *My Night With Reg*. This is not an AIDS play, like so many other shrill, hysterical Aids plays. It is first and foremost a great play. Its starting point is Aids, and the simple premise of a group of gay friends who have all at one time or another slept with Reg, a carrier of the virus. From there it spreads its exploratory grasp. A wonderfully delicate mixture of comedy, pathetic hope and vicious tragedy, it manages to skate over the deaths of many without ever cheating on their dignity. It achieves an extraordinary weightlessness, never belabouring its own depth of emotion. It manages to keep flying around, tracing delicate patterns over the ice, without succumbing to the pressure and the desire to tumble. Just as the gay community somehow managed during that extraordinary time, remaining light to the end.

A number of dramaturgical streams run into *Reg*. The device of picking an act up *in medias res* and letting the audience pick up where they are as they go along, owes a certain amount to Chekhov. The switching of sympathy around among the characters recalls Somerset Maugham and Rattigan. The domestic, flat-bound setting grows out of 1980s Bush naturalism (itself the angry grandchild of thirties drawing room comedy). And through it all runs an almost Japanese precision and formal beauty, a cool understatement. None of these sources are of course revealed. *Reg* looks completely original at every turn, its new content revealing a new form, but it is built on solid ground.

Elyot is no one-hit wonder. He wrote one of the earliest and most successful coming-out plays, *Coming Clean*, and a later beautiful time play, *The Day I Stood Still*, about falling in love, as well as much else. The same virtues of delicacy, formal experiment, exquisite characterization, inform each of those plays. In time, when and if the cloud that hangs over *My Night* recedes, they may prove to be greater achievements. But *Reg* caught its moment, and helped many to get through it.

Peter Flannery

The boundaries and limits of behaviour and power were a bit opaque to me when I began as Artistic Director at the Bush. I went to an awards do, early in my time there, sponsored by a drinks company who had come up with a new blend of whisky and ginger. They were handing it out free. Big mistake. In the course of an evening, I stole two plays off other theatres, offered about six people jobs (including to my eventual shame two people the same job), tried to seduce a critic, and, as the *coup de grâce*, offered the sexual favours of a member of the Bush team to Peter Flannery in return for a new play. Classy.

I had just seen and then read *Singer*. *Singer* was everything theatre wants to be. A big story, crossing decades and continents; a genuine hero, attracting and repelling sympathy; a rampaging narrative energy, sweeping up great and small in its wake; political bite, profound insights, wild humour, graceful language, acute characterization and sharp heartbreak. And it was all wrapped up in that impossible combination of complete mess and perfect form that theatre aspires to and hardly ever hits. A humdinger, and a natural extension of the glorious work in *Our Friends in the North*, which began as a stage play.

Nothing before or since has given me greater optimism about the future. Nothing has caused greater pessimism than the fact that he hasn't written another play since. I loathe the ceaseless whining about losing writers to television. Writers are grown-ups, and they go where they want to go (and where the money is). The choice is theirs, and to portray them constantly as naïve children being seduced by the evil demi-god of television does no service to anyone. Television can also be a distinguished and distinctive medium, as Flannery himself has proved. But still one hankers, and one yearns.

It always surprises me that more of a fuss was not made of *Singer* at the time, and that so little mention of it has been made since. A score of teeny, clever, neurotic plays that have been written since have been way over-praised as the Second Coming. It's almost as if it was too rich a meal, to sharp-sweet a flavour for jaded palates. As with Helen Edmondson's *The Clearing*, it suffered for its own achievement.

Brad Fraser

Brad Fraser was the early prophet, the John the Baptist of the brutalist school that flourished in the mid-nineties. A lot of the tricks that tired by the end of the nineties, the rimming, the sadism, the antibodies, the sexual frankness, the cool irony in the face of outrage, began with Fraser. His first play, *Unidentified Human Remains*, struck me as a glib bit of sado-masochistic chic on reading it. But both *Remains*, and his later work, *Poor Superman*, gained hugely in performance. In highly mobile, weightless productions, that approached the shock and horror with a deliberately lightweight disaffection, the plays gained immeasurable strength. They became high-definition cartoon soaps, with the capacity to twist mood on a sixpence. They could switch from camp to tragedy to frivolity with breathtaking speed. It was a style that many later imitated, without Fraser's casual freshness.

Poor Superman also boasted one of my favourite lines of the nineties, a perfect consummation of the folly of falling in love with someone younger. An elder artist stares balefully at his ex, a waiter who has just made a cheerfully incoherent speech about sorting his life out. He murmurs, 'How could I ever drown in such a puddle?'

The single most startling fact about Brad Fraser, given the shock, the wit, the imagination, the wildness, is a simple one. He's Canadian.

Michael Frayn

The best sort of delirious laughter is the type that induces a headache. When the noise around you, the noise travelling up your own jaw, the effort of shaking and the sheer *din* of it all just pounds into your cranium and makes it wince with pain. It's chaos at its best, and abandonment at its least dangerous. The whole theatrical dream of transforming a group of individuals into a tribe is never better achieved than by such laughter. Sentimentality can induce common tears, but is based on a lie; musicals can spread euphoria, but are undone by their own synthetic manipulation; tragedy can chill the bone, but isolates as much as it draws together. The one form that can truly gather folk together in a wild lawless naked dementia is a comedy or at best a farce.

That's how I remember *Noises Off*, surely one of the most perfect farces ever written. I saw it one night at the Savoy years ago, and remember the audience like a Hogarth drawing. Fat old fellows sweating and bug-eyed, women red-faced and weeping, young ones shrieking their heads off, buttons bursting, and throughout this incessant demented laughter. A group that arrived as a quiet timid Friday night shuffle of weariness, left as a wild exhilarated babble of Elizabethans.

The play follows the travails of a tacky provincial production of a second-rate play. The first act shows a less than happy rehearsal, the second act goes backstage at an early and even less happy show, and the third act shows a rapidly decomposing performance itself. The theatrical types on display are as stock as the characters in the play within the play, and the friction between the two sets of caricatures is delicious.

The glorious paradox, or trick of it, was that all this lunacy was achieved by the most rigorous intellectual control. *Noises Off* is the most beautiful construct. It is a tired old truism, but it is put together like an extraordinarily complex watch. Each part is perfectly calibrated, delicately integrated and complements perfectly each other part. Only the most coolly distant mind could have put together such a perfect imagining of insanity; only the most rigid control could create such unbridled madness.

A similar paradox ghosted around the heart of *Copenhagen*, Frayn's most recent success. A play on an egghead topic, it managed to achieve the most fiercely emotional effect. Centred around nuclear physics and the meeting between Niels Bohr and Heisenberg in Copenhagen in 1941, it touches on science, ethics, art and the whole shebang. The discussions are undiluted intellectual tussles, yet Frayn drafts in an extraordinary emotional power to fuse the thoughts together.

At his best Frayn performs the most dangerous highwire act. When he's not at his best he falls off. When there aren't any hidden currents of electricity running underneath the intellectual dryness, well, it's just dry. Some of his work can end up rather like a fashionable 1970s dish, called chicken in hay. Basically this was simply slowly cooking a chicken in a bed of hay. Whatever juice there was was drained out of the meat, which retained its flavour, somehow rendered even more delicate, yet lost its force. The taste was still there, but somehow at a distance. Desiccation abounds, both in style and content.

This fault is for me slightly more glaring in the Chekhov

translations. There's no doubting their fidelity to the original, nor their nuance, nor their poise. Yet they fatally lack the robustness, the edginess and the salt of Chekhov. The critical acceptance of Frayn's translations as the standard to be set has a lot to do with the way we have remade Chekhov in a false English middle-class genteel mould. In our stereotypical way, we are allowed the flavour, but only when it's been softened.

Yet when Frayn sings, he sings the song electric. When his perception is trained on the essential madness of the everyday, he unlocks the audience's sense of the lunacy that surrounds them. And that can release wild laughter, or a little gentle fear and trembling.

Brian Friel

What we cannot speak about we must pass over in silence.
  (Top man.)

Christopher Fry

Amazingly, the mid-century's brightest star, the man who was going to revive the fortunes of verse drama, and who then disappeared from our radar like a downed plane, is still going strong. Somewhere in a garden in Chichester.

I've very little acquaintance with the work, and have no claim to any authority on it. I've found access to its mysteries difficult after several attempts. Yet many of my father's generation, whose judgement I respect hugely, adore it and can quote chunks from memory. His Victorian decorativeness, the almost pre-Raphaelite piling on of imagery to burnish and re-burnish, is increasingly indigestible for palates that are so trained on the spare detail, the minimal flourish.

Fry fell foul of that lean spareness when Beckett rose to prominence. He fell foul of the raging of youth, when Osborne started commanding the front pages. Principally, though he got entangled in a meaningless argument about poetry and the theatre. The angry young man generation were all supposed to be reacting against the verse and verbal excesses of Fry and Eliot. There can be no argument here because there is one simple truth: there is no theatre without poetry. It matters naught if it's written in verse, prose or little words scattered about the page: if it isn't poetic, it has no place in the theatre. Anything in a show, from the lights to the props to the tunes to the words has to aspire to the condition of poetry. Its rhythm, colour, shape, size, mood, volume has got to balance, match and syncopate with the rhythm, colour, shape, size, mood and volume of whatever surrounds it. It don't mean a thing if it ain't got that swing.

Fry certainly has the swing. The fact that he used an archaic form to express it became a slightly unfair stick to beat him with.

Athol Fugard

One of my most forlorn evenings of the 1990s was watching Fugard's *Playland* at the Donmar. A tough, shrewd, unforgiving play, in a beautiful, austere production, with the majestic John Kani at its centre, the event had a dignity and a wisdom that you rarely see. This princely event had attracted an audience of about thirty people. The Donmar is a fun place when it's got a hit, but when it hasn't, all the wind goes out of its sails. Since it's a venue whose *raison d'être* is to be successful, when it's not, it loses its meaning. Sadly, when it puts on work of rigour or substance, much of its audience can be pretty unforgiving.

But it wasn't just the painful exposure, it was the sense that fashion had decided to leave Fugard behind. I overheard some fuckwit voicing the heart-piercingly crass: 'Doesn't he realize it's all over? That apartheid's finished? Can't he find a new subject?' As if that was all *Playland* or any of Fugard's work was about. One of the less pleasing aspects of the nineties was the patronizing contempt for anything deemed to be 'worthy'. The new slicks and style fascists scorned anything of substance, as if it brought disease with it. People printed manifestos eschewing 'worthiness' as if it was the equivalent of renouncing fascism. Michael Jackson said in an article that his Channel 4 wouldn't be worthy, as if that were the only way to persuade some people of its worth. It's as if everyone who was once ethical or political has to noisily disclaim any trace of commitment, or they won't be allowed into the club.

Now Fugard isn't worthy, but he certainly doesn't lack substance. To say his plays have no relevance beyond apartheid is like saying Chekhov has no relevance beyond the bourgeois intelligentsia of late-nineteenth-century Russia. His plays will of course have a particular pertinence wherever race is an issue, and wherever oppression is rife, and neither of those are going away in a hurry. But they also deal in love, freedom, friendship and the whole caboose. They are carved out of a burning sense of the importance of the spoken word, and the power of dramatic gesture. They will long outlast the fickleness of public taste, and the audience that re-invented itself in a new self-proclaimed and self-glorying heartlessness.

William Gaminara

The importance of timing. After writing a smoothly accomplished, but unambitious first play, *Back Up the Hearse and Smell the Flowers*, about salesmen, William Gaminara wrote a quite wonderful second, *According to Hoyle*. Unfortunately, it was about poker. It arrived shortly after Patrick Marber's *succès d'estime*, *Dealer's Choice*. Poker in the eyes of the world had been dealt with, and it was time to move on.

This was cruelly unfair. Gaminara's play is a mature, deft and surprising play about men failing to grow up, and hiding from the pressures of adulthood in a weekly poker school. It conveyed the thrill of the game, but remained unseduced by its fake glamour. Where Marber's play is an enthralling but essentially self-admiring piece of urban chic, with a whiff of danger, Gaminara's is a witheringly truthful picture of middle-class boys flailing. The first was written with its eyes on its image, the second with its eyes on its subject. The first took all the awards, the second got some nice reviews then faded away. So it goes . . .

Lucy Gannon

Lucy Gannon is now one of England's most thriving industries. It's extraordinary that a woman whose career began at a small RSC fringe festival, and then had her first full play on at the Bush, has since been responsible for *Soldier Soldier, Branwell, Peak Practice, TripTrap, Hope and Glory,* and tons more prime-time television. Her output is not only prolific; it is also of a uniformly high quality. The television series seem to go a little smelly after a certain amount of time, but in their inception, as with the single dramas, they are tough, humane and wise.

Lucy is an important proof for two arguments. The first is my oft-used Chicken Kiev argument. I frequently rolled this one out when asked to justify the subsidy for the Bush. It is that the Bush is a delicatessen. Twenty years ago the only place you could find Chicken Kiev was in a delicatessen or exclusive restaurant. Now it's as popular as steamed pudding. Last year's haute cuisine is this year's freezer food. What was once an elitist or exclusive flavour becomes over time disseminated into popular culture. So with Lucy (although I'm not sure how she'll feel about the comparison): a voice that first spoke to a fairly exclusive coterie of a hundred a night, within a few years was talking with alarming regularity to fifteen million a night, and with the same passion and insight.

Places like the Bush are the laboratories, the research and development centres. Through their discoveries, through the new flavours they unearth, they keep the soul of the mainstream culture alive.

The second argument Lucy proves, is that it's never too late to start. Her plays began to appear as she was approaching forty, just as she was finishing a long and full career as a social worker. The lessons she learnt, the stories she heard, the pain and the joy she saw, all these are the mulch from which she draws her prolific fictions. They didn't give her the talent to describe – that's something she was born with – but they gave her the stories to tell. Younger writers sometimes find themselves going back to the well for their third or fourth plays and finding it empty. Lucy's well was good and full before she began.

There's nothing remotely trendy about her choice of subject matter. Her first play for the Bush, *Raping the Gold*, was a lyrical imagistic play about the ravages of unemployment on a Derbyshire community. It used the metaphor of an archery club, and archery itself, with a wonderfully sure-footed lack of ostentation. Her second, *Dancing Attendance*, was about an armchair Lear, an ageing cripple who dominates and destroys the life of his devoted daughter. The themes of both – unemployment and tending for the sick – are not the stuff of the dreams of swinging Cool Britannia. But such realities are difficult to ignore. Television and the theatre are fortunate that Lucy has been around to keep them in view.

Pam Gems

The greatest living provider of turns for star actors, Pam Gems has hit on a formula that works. In biopic after biopic, from *Queen Christina*, through *Piaf*, *Camille* and *Marlene*, to *Stanley*, the pattern is the same. She takes a life, real or fictional or a bit of both, gobbles it up, picks out the saltiest, the smelliest and the most controversial moments, then dramatizes them fairly sketchily. She chucks down loosely whatever seems of inherent dramatic merit, then leaves the rest to the star. Intermittently she writes startlingly well, summoning up a period or an inner crisis with a casual phrase, and her plays have a wonderfully big-hearted rough energy, but they're not completely conceived.

It is the looseness of the conception that attracts the actors. They see holes that they can fill, spaces where they can strut their stuff. There is a certain type of actor – often trained early at the RSC – who will say in interviews, 'I don't do new plays, I can't find any that appeal to me', which translates as, 'The parts aren't big enough'. Or there is the even more flagrant type, who say, 'I hate to say this, but the new writing these days just isn't big enough, it's all so small, I need more to work with.' This translates as, 'There aren't enough big speeches where I can stand alone on stage, unrelated to any world or other people, and scream my head off.' For many, there is nothing scarier than a precisely imagined new play, since it forecloses showing off, and showing off, for many, is as necessary as oxygen. It is in part the fault of our response to the classics, where they have atrophied into opportunities for actors to dazzle, rather than the brilliantly imagined dramatic experiences that they are.

Yet Pam Gems provides the bones that the actors can dress with flesh. She has an understanding of outsize personalities, of outsiders, of those who live in conflict between the private and the public, which is rare. She understands stars. It's a reasonably noble calling, since the theatre needs heroes, and any tribe needs to watch the rise and fall, or fall and rise, of those who step outside its small games.

Peter Gill

Peter Gill is a fine proof of the pusillanimity of large parts of the contemporary theatre scene. Without doubt one of the finest directors in the country, no one understands the actor's process better than him, nor how to unleash an actor's energies and imagination. He is also one of our most original and particular writers. Yet for long periods he has been excluded from the centre of our theatre culture simply because he believes in intrinsic value rather than surface glitter. Because he believes that what happens on stage matters.

He fell victim of the ghastly 'theatre must be theatrical' age. The amount of rubbish that was peddled under the cover of this too-stupid-to-deserve-saying platitude beggars belief. Acres of Oxbridge graduates pretending to be chickens, frantic productions whirling around a vacuum, crap actors re-inventing themselves as 'performers', directors doing heavy-handed productions that write their own footnotes and writers who couldn't write a scene finding their inner epic. Theatre *is* theatrical, you nanas. It must be good, it must be wise, it must be truthful, it must be beautiful. Just as film must be, or television must, or poetry, novels, art, whatever. The moment any form starts saying that it must be more itself is the moment that it starts to lose contact with its own task, and, for that matter, reality. And it's at that same moment that it starts to marginalize its own real talents.

Peter hardly helped himself by delivering regular jeremiads about how the theatre world was going steadily to pot. In print, in public and in private, he can be both savage and long. A decent monologue of his can continue carving up the competition for a couple of hours, without even pausing for breath, let alone interruption. And a day after you've listened with rich appreciation to his denunciation of an institution or an individual, you'll hear that he went on to another gathering where he cheerily murdered you. Or you'll read something tart in a paper. But if we can't take a bit of abuse, we're in the wrong game.

The prime virtue of Peter's writing is his dialogue. It is quite extraordinary. It is the definition of the word buoyant. Although studiedly naturalistic, and frequently fastidiously demotic, it has the most wonderful internal rhythm. Scraps of speech, phrases, non sequiturs, repetitions combine to form a music that is both utterly real and strangely operatic. It is the verbal equivalent of a sprung floor. Any dancer will tell you the difference between working on a properly sprung floor, and working on concrete. Similarly, any actor will tell you the difference between speaking lines that have life, and those that are dead. Peter's have an extraordinary bustle of life.

If his plays have one area of difficulty, it is their tribalism. Whatever community he is presenting, whether the gay one, or the Cardiff working-class one which he returns to most frequently, it can sometimes feel as if the audience is being deliberately excluded. There's a sense of anthropology, of watching a group rather than becoming part of them. The tribes aren't just enclosed, they often seem to be actively driving people away. For many, this will be an additional virtue. For me, it's a problem.

The common perception of Gill's work is that it is utterly naturalistic. This is wrong. He uses naturalistic paint, and then splashes it around the theatre in a series of extravagant

Jackson Pollock brushstrokes. The result is a genuine expressionism, rather than the mess that habitually masquerades as such. But the heart of his work is people, and people talking, the heart of all good theatre. And it's that reminder of what theatre should be, that makes people turn away from him in the dog days.

John Godber

Wherever you are in the world, if you're with a group of more than ten male actors, it's a fair bet that two of them will have been in a production of *Bouncers* by John Godber. And that they will still remember it as if it was printed on their genetic code. And that at some point they may well launch into a routine from it. It's almost like a complicated dance routine – once it's ground into the fabric of your muscles, it's impossible to forget.

We're constantly being force fed the blah blah about Godber being the third most performed playwright in Britain (behind Shakespeare and Ayckbourn), without acknowledging that he has a considerable international impact as well. The same virtues must work all over – energy, storytelling, street poetry, pumped up rhythm, exuberant physicality, broad humour and the pathos of deflated masculinity. He is a deliberate, successful and triumphant populist.

Regionalism is of course a virtue, up to a point. It is important for any writer to find a world, whether real or imaginary or a blend, to create it truthfully and with care, and thus use it as a microcosm for the wider world. It's the amplifier through which a writer creates volume from some small electrical impulse. It's vital for a writer to be true to that region. Without it, writing soon becomes pale and bland. There's a sort of Eurowriting, which began on the continent and is creeping in over here, where faceless people meet in some nameless location, and spout phrases at each other. This is about as boring as it's possible for writing to be. Flavourless and pretentious at the same time.

So truth to the particular is a good thing. But aggressive regionalism is something else, and this is where Godber's work for me hits its boundaries. There's an underlying suspicion of the wider world, a discreet 'fook you and all your poncey nonsense', which diminishes everybody. It's a sort of cultural Serbery, an inverse snobbery tied up with a large-scale inferiority/superiority complex. When challenged this often boils down to an 'I know what I like' defence, which is as good a definition as any of the death of culture. Any cultural artefact has to absorb as wide a range of influences as possible, while retaining its own character. The contradiction between those two acts is one of the many tensions that make it live. Respecting the impulse and respecting the education. The greatest works of art achieve a balance between the two. Occasionally, for me, Godber leans too heavily on the impulse.

Murray Gold

Sometimes directing and producing a play can be pure, unmitigated joy – a blend of Plato's ideal kindergarten with drink, drugs and sex sprinkled on top. And sometimes it can be long, slow, unmitigated torture – like eternal rehab, a babble or a Babel of screeching egos. For some unknown reason, it is a frequent and general truth that it is almost always the unhappy experiences that lead to success, and the joyous ones that lead to failure.

Although this truth is generally known in the theatre, it is rarely admitted to. The consequences are too appalling. It opens the door on a level of cosmic injustice we can't bear the thought of. Why is it that when we're surrounded by good, kind colleagues, we always feel a tremor of fear, and when we're working with monsters, we often feel security? Is it some inner apprehension of the fact that the bad and the greedy will always be rewarded, and the good stepped on? The cruel and vicious often seem to die smoothly in their sleep at a ripe old age, while those full of love and kindness and modesty are snapped at the twig stage. We've waited an awfully long time for the meek to inherit the earth, and we're still stuck with David Hare.

Anyway producing Murray Gold's play *50 Revolutions* in the boldest manner possible – opening a new play by an unknown writer with a cast of sixteen in the West End doesn't happen every day – was one of the most joyous experiences I've had in the theatre. True to the above truth, it got reasonably bullied by the critics, did poor business, attracted a passionate cult following and remained very pleasingly proud of itself. And none of the silly game of success or failure had anything to do with the inherent quality of the experience. It remained a bright and brilliant play, beautifully acted (in a rather lumpen production).

The reasons why directors choose to direct particular plays remain multifarious. Some do it because they're unemployed, and need to earn some money; some because they can spy a commercial hit; some because they see a shrewd career move ('I've just done a musical, I'll do a Beckett. That'll keep them guessing'); some because they want an adventure; many because they want to meet large numbers of their desired sex in undomestic environments.

Those who are lucky enough to be able to make reasonably pure choices, fall into two camps. There are those who read something and think 'Ah, I see what I can do *with* this', and those who think 'Ah, I see what I can do *for* this'. The former are those endowed with the vision thing, theatreati who like to stamp their mark all over their work. Their signature doesn't appear discreetly in the bottom right hand corner, it's scrawled all over the middle, often obscuring what the picture is of, shrieking 'Me. Me. All my own work!' The latter frequently don't know why they decide to do something, they just feel a tug or a twitch in the heart or stomach, a small tightness like the beginning of a fever that tells them simply, 'You have to follow this through to the end.' After that there's no choice, you simply have to get that work on stage. It doesn't mean you'll do it well, it just means you have to get it on.

Like a painter when he sees a particular fall of light, or nature caught in an object, or the harmony in an arrangement of life. Or the musician when his mind burps up a chord sequence from nowhere, or when the happy accidence of the world fuses some sounds to set off a rhythm or a melody. Or the writer when scattered images in the storehouse of the mind start to coincide into the mystery that is a story, when those images start to relate in a way that is just and true to themselves and surprising to their creator. It is the same peril or thrill as falling in love – the same walk into the basement with the flickering lightbulb. Feeling the twitch doesn't mean you're an artist. You need all the accessories to get you to the end – talent, gift, ambition, need, tradition, ruthlessness, monomania, generosity, industry, courage – but the twitch is the right place to begin.

Anyway all this guff about the self-effacement of the director, it's probably time to mention the play. So. I'd been aware of Murray's writing for some time, having read a couple of his early plays, and seen his light and delightful adaptation of the *Candide* at the Gate. But I was entirely unprepared for *50 Revolutions* when I first read it.

It's a lawless play. With a Jacobean vigour, and a Jane Austenish lightness of touch, it roams through the streets of London on a Friday and a Saturday night. Seamlessly segueing from sharp naturalistic dialogue to rich rhetoric to surreal invention to the angst-ridden techno-jargon of relationship speak, Murray's play includes homeless drifters, actors, musicians, managers, doctors, nurses, bouncers, stars, producers in its large embrace. He even, with an expressionist flourish, fractures a bouncer and brings on stage his feminine side and his conscience. It's a play that looks at the wild variety of contemporary life, and of contemporary theatre tradition, and happily cackles, 'Come on in, there's room for all of you here.' It's not easy to be inclusive at the end of such an exploded century, but Murray manages it. And he does it all while retaining a classic comic structure, ending at a church as a funeral competes with a wedding for the attentions of a vicar. Big and beautiful.

Because of the exigencies of British culture there was only one way to put it on. In Germany, you'd have six months, thirty actors, an orchestra and a truckload of money for the set. In England, the only way to do it was in three weeks, at a charge and on a prayer. It hadn't quite found its necessary lightness of touch in time for press night – almost entirely through wrong choices of mine – so it wasn't seen for what it is – the first play of the twenty-first century. But once it had, it was greatly and widely adored.

And was it the hybrid vigour, the effusion that twanged my heartstrings, and made me have to do it? No. It was one simple exchange. A muted love story between two young homeless girls is threaded through the play. At the end one of them dies, and in the final Mozartian act outside a church her ghost appears to her friend. The deserted quizzes the departed: 'Lou? / Yeah . . . / I thought you said you'd never leave me./ Ah, well . . . / I don't like it on my own.' It's a beautiful simplicity arrived at through a sea of mess. It's a distillation of painful experience for Murray, and so for many of the rest of us. It meant that I had to get it on.

Simon Gray

The poet laureate of dyspepsia. Simon Gray has produced an enormous oeuvre, possibly too large a one. Hardly a year goes by without a new West End play popping up, together with a book about the experience, followed by a televisualization of the book. All that, and an original teleplay or screenplay on top. Since he's clearly a man who's not at a loss when it comes to enjoying himself, one wonders where he finds time for all the writing. I say too large an oeuvre, since his gift is clear and enormous, and it would have been good to have seen it more purely distilled.

The books are unmatched as records of contemporary theatre-making. He writes with an easy, gentle and compelling prose style. He catches brilliantly the mix of booze, elation and paranoia that provide the rocket fuel to launch a show. Without adopting a moral tone, he observes with a gentle acerbity the vanities, hypocrisies and lies of most involved in theatre. It's a shame that he has spent less time in the subsidized sector, since it would have been enjoyable to read his reflections.

The plays, a long list from *Butley* through to *Life Support*, live in an exclusive, cosmopolitan world. They are delightful entertainments, warm inquisitions into the pampered. There have been the occasional excursions, including the wonderful *Rear Column*, set in the back of Stanley's expedition to find Livingstone in Africa, but by and large they have inhabited the liberal, boho intelligentsia of

London. There is, of course, nothing wrong per se with taking a limited world and observing it minutely. A miniature can be just as revealing as a wide canvas. And Gray observes this clan, with its disaffiliation, ennui and casual appetites, beautifully. There's no hysterical condemnation, nor is there any soft-soaping. He writes with the truth of understanding. The people come to life, the world is real, the stories are natural. So why do the plays leave me slightly peckish?

It's probably more than anything the subject matter itself. Literary London or media London has only a limited dramatic potential. You can ardently believe in the virtures of presenting life under the microscope, but the choice of specimen on the slide still has a profound effect.

Career envy, sexual betrayal, bisexual power games and emotional desiccation will only stretch an evening so far. Headaches, hangovers and the occasional bout of inner emptiness are without doubt the substance of most of our lives, but make for slightly thin drama. This is not to say that theatre has to live exclusively in a zone of myth. There's nothing scarier than the thin-voiced and bespectacled fascist who talks about the return to verse drama, and exploring our Arthurian heritage. But it can't veer too far the other way either, into an entirely sublunary world. Myth and malt whisky, magic and make-up, should be allowed to walk hand-in-hand in a theatre.

There is also a tiny arrogance in their claims for universality. Loss of feeling, and lack of connection, are privileges for a few, not paradigms for humanity. Hampstead may be living in a perpetual state of the *Four Quartets*, tiny echoes of redemption in an empty sounding chamber, but Somalia certainly isn't, and nor, for that matter, is Weston-Super-Mare.

Where Simon Gray scores most is with his television work. For my money, he is up there with Dennis Potter,

Alan Bleasdale and Jimmy McGovern, as an innovator for
and exploiter of that medium. There is something about
television, its squashed aesthetic and its need for quotidian
accuracy, which suits these writers best. On television,
Gray can be frightening, magical, spiritual, wise and
passionate. This looks like a back-handed compliment, but
in fact there are far fewer writers whose talents are released
in this way by television, than by either theatre or cinema.
More than anything television is a chronicle of our times,
and Gray one of its few Bedes.

Trevor Griffiths

How many people these days could get away with leaving a pub after a convivial night, turning around at the door and raising a clenched fist in farewell salute? Without looking like a complete twonk. Precious few. Trevor Griffiths is one of them. There's no shortage of old playwrights with clenched fists, making youth blush by shouting 'Right on' at them, clutching Chilean poets to their breasts like ideological trusses. Few of them can carry it off. Griffiths can. By maintaining and living up to his youthful ideals – not with ease certainly, with a labyrinthine complexity, but with magnificent heart – Griffiths has survived as a beacon, lighting the way backwards to the fierce passions of the late sixties and early seventies, and forward to what still could be a better future.

We had the privilege of presenting his most recent play *Who Shall Be Happy . . . ?* towards the end of my time at the Bush. After bringing through and introducing so many young cubs, it was a surprising pleasure to allow room for the gentle roar of a senior from the pride. *Who Shall Be Happy . . . ?* is a passionate and playful entertainment. It places Danton in a cell awaiting his execution. He teases his guard, keeping him uncertain as to whether he really is Danton or an actor pretending to be him. A friendship grows between them as the execution approaches. All the while, Danton, lost in a miasma of sex, sense and the lies of power, tries to reach back into his past to discover some truth he can cling to. A brilliant portrait of a grizzled and ageing revolutionary, he spends the time the play observes trying to rediscover the germ that grew into the desire to change the world.

A question haunts him, 'Who shall be happy . . . ?' It keeps returning to him; 'Who shall be happy if . . . ?', and growing all the while, 'Who shall be hapy if not . . . ?', until finally the memory appears clear as a crisp, spring day. As a young lawyer, flushed with success and hope, on the way to a public meeting, a figure from a crowd had grasped him, looked square into his soul, and asked the only question: 'Who shall be happy if not everyone?' With that memory clear in his mind, Danton can walk a little easier to his death.

It is a wonderfully structured rhetorical, political and emotional climax when that question appears, and a wonderful trick to present a question as a defining truth. Griffiths is not daft, nor is he doctrinaire. He doesn't believe that everyone can be happy. But maybe he does believe that a man can only live easy if he *wants* happiness for everyone. Not for a caste or a class or a race or a group or an individual, but for everyone. This is no glib political message, this is the journey and the resolution that Lear describes, and in a different way Hamlet. The resolution is a glorious one, but too glorious for this day and age, where any idea of the greater happiness of the community is treated as a form of revived Stalinism. But at the end of the day, the question is perfect. Who *shall* be happy, if not everyone?

Once you've written a play as great as *Comedians*, there's little else that you have to do in a life. That play's perfection of form, its completely credible specificity and its strength as a metaphor on a variety of levels need no legitimizing here. It stands happily for itself. After that Griffiths could have quite easily shut up shop, and spent a happy life watching revivals and touring the world's universities. The other great temptation having hit that height would have been to have repeated it in some form, subtly adjusting the shape but essentially dancing the same dance. But Griffiths' great adventure has been his continual desire to experiment in form. Time and again since his first big hit, *Occupations*, and through to *The Gulf Between Us*, *Thatcher's Children* and *Who Shall Be Happy . . . ?*, Griffiths has sought out new forms and new structures to encase and liberate new content.

One of my first glimpses of the inadequacy of critical response in this country was when I saw Griffiths being interrogated by two critics on a late-night TV programme. He was on low and meek form, the critics sensed his weakness, and they moved in for the kill. For twenty minutes they bullied him, lecturing him on dramatic structure and telling him how the masters wrote their plays. These two journalists, who had never written anything remembered for longer than a day, were lecturing and patronizing the man who wrote *Comedians* and *The Party* about dramatic structure. I literally boggled. It was one of the most distasteful things I've ever seen on the telly, worse than the worst German porn. It was as if they thought he had no idea what he was doing, and was incapable of making his own dramatic choices. They wanted him to continue in the two or three act Ibsenite mould, to have become a boulevard-with-chic-frisson merchant like David Hare. Griffiths is braver, and seeks out the new. Such courage is rarely rewarded in its own lifetime.

And he made it a joy to participate with him. It's often a jumpy relationship between a producer or a presenter and the director of a show. As the former, you'll generally have the best sense of what works in your own space, as the latter you'll always have the best sense of how to retain and enhance the spirit of your own show. It's a potential minefield in terms of accommodating both, although the director, unless he or she is an idiot, should always be allowed pole position. This relationship was never easier in my experience than with Trevor Griffiths. He has a beguiling natural modesty and enquiry that made him seek out comments, suggestions and notes from everyone around. Humility, as Eliot said, is endless.

Griffiths hasn't arrived at such creative generosity easily. He's been on a difficult path. He doesn't ask 'Who shall be happy . . . ?' with any glib presumption, he lets you know you have to earn the right to ask it. But having walked the path, and earned the right, we can only hope he continues to do so. What is? Struggle.

Nick Grosso

Nick Grosso is one of the few playwrights around who writes in Chinese. By which I don't mean indecipherable script, but Chinese style. He writes still pools. He writes a series of them. They become a play. Those pools don't have to carry significance, they don't have to act as symbols, they don't have to follow all those tired old western civilization moves – crisis, resolution, self-knowledge, catharsis – that come at you across the dancefloor on an evening out like some sweaty old seducer. Grosso's still pools don't have to do any of that. They simply have to be. And be simple.

In his three plays so far, *Peaches*, *Sweetheart* and *A Real Classy Affair*, there are no rampaging plots, no enormous situations, no conflated dramatic scenes. He finds simple, quiet, but significant moments in the lives of young people, and presents them in all their unexceptional banality. There is a limpid, banal music to the dialogue, although less so in *A Real Classy Affair*, which has a shade more testosterone than the other two, possibly too much for the delicate Chinese pastels that surround it.

His work is beautiful in its lack of ambition, and hugely ambitious. Like a miniature, an icon or a Chinese watercolour, the fascination is in the detail. Everything has to be perfectly placed. Nothing can desire an effect, it has to just be. Critics and others chivvy Grosso for not being ambitious, for not writing some mythical state of the nation piece that doesn't exist and nobody wants. Some of that strain seemed to appear in *Classy Affair*. He should forget the others and just follow his own star. It's fairly special.

John Guare

I can't claim any more profound acquaintance with John Guare than *Six Degrees of Separation*, nor any more profound feelings than simply awe and delight at such a wonderful play.

Rather like one of those microlite airplanes, it glides over huge acres of territory – through race, contemporary identity, class, ideas about art, the sickness of aspiration, and the necessity of imagination – without revealing the faintest trace of a motor or an engine. It achieves the condition which so much modern art dreams of attaining. It is effortless.

It also contains a speech that can rank alongside 'O reason not the need . . .' as a definition of the difficulty of being human, one of the most probing questions about our contemporary culture:

'The imagination has been so debased that imagination –
being imaginative – rather than the linchpin of our
existence now stands as a synonym for something
outside ourselves like science fiction or some new use for
tangerine slices on raw pork chops . . . The imagination
has moved out of the realm of being our link, our most
personal link, with our inner lives and the world outside
that world – this world we share.
    Why has imagination become a synonym for style?
    I believe that the imagination is the passport we create
to take us into the real world.

I believe the imagination is another phrase for what is most uniquely us.'

If you substitute the word vision for imagination, you get much of what is wrong with contemporary theatre. Vision, instead of a means of understanding the self, or the world, or the relationship between the two, has become a few moody lighting states, or making a house fall down, or making everything purple. Vision, the quality that makes theatre necessary and health-giving and important, has been substituted by display. And as long as it stays that way theatre will wither.

There is no shortage of vision in *Six Degrees*. It reveals truths with the most elegant insouciance. How you get a play to bounce on the winds of its own invention, floating dizzily above its source material, is a mystery known only to a few – to Aristophanes, to Plautus, to Shakespeare, to Sheridan, to Wilde, to Coward and, from the evidence of this play, to Guare.

Lee Hall

Captain Fantastic. At present the most prolific authorial presence in England – an adaptation here, a version there, a monologue in the studio, a farce in the West End, a new film at Cannes. Young writers are often given stern lectures by theatres and agents about the dangers of over-commissioning, about taking on too much responsibility and burning out too fast. Lee Hall has blown all such expectations in the air. Somehow he manages to keep many thousands of hungry mouths happy with a few loaves of a talent.

Hall's versions are a chutzpah–soaked mix of a lot of coasting, a few good jokes, a nice turn of phrase and an ability to get away with bald sentimentality. It's an effective pot noodle formula that has delivered lively adaptations of *The Servant of Two Masters*, *Puntila and His Man Matti*, *Mother Courage* and will work for probably about fifteen others. Much the same mixture of qualities informs his own work, about which I feel an unease that I can't quite identify.

He is an unabashed populist. His comedy, *Cooking With Elvis*, is as broad as a comedy can get, piling sex on dirty jokes on cripples on naked men. There's a glorious abandon to it, and the deliberate tastelessness gives it a sort of modernity, but there's some lack of centre. Farce is meant to be a whirl of activity around a vacuum. But that vacuum is defined by a strong sense of the humanity it lacks. The madness of what ensues in the best farce is the denial of a sensibility that may not be present, but has to be felt. I don't see that in this play, I just see a spiral of madness that serves itself. It just wants to be funny.

In a similar way but a different key, with *Spoonface Steinberg*, it is hard to perceive the centre. This began as a radio monologue, then became a television film, then a stage play. It is the painfully sad story of an autistic Jewish child dying of cancer, and a display of her courage in dealing with it, and her discovery of a sort of redemption. Everything that's meant to be there is there. It's fresh, idiomatic, deeply sad, then it journeys towards the light. Again, it's just hard to perceive a centre. There's something profoundly inauthentic going on. It borrows pain (even partaking in some minor larceny from the Holocaust) to weigh the spirits. It manufactures redemption to lighten them. As an exercise in low-level tragedy, it's perfect. As a work of art, it's nowhere. It's hard or impossible to tell where it comes from. It just wants to be tragic.

To be a populist is an entirely creditable occupation. Lee Hall is also wonderfully talented. Thus far it's hard to tell if he wants anything more than success. But if that is all he wants, in this world, he'll almost certainly get it.

Christopher Hampton

The invisible man. Christopher Hampton disappears into his work more effectively than any other writer. No other has covered such a range of genres or content, nor has any other remained so brilliantly hidden from view. Consider the variety. He makes David Bowie look as protean as Rolf Harris.

There's the first play of untidy adolescent passion, *Total Eclipse* – the story of the destructive love of Verlaine and Rimbaud. There's the play of political anger, with Brechtian freedom of construction, *Savages* – a cautionary tale of the first and third worlds butting up against each other. There's the well-made West End play with boulevard polish, *The Philanthropist* – an intellectual high jinks piece about an academic undone by his childish love for all. There's the study in Strindbergian intensity, *Treats* – a rather 1970s tale of adultery and control in a pained triangle. And most famously there's the Restoration recreation with high, light and biting wit, *Les Liaisons Dangereuses* – the adaptation of the Laclos novel. In addition to this, there's a slew of translations and adaptations, climaxing most happily for his bank balance in *Art*.

It's almost as if he's an actor in a permanent state of audition, looking for the perfect role that will fit him like a glove. Yet every time he tries a costume on, it fits. He brings it off so easily and so well, he gets bored and has to look elsewhere. The search for the personality is more intriguing than the discovery.

Amazingly he even managed to write an autobiographical play, *The White Hotel*, about his childhood in Egypt, and yet still to give nothing away. It was an excellent play – all his work is excellent – but he assumed the role of the writer revealing himself so deftly, that he managed to give the impression of not actually revealing much about himself, after all.

He is the supreme technician, the supreme playwright in the sense of a maker of plays. His writing is always fiendishly clever, exquisitely light of touch and almost perfectly constructed. His art is that of the Wedgwood or the Chippendale or the Stradivarius. It is about making perfect objects that accidentally attain art, rather than the full-out assault on art with the personal statement and the large ego. It's the 'look at this' approach rather than 'listen to me'. His craft is an example to all.

Chris Hannan

How can you account for or explain talent of this order? Chris Hannan had the archetypal late-twentieth-century romantic beginnings, a working-class Glaswegian who became a star Oxford scholar. But even that can't explain a gift of his magnitude.

The traces of many different sources infect his work – wild, dark humour, a probing philosophical mind, a deep sense of literary tradition, a political anger. But that doesn't make him a scattered blend of 7:84, Plato, T. S. Eliot and Jimmy Logan. He is a mature artist and as such he absorbs influences into his marrow, then lets them talk through him, rather than displaying then on the surface. The voice that results, a high confection of burlesque and blood, is uniquely his own, and all the buried and invisible influences add depth and flavour.

Chris has written four plays to match the world: *Elizabeth Gordon Quinn*, an invigorating blend of Brecht and high farce, about an insanely genteel matriarch in a 1920s Glasgow tenement; *The Evil Doers*, a lacerating and hilarious portrait of a family in meltdown as they blunder their way through one day in a postmodern Glasgow celebrating its European year of culture; *The Baby*, a play set in Pompey's Rome (you don't get many of those), following a group of professional mourners and the mission of one to take revenge for the death of her child; and *Shining Souls*, a despairing existential city comedy, set in a contemporary Glasgow, centred on one woman's attempt to choose which of two Billys, named Billy One and Billy Two, to wed.

These descriptions do scant justice to the plays and their level of ambition. Each is tightly and carefully plotted; each is written with care and truth; each is written in a uniquely rich style that can crack a joke, reveal a soul, break a heart, soar and swoop without drawing breath. But within a framework of supercharged lyrical naturalism, how far he travels. *The Evil Doers*, within the paranoid ramblings of a young, highly stressed loan shark, opens up visions of chaos way beyond that inside the man's head. Entire cosmologies are invoked both of the universe and a single atom. In *The Baby*, an epic piece of storytelling to match any play of Brecht's, the death of socialism walks as a third alongside the play never revealing itself but ever present. In *Shining Souls*, questions of identity and of the nature of truth fall into a stew heated by the sun god.

No one has looked harder into the new non-political world than Chris; no one has more probing questions about identity and gender in the new shiny kingdom; no one has worried so fiercely over what it means to do good now; and no one has made manifest more completely the enduring necessity of God and love.

So why is he not more celebrated? His plays have played to large houses, but he's never been brought into the centre of the canon. Partly because he offers too rich a meal. We are not robust in our appetites any more. We prefer a glib salad of entertainment – some trite pseudo-shocking sex comedy – to a full rich meal. As ever we worship achievement, no matter how small, and loathe aspiration. We love a finely turned elm burr bowl, and are scared of the woods.

Due to a discreet racism in some of the critical fraternity, there's a thinly concealed presumption that the Scots are best at jokes, music hall and blunt political statement. When they reveal themselves to be more subtle and sophisticated than the Sassenachs, the critical trend is to patronize. The first production of *Shining Souls*, a broad and upbeat affair, was predominantly praised on its first outing in Edinburgh. Its upfront exuberance was celebrated. When Chris himself redirected it in London, drawing out its strains of romance and quest, it was treated as if he had let the side down somehow.

But principally, and this will sound naff, he's too good for us. Some writers catch on immediately because they write what people want, some take longer to find their audience, because they write what people need. When Peter Hall revived *Waiting for Godot* in 1998, forty-two years after his first production of the play, it proved the first time it had been commercially successful. People don't always like to be reminded of what they need. They often prefer to be manipulated through shallow ponds than to be chidden into jumping into the sea.

The lack of celebration pisses Chris off, and rightly so. He believes in popular art, he writes popular plays, but the true and deep generosity which he pours into his work, is not always matched in the response. He's a delightful man with an enormous zeal for life. Before he settled down, it would be a bold man who could predict at the beginning of an evening with Chris where he would be at its conclusion. He floats with enthusiasm (if that's possible) wherever the tide of life takes him, whether it be a country house or a crack den. The same detached vivacity electrifies his work.

David Hare

I'm always reminded of David Hare whenever I attend a children's birthday party, and it's time to go. Just in case the children haven't enjoyed themselves enough, they're always given a brightly coloured plastic bag, containing a sweet, a puzzle and a toy. It's called a 'going home' present. It's not dissimilar to a David Hare play – a couple of hours of stimulation and excitement, then, to take home, three aphorisms, an issue and a moral, all synthetically wrapped up.

The most intriguing question about David Hare is how such a flat writer has come to be afforded such a mountainous reputation. It still baffles me. I presume the answer can only be a matter of desperate ambition. He simply wanted it badly. Which is all the more surprising given where he began.

Tumbling along the pot-holed A-roads of Britain, throughout much of 1972, there must have been a dirty van, in the back of which sat the creative nucleus of Portable Theatre: Snoo Wilson, Howard Brenton and David Hare. Big hair, big sideburns, big Marx, big Gramsci. These were the classic over-educated firebrands, desperate to transform the world and find theatre a new role within it.

Each in a way exemplified a different facet of the emotions that fund any form of utopianism. Snoo was the righteous soldier of Imagination, the great cloudburst of fancy, who could reconfigure history, society and matter with his deranged conceptions. Howard Brenton fought the good fight for Romance, reaching down into hearts and souls to uncover goodness and wickedness, seeing heroes and villains all around, with Shelley and Byron floating over them all. And David Hare saw to the heart of Power. And having diagnosed its mechanisms, he decided that he wanted some for himself.

Portable Theatre didn't last long. Its mutual contradictions were no doubt too great. But it's fascinating to remember it, and to see the distance travelled since. So how did the radical long hair of Portable become the dramatic laureate of the establishment? How did the co-conspirator of Brenton and Wilson against the state, become the purveyor of T.I.E to the haute bourgeoisie in the form of *Via Dolorosa*?

This was an astonishing case of the distance travelled by the old British left. Here was the old scourge of the establishment, who had now become Sir David, a millionaire, delivering his own monologue, to the great and good, about how the Palestine situation is an incurable muddle, in a theatre (the Royal Court) whose development director was the heir apparent to the Murdoch empire. Now any one of those bits of moral tergiversation would be easy to take, two would be perfectly possible, three would be difficult but *six*?

And how did the writer of *Fanshen* – one of the purest, most original and cleanest works of the post-war period, end up creating the stomach–churning spectacle that was *The Blue Room*?

This re-working of *La Ronde* was the last word in one strand of nineties theatre, the theatre of success. It was an event that was almost Roman in its exclusive decadence. Conceived by millionaires, performed by millionaires, and watched almost exclusively by others, the entire event was about success – successful people watching very successful people in something that must ipso facto be a success. It's a long way from Grotowski. It's almost beautiful in its conception, as any fruit is beautiful just before it goes rotten. If there was another reason to go, it was the off chance of catching a glimpse of Nicole Kidman's butt. How classy is that? How gracefully capitalism matures.

Having failed to catch up with *Amy's View* in London, I eventually stumbled across it in Berlin. I'm as confident in German as I am in Mandarin, but if you're in the right mood, no theatrical experience is ever wasted. So I bought a ticket.

The audience was an almost precise replica of the British David Hare audience. The chaps might have had bigger beer bellies, but there they all were – over fifty-five, besuited or be-pearled, concerned, moderately sophisticated and quintessentially bourgeois. (In interviews, Hare always rather cattily blames Richard Eyre for failing to bring a young audience into the National, seemingly blind to the fact that most of the new work Richard Eyre did was by David Hare.) And there they all were in Berlin, the doughy, unleavened, squat establishment.

When we sat down, the first thing that we were presented with was a giant TV set – a huge perspex rim around a gauze screen. Before the play began, there was a blown-up video projection of an English country house, a slow zoom in on it, underscored by a jaunty and profoundly cheesy tune, then titles appeared in soft white cosy lettering. Titles, for god's sake, began a play! It was the carbon copy of the beginning of any 1970s sitcom. I half-expected Wendy Craig to appear, and then lo, there she was, or the German equivalent. The gauze flew up and the play began, although the perspex rim remained framing the action irredeemably as a teleplay. To rub salt in, between the acts the gauze returned and showed adverts.

Now David Hare can't be blamed for the insane caprices of a German director. I can only half guess at the mixture of rage and depression that must have swelled through the author when he saw this production, if he saw it. But the fact that this was the way he was re-interpreted seems telling. If you're going to be crassly re-interpreted there are more flattering ways to have it done. A monumental crucifix, a post-nuclear landscape, a large inflated penis or, for that matter, a vulva, anything would be better than a TV set.

How did all this happen? How did the revolutionary become encased in a TV set? I haven't a clue. I know little or nothing about David Hare beyond a knowledge of his work. It's not hard to discern a clear pattern, a certain dualism in his later plays. For every clumpy, clod-hopping do-gooder in his plays who has to spout dull, liberal cliché, there has always been a sparkly, witty, devil-may-care enrager of the *bien-pensant* nexus. Think of the unequal battle in *Skylight*, the elegant put-downs in *Plenty*, the urbane Shadow Chancellor decimating the good-hearted opposition leader in *The Absence of War*, the worldly bishop smoteing and slaying all the ill-educated earnest in *Racing Demon*, Esme outshining the serious in *Amy's View*. There's giving the devil the best lines, and there's wiping the floor with the competition. The two things are distinct.

You get the feeling that somewhere in David Hare's heart he not only sympathises with the enemy, he wants them to win. And that is why he carries his audience with him. It's the not-so-covert conservative conspiracy. They too long for the world to be liberal. On the condition that it remains a matter of longing. As long as the devils are still in charge. That's where their security lies, and that's where they find reassurance in David Hare. It's the perennial conservative reassurance that there will always be hapless idealists who will suffer in agony to help nudge the world forward, so the fat, rich and complacent can continue to coast along getting cheap laughs at their expense. They want to see liberals battling, but most crucially, they want the romance of liberals losing.

Why should we mind? Partly because it is such an irritating con trick. Partly because we have had to put up with so many sneers from David Hare about younger writers (bar his not so surprising crush on Patrick Marber). Partly because he is constantly telling us via the newspapers what a musical, fluent writer he is, when he's as musical as a cement mixer. Largely because of the tortured writhings we had to endure about his acceptance of his knighthood, when it's obvious he's been dreaming of it for thirty years, and waking up with a hard-on.

Why should we care? Because of *Fanshen*, which was a truly magnificent achievement – a cool, pure, distillation of Hinton's tome about the Chinese revolution. In a series of Brechtian tableaux, written with a luminous simplicity, he showed the trials and rewards involved in a community and individuals attempting genuine change. Because of the anger and wit of *Knuckle*, which used the detective story format to reveal the breadth and width of British corruption. Because of *Plenty* which created in its heroine a genuinely romantic and complex woman who could expose the torpor and pettiness of post-war Britain.

And because of two heart-stopping moments of emotion – the ending of *Secret Rapture* and the last act of *Amy's View*. Both unpeel a sense of staggering loss. They do so with grace and dignity. And in both cases the loss, by death, is the same. It is of something female, something virtuous, something too young, something endlessly accommodating, something good. Now, I wonder what that was . . .

At the end of *Amy's View*, when the old West End dame descends to the stage to appear in her fringe hit, there is a tantalizing glimpse of the writer Hare could have been. It's intended as a parody of clumsy theatre, involving light and water and something semi-religious, but in fact it looks considerably more interesting than everything that preceded it. It's the theatre of infinite possibilities that Hare could have explored rather than the conventions that he chose.

Perhaps the early enemy proved too seductive, and what began as a target became a lifestyle. Or maybe the real enemy all along was vanity, and that eventually couldn't be defeated. For someone who complains about harsh treatment from the media, he doesn't half do a lot of interviews. No J.D. Salinger he. It is this assiduous hard work on his own behalf, which has finally got him what he wants – status and Power. Good luck to him. I think history will be kinder to Romance and Imagination.

Tony Harrison

The vernacular virtuoso behind three of the greatest theatrical events of the last thirty years – *The Oresteia, The Mysteries* and *The Trackers of Oxyrynchus*. Harrison's verse has a vigour, a publicity, a vulgarity that makes it ideal for the theatre. The central problem with verse in the theatre is its instant sense of its own cleverness and the alienation that ensues. The whiff of academia and elitism floats too close and drives sympathy away. That's no problem with Harrison. 'Look at me, I'm in metre', his verse noisily boasts at you, 'and I rhyme too', and the Byronic brio of it all enchants. The thump and the heft of it works perfectly for the grand stories he assails. The rhythm democratizes wherever it touches – bringing God, Jesus, Agamemnon, Orestes, whoever, onto our streets. It's the Harrison touch; he takes legends and makes people.

The most pressing question raised by Harrison's work, is when shall we see his like again? He is a product of a particular age, when a certain class saw culture as the stuff of life. They ate, drank, breathed it in, as if their lives depended on it. A Greek myth was a means of salvation, not a pretty artefact, nor a luxury. A Shakespeare play was a path to greater health, not a numbing evening of noise and display. Harrison and his generation revered their culture, and included it in themselves. They made it part of their centre, rather than wearing it as a dazzling coat, or exploiting it to change themselves and gain power over others. So he can balance his roots with his esoteric knowledge, his nature with his nurture. He can hold the two together, and from the tension between the two comes the life of his every single word.

Now we have a world where culture is spat on by every class, where the educated pretend to be street, the middle of the road pretend to be funky, the street pretend to be what's happening, and the artists seek nothing but sensation. Where an entire Saturday evening is given over by Channel 4 to a list of the hundred greatest ads, punctuated by self-styled cultural commentators, lathering over the crumbliness of chocolate. We spent so long deriding the middle-class man sitting with a glass of sherry listening to Beethoven, no one imagined the vacuum there would be without him. Without the thirst for culture that distinguished the Peter Hall, Tony Harrison, David Storey, Dennis Potter generation, we build our works on very flimsy stilts.

We should count our lucky stars that that moment gave us Tony Harrison, as well as so many others, and that he chose to breathe his particular brand of fire in the theatre.

David Harrower

'Category-smashers, every one' is how Snoo Wilson used to describe his work. It is a state greatly to be desired. Nothing bedevils any modern career in the arts so profoundly as the peril of being pigeonholed. From the first moment you do anything as a writer, or a director, or an actor, you have to contend with the world's desire to parcel you up into a box, slap a label on you, bung you in place with all the other boxes, then move on to the job of neutering the next unruly talent.

At the vanguard of this movement are the critics, one of the more conservative forces in the culture. Sitting, night after night, watching a variable phantasmagoria pass by, isn't the ideal prescription for a balanced world view, and their barely contained schizophrenia is only held together with a fragile thread at the best of times. The patterns they create to crab in and confine a world of chaos, however false they may be, are crucial to the maintenance of their sanity. When people start jumping out of their pigeonholes and dancing about, they squawk and shriek as if the barbarians were at the gates.

You get quite a lot of this as a director. If you begin, as I did, directing new plays in small rooms, then that's what you do. If you then direct new plays in large rooms (the Old Vic), as I did, you're told that you can't adjust to the size of the space. No matter that the audiences are happy and large and growing, you can't adjust. If you then direct a classic, in my case Chekhov, you're told there are certain rules which you're not observing. No matter that it's a sell-out, and the audience are being awoken by Chekov's life in a way they'd forgotten was meant, the rules aren't being observed. If you then direct a Shakespeare, well, you ought to be arrested.

Although, it's hard for directors, it's nothing compared to the difficulty for writers. This is the essence of the 'second-play syndrome'. This much talked-of syndrome is generally described as writers' difficulty in measuring up to the achievements of their first play. That's crap. The difficulty is in circumventing the critics' and some of the audience's desire for the writer to write the same play over and over again for the rest of their lives. It is almost impossible to have a second play seen as itself. It is almost always seen through the filter of the first.

David Harrower suffered acutely from this with his wonderful second play *Kill the Old, Torture the Young*, a mordant, funny, despairing take on modern urban life. It was wholly original and wholly refreshing. Following the travails of a panoramic sweep of characters from a rock star through a birdwatcher to a couple of young lovers, it was held together by the story of a documentary maker's return to the streets of his youth. It used the city they all inhabited as an extra character, a character of endless fascination to each of them, but also a prism through which we understood them in return. Held together by a laconic calm, it embraced a huge variety of moods from romance to despair.

Had it been a first play, it would have been hailed as staggeringly promising, or some such idiotic epithet – 'a voice to watch' – and the critics would have looked forward to many new 'bulletins from the frontline of urban life'. As it was, it was declared a disappointment, since it diverged so far from Harrower's first play. And David did himself no favours by making his first play, *Knives in Hens*, a masterpiece.

It could not have been placed in a more different milieu to *Kill The Old*. *Knives in Hens* takes place in the countryside, in a pre-industrial Scotland. It is a three-hander, observing the tensions between a farmer, his new wife and the village miller. Its spartan simplicity and rude brevity of language create a powerful sense of the earth, stone and wood of their lives. Its overwhelming impression of loneliness and silence creates a tremendous sexual electricity.

The story is at its most obvious level a thriller, describing how love turns sour between the husband and wife, and as passion grows between the wife and the miller, it becomes imperative that the husband should be killed. It is also a parable about the desire for knowledge, the power of language, female enfranchisement, and a whole bucket of stuff. Yet it achieves its ripples without ever losing the extraordinary strength of its own specificity.

It is rock solid, full of the strength of something that is nine parts imagination. Harrower understands that the vast majority of an atom is space. He fills in only as much detail as is necessary to trigger the imagination to create more. That is what makes his edifice so much more sturdy than many more baroque and brittle creations. The work of art's faith in itself is demonstrated by its own economy. Frills, tassles and decorations would detract from its own power-ful Protestant modesty.

Knives in Hens was a huge hit at the Traverse and the Bush, and in the new repertory, the repertory of Europe. Sarah Kane and I once joined a silly radio discussion to defend new writing against the feeble ravages of a middle-aged critic. He and his cohorts were bemoaning the breakdown of the repertory system which used to give a further life to London successes. While there's certainly a truth in that, the result of long-term underfunding and a failure of heart, we quickly retorted that there is a new repertory for new work.

Sarah's work, Mark Ravenhill's, Gregory Motton's and Martin Crimp's and many others has enjoyed the most enormous exposure around Europe. It's one of the peculiar intoxications for modern playwrights to graduate from a first production in a smelly black box to a second in a gleaming great state-of-the-art German playhouse. When we staged Roy MacGregor's first play at the Bush we could only just manage the technology of a speaker in a radio. When the same play was produced in Frankfurt they had a live band to play showtunes whenever the radio was turned on. Germany in particular is an enormous consumer of new British plays, and no play is more popular there than *Knives in Hens*.

Jonathan Harvey

It was an extraordinary night. First previews at the Bush were always fairly wired events, fairly gladiatorial, with more adrenalin than beer sluicing round the building.

Sometimes they would go off half-cock; a taut mixture of missed cues, technical fumbling and tight acting. Everyone would stand around in the dressing room afterwards swilling Australian Chardonnay and mouthing the right platitudes; 'that's-what-previews-are-for' and 'you've-got-to-miss-them-to-score-them'.

Sometimes they'd be disasters. A new play would meet a living, breathing audience for the first time, and the living, breathing audience would utter a silent, but resounding NO. The pub would be empty when you came downstairs, and all the staff would be wearing insane grins, like old skulls. They knew there was six weeks more of self-denial to come. 'No, the show's great, the critics just didn't understand it, houses are good-ish . . . really, where did you hear that from? . . .'

And sometimes they would fly. And none has ever flown farther or higher than the first preview of Jonathan Harvey's *Beautiful Thing*.

It would be wrong to say you could feel the ground moving, it wasn't like that. It was more as if some large hand took hold of the little black box the hundred people sat in, wrenched it out of the old Victorian building that surrounded it, took it out above London, above its theatrical and social context, and chucked it hard and high up into the stars, where it floated around for a couple of hours, exhilarated by the view.

It was largely the laughter, which pounded out of everyone, until your eyes wept and your head ached from the sheer noise. But it was more than that, there was a quality of joy, pure joy, which surprised as much as it pleased. Nobody could believe they were allowed to be that happy. Or that a modern story, a modern play could so deftly, truthfully and skilfully take them up rather than down.

Of course press night wasn't the same. All the fashionable madmen came, and raised their pedantic cry – 'Life's not like that', 'Where's the pain?', 'It's wish fulfilment'. But once they'd cleared out of the way, the amyl-nitrate in the heart of the play gushed back into the auditorium, and every night would be the same glee-filled trip to the stars.

It was never regarded as such, but for me, the first preview of *Beautiful Thing* was one of the more significant nights in post-war theatre. In one night, the empty space became the full room. New writing, and particularly, political new writing would never be the same again. *Beautiful Thing* was the crash of a wave that had been rising for several years. It was a wave of reaction to the miserabilist tendency that had predominated for almost a decade before.

This dry, dusty hideaway housed a ton of dead drama: state of the nation plays rehearsing arguments already settled long before the audience arrived; journalistic plays on single issues; work plays exploring the tensions in a DHSS/minicab/newspaper office; ghastly plays of opinions; autobiographical therapy theatre dressed up as confession, and the long endless nights where the left would argue all night with the radical left, and dawn would break, and someone would burst out crying. Small subjects, small plays.

Two principal sins bedevilled this school of writing. First was the odd twentieth-century idea that argument is at the centre of theatre. This is a peculiarly British phenomenon which seems to result from too much exposure to George Bernard Shaw at an early age. The marriage between philosophy and theatre always struck me as deeply uneasy, but for a while, for a couple of decades, any play that didn't sport a loud and long thesis was seen as deeply illegitimate. You needed a point to survive. No wonder audiences dwindled, tired of being lectured at, or having things explained to them.

The other great sin in many of the new plays of this period, and other forms of theatre, was fake pain. We live in a world of rampant cruelty, waste and injustice; we see it in every place, at every level. It's a given. We also, especially in this country, live in great comfort, surrounded by tolerance, generosity and compassion. We often seem to find this harder to deal with than the downside. We certainly hate to admit it.

It's not perfect, it's far from perfect, it's often hideously imperfect, but show it to a Romanian, or a Georgian, or a Peruvian, or a Moroccan, and tell them about how much suffering there is here, and you'll notice a funny look creep into their eye. Yet, in theatre, this didn't stop wealthy, healthy, middle-class folk looking at some inane subject like pensions or architecture or spying or newspapers and finding more rottenness than in any Denmark, more pain than in any Holocaust, more apocalypse than any Hiroshima.

Our suffering is of course legitimate, but it is not the only thing that legitimizes us: our joy does too.

Those who did have something genuine to complain about, the gay community, the ethnic minorities and, not to baulk at an enormous generalization, women, managed to produce some of the best work of this period. They also managed to move in from the edges to become the mainstream. One of the reasons was they wrote stories. Another was they knew enough about real pain not to need to fictify it.

With *Beautiful Thing*, Jonathan Harvey bravely went into classic old miserabilist territory. With young gay love as his theme he went on to a housing estate in a working-class enclave, and there he found joy and love and wit and tolerance and compassion and justice. He didn't ignore the difficulties that surrounded these people, but was happy to show they could triumph over them. He also wrote a simple story simply – there was no argument, no analysis, just sympathy and truth.

Of course the old miserabilists found it very hard to take this seriously. If they did they were out of a job. So all the people who spent their lives attending conferences rallied round to diminish Jonathan's achievement. They called it over-rosy or unintellectual. What they couldn't stomach was that this was genuine populist theatre – not dire Marxist cabaret, nor sentimental gluck – but an evening that everyone could love. Nor could they abide its scintillating quickness of wit. This wasn't theses delivered at the pace of continental drift. This was streetsmart writing, sharp, compressed and lively. Many simply couldn't keep up.

Of course *Beautiful Thing* wasn't the only play that put life before argument, nor is it necessarily the greatest. There was a whole host of writers who preceded Jonathan in breaking the shackles of Marxist critique or reductionist pointmaking. But it arrived happily at the crucial moment when the old conventions were crumbling, and something had to give to allow the new state of feeling its necessary space.

Of course, this is not a prescription for everyone to go out and write Happy Plays. Jonathan Harvey himself went on to write a savagely dark tragi-comedy *The Rupert Street Lonely Hearts Club*, a bitter-sour Eurovision farce, *Boom Bang-a-Bang*, and a beautiful and warm meditation on life and death, *Hushabye Mountain*. Nor is there a necessity to do away with analysis altogether. All the best plays are hard as well as easy, they have insights that are not immediately apparent, nuggets of difficulty that keep the plays out of the audience's greedy grasp. The dangers of going too far towards life and story are obvious – conflated potboilers get talked up as major works of art.

Beautiful Thing was the tip of the battering ram that knocked down the wall of dogma and defeatism which had surrounded theatre. It was the brightest colour of a whole host of colours and shades and hues that had been trying to infuse some variety into what had become a very grey room. Happily they succeeded.

Robert Holman

There was no happier sight for me in 1999 than the hunched figure of Robert Holman, shrouded in his anorak, standing in the foyer of the Oxford Playhouse. His eyes were popping, and his grin looked as if it would break his face. Outside two coaches were drawing up, and disgorging middle England to watch the first night of his play, *Making Noise Quietly*. To have his play revived was one thing. To be in big theatres was another. To be on a tour before the West End was yet another. But coaches were something different altogether. It was a writer's daydream writ large.

No one has suffered more from cultural ghettoization than Robert. There is a creed that some writers work in small spaces and some in large. Big public plays teeming with people are suited to large stages, small private work is for the studios. This is of course a ludicrous canard or to put it more bluntly, bollocks. Much of the last ten years has come to prove this. A new school of chamber epics has come to dominate all auditoria. The biggest commercial successes of the late nineties – *Art, The Weir, The Beauty Queen of Leenane, Copenhagen* – have all been ostensibly miniatures. Yet there is still a critical preconception that without a bit of pageantry, or its contemporary equivalent, then plays should be kept in small black boxes. With the lid firmly on. Most of the critics have now outgrown this, but there are still stubborn pockets of resistance.

Size is a subtle and peculiar quality. A single action, the

striking of a match, the fall of a tear, the undoing of a button, can fill an enormous theatre with joy or pity or fear. It is all a question of resonance from a particular context. If the context is sufficiently well created, the resonance ripples out into the imaginations, the understanding and the heart of everyone watching. And if the writer has invested sufficient imagination, understanding and heart in his work, the resonances can fill Wembley Stadium.

No one achieves this with greater purity than Robert Holman. *Making Noise Quietly* is a triptych of exquisite miniatures, studded with unostentatious but perfect detail, which meditate on the nature of man in a time of war. In the first, *Being Friends*, set in a Kent field in 1943, a London aesthete meets a northern Quaker. They talk of their reasons for not fighting, two doodlebugs pass overhead, they share a picnic, then finally undress as a prelude to swimming. In twenty-five brief shimmering minutes, without straining for any rhetoric, Holman packs two novels' worth of humour, light and emotional force.

The second play, *Lost*, portrays with equal brevity a naval officer, during the Falklands War, reporting the death of a friend and colleague to the bereaved mother. As both relate how difficult they found the dead man, how arrogant and dislikable he was, the small Cleveland sitting room in which the encounter takes place becomes a crucible of repressed pain, exemplifying too many millions of such encounters through history. Some find this play impressive but resistible, some such as myself find it very hard to recover from.

The third play, *Making Noise Quietly*, set in the Black Forest in 1986, posits an encounter between an English private gone AWOL with his disturbed stepson, and a wealthy, elderly German Holocaust survivor. This is a looser, more discursive exploration of the themes set up in the first two plays, but no less impressive for that. The action of the play is principally the effort to make the small boy speak, an effort in which both adults get drawn into increasingly violent behaviour. The play opens several cans stuffed with an embarrassment of worms, yet it never loses its extraordinary specificity, remaining resolutely in the here and now of its own world.

Each play is a marvel. Put together they make a masterpiece. Discussion of this one work (the one I know best) shouldn't give the impression that Holman just does the one thing – social realism with echoes. An extraordinary strain of fantasy pulses through his work. Another play, *Rafts and Dreams*, takes off from a suburban setting, after a casual ten-minute monologue from one character about being drawn into the child sex trade, into a weird fantasia. Two men uproot a tree in a London back garden, and trigger a flood of the entire world. Cast adrift on makeshift rafts one couple land in Africa, where a woman who suffers from a pathological fear of touching anything cures herself by being forced to cuddle a dirty chicken. It sounds laughable in précis, but on stage in the Royal Court Upstairs, it afforded a vision of late-twentieth-century dissociation from nature and the world that I've never seen equalled. It was truly a large play, in imagination, in philosophy, in heart.

Robert Holman has been writing for twenty-seven years – a consistent and distinguished record that I've done no justice to here – yet he has never acquired fame or all the crapology that walks alongside it. Why? Partly because he genuinely is too good. Some flavours are simply too exotic and too strong to be accepted immediately. Partly because he writes so slowly. He ekes out his plays. They only appear once every two or three years. But this means they are written with infinite care, and it is that, in part, which makes them so good.

Declan Hughes

'Oh, spare me the North,' an urban sophisticate drawls in exasperation, as a group of Dublin thirtysomethings settle for big drinks and a natter. It was a small line, but perfectly pitched, perfectly placed and perfectly delivered, it marked a turning point for Irish drama. And it got a big laugh to boot.

The play was *Digging for Fire*, the year was 1992. It was produced by Rough Magic, a company that for ten years had been bucking many trends in Irish theatre, introducing a wide range of new voices. This was their first big success with a new play, and what a success. Playing in the Project in Temple Bar, when it was still reasonably cool (before the whole area became Club Craic, and Dublin became the stag/hen night capital of Europe), people fought to get in. Even the President showed up. It subsequently toured with great success, came to the Bush and did boffo there, and almost barged its way into the West End.

The play is itself of value, separate from the effect it had. Although as with many other signpost plays – *Look Back*, *Godot*, *Bent*, *Cloud Nine*, *Beautiful Thing* – the effect develops a strange ulterior life that constantly haunts the play itself, a ghost that walks beside it, obscuring its worth.

Digging for Fire is a variant of the *Big Chill* theme, with a smattering of the old Bran myth (where the wandering prodigal returns) thrown in. The return from New York of a greatly loved firebrand provokes a gathering of old university friends. They chat, they drink, they tell lies, they drink, they go to the pub, they drink, they tell secrets, they drink, they come home, they drink, the secrets are out, they drink, they fight, they drink, they sleep, they wake up, they're hungover, painful truths are spoken, they leave. For a drink. It's a fairly classic set-up. But each character was beautifully etched, the plot was tightly sprung, the jokes were bracing, caustic and very funny, and the whole had a remarkable Restoration vigour. There was an energy here that dazzled.

Largely that energy was the result of Declan's own wit, and his knowledge and love of Restoration drama; but it was also the subterranean energy of a historical moment. Here was a slice of Irish culture saying with a controlled ferocity, 'Look we're not farmers, we're not bombers, we're not full of sorrow, we don't weep at the sight of a river, we couldn't give a shit about old tribal politics, we have no dreams of leaving. We are sharp, savvy, cultured modern Europeans. Watch us burn.'

This is of course, not so surprising now, when every other commercial is full of some cod version of Dub dudery, but at the time it was an immense surprise. So much Irish drama before had been so determinedly miserabilist and full of its own agony, shrouded in the dark cloud of the North, *Digging for Fire* announced the arrival of more than just a talented writer. 'Spare me the North', with its brutal indifference, helped push open the door for the cultural tiger.

Declan won't thank me for writing so much about the one play, since he's probably bored by the shadow it has cast. He has written several plays since, including another for the Bush, *New Morning*, a light and subtle variation on the town/country, primitive/modern theme, where two sisters go for a camping weekend. But he has largely been dicked around by television and film companies since. No matter, *Digging for Fire* didn't write itself. It took rare insight to understand its world, and rare wit to express it. That insight and that wit should help make for more events in the future.

Catherine Johnson

One of my purest moments of joy at the Bush was breaking into a block of Bayswater flats at 6:30 in the morning with an old credit card trick, kicking a writer awake, and reading her a rave *Guardian* review that ensured the success of her play.

One of my greatest moments of shame was frightening a writer so badly with some drunken lurching, that she deserted her coat, bag and address book, ran out into Westbourne Grove and hailed a black cab for Bristol, thus spending all the £250 prize money she'd won earlier that evening.

One of my greatest moments of terror was on a disastrous field trip in the country, when I had to organise for a deeply sozzled writer, belting out 'Anarchy in the UK', to be poured into a car, while I poured a gallon of mead down the throat of an even more sozzled director, and tried to keep a cast from deserting the production.

Oddly enough, the writer in all three cases was the same, Catherine Johnson, and each story could come out of one of her plays. She is Mrs Chaos. She lives in an extraordinarily merry and healthy state of chaos, she brings chaos to wherever she finds boredom, and she describes chaos in her plays better than anyone. She has lived most of her life in the murky depths of Bristol, and, though not a guttersnipe herself, is living proof of the Strummer line, 'They think they're so clever/ They think they're so right/ The truth is only known by guttersnipes'.

Ragdoll, her first, is about an epicly awful West Country family, who live in a council house and merrily bang each other's brains out while keeping their eyes glued to the television. Mother, son, brother, sister, father, daughter, they're all absent-mindedly in and out of each other's orifices, and all think morality is a village in the Cotswolds. It's monstrous, gothic and if you were brought up in the West Country, frighteningly real. Now we know some of the culture that created Fred West, it also turns out to be horribly prescient.

Boys Mean Business is set on the faded splendour of Weston-Super-Mare pier, a sad relic of its fifties heyday. In a light-hearted drifty atmosphere, two brothers, washed up at thirty, fight for focus and remember their glory days in a failed punk band. A local small-time drug dealer pops in and out and eventually engineers a violent ruck. *Dead Sheep*, her next, is a savage inversion of redemption drama. A group of casualties from a rehab clinic are taken up a mountain by a born-again dwarf and a half-witted Rambo wannabe. Viciously funny, they all expect the mountain to bring glimpses of God and the good life, but all they get is an even greater darkness. *Shang A Lang*, her latest, depicts the wild, drunken excesses of three women hitting forty like a train crash, on a weekend at Butlin's, trying to revive the ghosts of their slaggy youth.

Catherine is the playwriting equivalent of a Maupassant. She creates situations that have a potential for chaos and disaster, winds up the spring to an unbearable tension, and then lets it unwind where it must go. She's not only unsentimental, she takes a positive punky pleasure in gobbing in the eye of the feel-good faction. Her compassion is expressed through her accuracy. She doesn't let people off the hook, nor does she glamorize their cruelty. She just hits the target, and honours the world that way.

For a while, television and film were wiser to her talent than theatre management. Then she struck gold, and parlayed her gift for accuracy and for organized chaos into the equivalent of winning the lottery. She was given the hopelessly difficult task of creating a story and a book to string together the songs of Abba. The result was *Mamma Mia*. Few could have managed it. Very few with such raucous, unpretentious generosity. None, bar Catherine, could have deserved its success so fully.

I hope she continues to surprise with her graceless grace and her artless art. I hope she finds a better behaved, more couth, artistic director than me to look after her.

Judith Johnson

An assured, still and sane voice, Judith Johnson was swamped by the explosion of boys plays that appeared at the same time as her. She wrote one unassuming modest slice of young working-class life, *Somewhere*, and another gentle and heart-rending family play, *Uganda*. The second was a beautiful achievement, managing to shoehorn a sense of modern global consciousness into a sitting-room domestic drama. She did this without any grandstanding, no big speeches or theatrical coups. She simply created a very strong and consistent sense of what is normal and then quietly infiltrated a sense of the larger world outside. Few plays have caught the disjunction between the modern and the old as eloquently.

Unfortunately just as these plays were appearing in the mid-nineties, the boys ran in to the playground with their zippety-zappety language, their violence, their sexuality, their big plots and their souped-up despair, and frightened everyone else into hiding. Once the noise from the shouters has died down, it will be those who talk who will be listened to, and Judith Johnson is in their first rank.

Terry Johnson

In *Hysteria*, Terry Johnson's surreal fantasia on psychother-
apy and the Holocaust, there is a beautiful and elegant
exchange between Salvador Dali and Sigmund Freud in
Freud's consulting rooms in Hampstead. Dali urgently
requests Freud's opinion of his work:

DALI: But have I caught what we are chasing, you and I?
Can you see the unconscious?

FREUD: Oh, Mr Dali. When I look at a Rembrandt, or a
classical landscape or a still life by Vermeer, I see a world
of conscious activity. A fountain of hidden dreams.

DALI: Si?

FREUD: But when I look at your work I'm afraid all I see is
what is conscious. Your ideas, your conceit, your meticu-
lous technique. The conscious rendition of conscious
thoughts.

DALI: Then this . . . He . . . I see.

FREUD: You murder dreams. You understand?

It's a valuable insight into all art, the importance of letting
the unconscious, the hidden, reveal itself and resisting the
temptation to render it. It's also an essential key to
understanding Johnson's own art.

A large part of him would love to be nothing but a realist,
if that is the right word, an evoker of life. He would love to
do simple portraiture, plain landscapes, unadorned still
lives. Just as Lucian Freud can reveal a history in the skin

tones of a cheek, or Alan Bennett can summon up years of self-denial with a turn of phrase, so any dramatist wants their characters to come to resonant life. Just as Van Gogh can giddy our spirits with a field of yellow and green, or David Storey can evoke the blighted march of progress in a valley, so any dramatist would like to encase their stories in charged and truthful worlds. Just as Chardin can summon whole childhoods with the shine on an apple, or Pinter can let a rickety dumb waiter summon up all our nightmares, so any dramatist wants all their objects to become real and numinous. The modesty is all.

It is hard enough to achieve such weighted truth. What is harder still is to leave it alone. A writer like any artist wants the receiver to see the world, but often they also want to help the receiver to *get it*. They want everyone to understand the impulse that led to its creation. This desire to explain is all the more acute with playwrights, since their prime building brick is by nature discursive and explanatory, conversation. Since Plato's dialogues, philosophy and drama have been peculiar bedfellows. The hardest task of all is to resist that desire to explain, to leave the world plain, unadorned, itself.

As a director Terry Johnson has worked with many realists, as a dramaturg he has brought on many others. He appreciates writers who paint truthful, modest portraits of people, individuals or a world; who let history, ideas and subtext lurk unseen beneath the brilliantly achieved surface. As Freud would appreciate the held grace in a bowl of sunflowers.

But this is not his way. His subtexts can't remain hidden. They burp and belch their way up to the surface. His realities are constantly being invaded by his insights into his own realities. You get the life, and you get the explanation. Like Dali, he throws dreams and realities into the blender and sees what results. If he wasn't aware of this himself, the results would be disastrous, a clumsy mishmash of realism, poetry and philosophy. It would be exactly the sort of hodgepodge that most students write. But Johnson is aware of it. Like every true artist, he knows his strengths, his peculiarities and his weaknesses and he uses each. He has the gifts described above, portraiture, still life, landscape. But he can't just do that. He has to do more. He has to frame. He has to curate. He is profuse in that way. And he has manipulated his peculiar gift to create a body of work that is entirely original, entirely truthful and enormously entertaining.

Hysteria and *Insignificance* are the most obvious examples. Two tightly observed worlds, Freud's Hampstead consulting room and Marilyn Monroe's New York hotel room are invaded by figures from the twentieth-century hall of fame. Dali in the first case, together with an almost exemplary patient, and Einstein, Joe Di Maggio and a McCarthy-like senator in the second. These figures of reality/myth, pitched in a peculiar place between character and caricature (yet always alive), enable Johnson to segue easily into large discussions of relativity, freedom of thought, psychoanalysis and genocide. They are twentieth-century Homeric adventures of the mind, trammelled into single rooms.

In other plays, Johnson has dissolved the dividing line between reality and dream, by observing the lives of people who live in a divided world themselves. In *Dead Funny* – his acid (almost too acid) dissection of failed suburban marriages – his characters are all lifted out of the ordinary by their fanatical devotion to comedians past and present. The death of Benny Hill is the release for the play. A straight portraitist would have simply observed the failed relationship at the centre: Johnson's addition of the comedian's fan club allows room for a freer jaunt through comedy and sexuality, and creates the room for some dazzling farce at the end.

In *Unsuitable for Adults*, a brilliant take on feminism and the sex war, we watch the collapse of a relationship between a mimic and a feminist comedian, brought on by the appearance of a stripper. Set in the beautifully observed world of alternative comedy, with all its petty passions and sordid grandiosity, the mimic's endless ability to take on different persona opens up questions of identity. While in *Cleo, Camping, Emmanuel and Dick*, Johnson introduces us with an accurate but warm eye to the strange netherworld of the celebrity, in this case the *Carry On* team. The portrayal of characters we already know somehow frees Johnson up to write with a barbed lyricism and a ruefully pained comedy. His subject here is the horrors attendant on the love of an old man for a younger woman, its squalor, its desperation, its joy and its light handshake with mortality. He treats it beautifully, without bitterness and with sympathy evenly apportioned throughout. It's a peerless creation.

Even when he comes off the rails a little his work is still fascinating. *Imagine Drowning*, a bit of Cumbrian gothic, which took on as much as it could of the environment, passing by abusive violence and astronauts along the way, occasionally stuffs too much in for its own good. But still in its awkwardness and its open honesty, it acquires a huge charm.

Terry Johnson has successfully created his own reality, a blend of what we know and what we dream, where he has the freedom to be truthful, to be philosophical, to be rhetorical and to let his own concerns, his own cruelties and his own cares float free. It is a huge achievement.

Charlotte Jones

Charlotte Jones may represent the future of a form of populist theatre. To date she has written two highly successful comedies, *In Flame* and *Martha, Josie and the Chinese Elvis*. The first is an elegantly put together time play, juxtaposing incidents from the beginning of the twentieth century against events from its end, in the life of a particular family. There are show-stopping routines, dances, romance, historical echoes, a bundle of jokes and throughout a teased-out mystery which is only solved at the very end. It's a full and bulging bag, not especially shapely, occasionally a bit soapy and always broad, but redeemed by its warmth of heart, its lack of pretension and a remarkably uncloying sweetness of tone.

Martha, Josie . . . is less original in its construction, a farce set in a single room with a dotty cleaner, a smart prostitute, her daughter and a Chinese Elvis impersonator. Although the texture is naturalistic, the writing is always too public, too turned, too theatrical for that. The plot is a pleasantly unsurprising mix of farce and sentiment. What keeps it particular is a concurrent weirdness, an atmosphere of madness in the air which infects everyone, and keeps every exchange surprising and somehow true. Hers is the magic realism that reflects life. It owes a small debt to the contemporary gothic style of the American writers, Beth Henley and Wendy McLeod. They carved out a form of gently twisted feminine loopiness that exerts an incredible charm. This is not the aggressive weird of the boys, the 'look-at-me-I'm-mad' writing, the many wacky children of the dead parrot sketch, which quickly tires. It's more a pervasive warping of the world, practised with heartfelt affection.

Jones is naturally a public writer, and the theatre desperately needs talent like hers. Writers who can talk to an audience, engage them without begging for favour, and gently change their perceptions.

Sarah Kane

The following was written before Sarah died. I've read it and re-read it many times, thinking I should change it for this book, but since it captures a moment for me when she was still alive, I've decided to record it exactly as it is, and then add something, rather than practise any revisionism.

Sarah first hoved into view when she applied for the assistant director job at the Bush. In her letter, instead of the usual two-paragraph cocktail of smarminess and arrogance, she sent in a four-page essay about the future of British theatre and hence the world. It was original, unremittingly bleak, and highly compelling. Still at university, she appeared for her interview dressed in a lot of black, scowled a lot and got angry with us for our failures to communicate with her. We liked her. We interviewed her again, but couldn't offer her the job. Her intelligence and judgement were clearly extraordinary, but we worried that her non-stop intensity might drag a little in rehearsal. We felt she might gain from a bit of leavening.

She spent the next year on David Edgar's playwriting course at Birmingham, where how to lighten up isn't, apparently, a module. Occasionally she would appear at the Bush, go in to see a show, then walk out at half-time. Instead of the usual discreet slipping away with head lowered, Sarah would sit on the stairs and lecture the theatre staff and anyone hanging around, including on one occasion the actors waiting to make their entrances in the second half, on what was wrong with the show. This was something we had to forcibly discourage. She had adopted us as parents to rebel against.

A year later she applied for the same job again. She still wasn't right, but we wanted her in the fold, so we created a job for her, literary associate. She had a voracious appetite for scripts – much like Edward Bond in the Court's early days – and was an excellent reader – shrewd, pluralistic, generous and tough. Nothing we did caused her anything but rage. Her permanent attitude was exasperated affection. She would frequently stomp out for brief periods, and then one day disappeared altogether. It was only a couple of days later that we realized she'd walked out. She'd left an indignant note, but unfortunately none of us had ever found it.

Sarah has the best theatre mind, bar Peter Hall, that I have ever come across. She has a comprehensive knowledge of theatre history, ancient and modern; she has extraordinary intuition and cool judgement. She is passionate about the form and cares deeply about the role of theatre in society and in the individual's heart. Success matters little to her, but the effect of her work is sacrosanct. In a world, and particularly a generation, which cares for little but box-office returns, this is a real relief.

She also has an acute understanding, both philosophical and quotidian, of the fabric of the modern world. She sees it with a clarity that is startling, at the same time as being startlingly true. If she leans towards the dark and the cruel, that is a perfectly honourable thing to do. Our cultural opposition to it is only the result of our terror of tragedy. *We* lean too much towards good news for Sarah.

The only problem with Sarah, in my view, is that I'm not sure she's a natural writer. The *sturm und drang* and the savagery; the shitting and the fucking; the deconstruction and the erudition, the whole feast that's on offer tends to distract from the lack of simpler, quieter virtues. Relaxed human dialogue; characterization that is vivid, surprising and true; the creation of worlds both recognizable and new; narrative lines that both support and surprise; a fidelity to life – all these virtues are harder to find in Sarah's work. Her supporters, and many doctrinaire Brechtians, will say that these are the petit-bourgeois virtues, the staples of human interest drama. They will say that these are the very values that she is trying to subvert. But no one has yet survived without them, and I doubt that anyone ever will. They are the foundation stones of the whole kit and caboodle, including Brecht.

Theatre thirsts for ideas, for new forms, for a strong ludic sense, for a sense of its own deconstruction. Without this it becomes redundant. But they are not its heart. Its centre is stories by people about people for other people. Even a form as weirdly abstract as Caryl Churchill's *Blue Kettle* encloses a piercingly painful and human story. People and life is what I miss with Sarah.

History may laugh at the people who underestimate Sarah. It may laugh at the people who have so hysterically defended her. I hope that she goes on to prove everyone wrong. There are quiet conversational moments at the beginning of *Blasted*, theatrical images in *Cleansed*, and arias in *Crave*, where she looks like the real thing. *Crave* was a change of direction, but its self-conscious intertextuality drowned its real life. Sarah could well turn out to be the business, if she can escape from her own fan club. But at the moment, driven by ideologues, she is taking too many risks, and neglecting to develop her safe ground.

Whatever she writes, her commitment to the theatre and its possibilities is one of our culture's great assets. A future in which she was running the Royal Court is a very rosy one indeed. A future in which she was galvanizing some sleepy old pile of flab like the Royal Shakespeare Company would be close to a utopia. The best of luck to her.

Ah well, ah well . . . Sarah's grand larceny of her life left a long black cloud hanging over many. A huge amount of anger was felt. Anger at her for robbing us of what we so loved. Anger at those who maltreated her. Not actually the press, who have been held up so easily as scapegoats, but more at certain people in the profession. There were a lot of timid souls who dared not, who forced Sarah to dare on their behalf. She enacted their fantasies of outrage for them.

There is always one child in the class who will do the things others fear to. That is what marks them out, their courage, and their will. The good friends of that child will help her to harness it for her own benefit. The bad friends will use it as a form of entertainment. 'Go on, jump over that', 'Say that to the bully', 'Go on cut yourself'. Sarah was that child, and where some reined her back, others let her go, even encouraged her.

And then anger directed inward, for failing to help her. I still saw her occasionally, and spoke on the phone, but I had no idea of the inkiness of her black dog. We weren't as close as we'd once been, and we all always forget how large London is, how lonely, and how easy to get lost in. Backtracking obsessively over our correspondence, and our friendship, trying to find clues, resolutions, and blames and ways to ignore blame, it's hard to think one was a good friend, or a worthy friend. Or much of a friend at all.

But anger is a nonsense, and hardly worth the breath in the face of such loss. She was a magnificent girl; she was Cantona and Rimbaud; she was seven pints and puritan water; she was a ferocious vegan who wore leather trousers; she was the most scary scowl and the world's sweetest smile; she was gay and she loved men; she was a frozen stare and a peal of laughter; she was alive. She was alive.

On the day of her memorial service, I was walking back through the park with my two daughters, and trying to explain to them why I couldn't look after them that night. I explained where I was going, and my three-year-old attacked the subject with her usual grave seriousness:

'I'm going to say goodbye to a friend who has died, and we're all getting together to say goodbye to her.'

'Oh.'

'She was someone who knew you when you were young. She loved you very much.'

'Oh. (*Pause.*) Did she want me to get stronger?'

'Yes. Yes she did.'

'Well, I am stronger now, aren't I?'

'Yes. Yes you are.'

'And I can tell her that through my heart. Can't I?'

'Yes, you can.'

'I will. I will tell her that through my heart.'

We all behaved a bit strangely after Sarah's death. It awoke old despairs, and morbidities, and adolescent terrors. I went back to *The Waste Land*, which I can't have read for almost twenty years. The epigraph struck me like a baseball bat:

'Nam Sibyllam quidem Cumis ego ipse oculis meis vidi in ampulla pendere, et cum illi pueri dicerent: Σίβυλλα τί θελειζ; respondebat illa: ὰποθαυεῖυ θελω.'

Once I saw with my own eyes the Sibyl hanging in a cage, and when the boys asked her, 'Sibyl, what do you want'; she replied, 'I want to die'.

Ah well, goodnight sweet princess, and flights of angels . . .

Charlotte Keatley

To have one's first major play turn into a phenomenon is a sort of disaster. *My Mother Said I Never Should* is a wonderfully constructed, warmly written saga about the chains and the keys of inheritance through four generations of women. It conjures up moments in the twentieth century with deft ease, its narrative is an artful compendium of coincidence, suspense and truthful clumsiness, its dialogue is tight with repression and tension, which renders the moments of relaxation and sentiment all the more disarming. It doesn't so much touch chords in people, as twang them.

Charlotte could not have known the effect her child would have, when she left it at the playground gates. It was a huge hit in Manchester, in London, then all over the country, then all over the world. Now, it's a set text. It says a lot about the prevailing aridity of the playwriting culture when it appeared (late eighties), that everybody rushed so eagerly to drink from this oasis. Heart, story and humour weren't exactly à la mode then. As well as those features, its small cast, mobility and popularity make it a favourite for theatres everywhere.

The success of the play unfortunately left Charlotte prey to the conference circuit. They grabbed her, successful, young and a *woman*, and dragged her along to panel after symposium after talk after platform, to talk about this and that and the other. This is a peculiar way that the English have of clipping the wings off their peacocks. They find a talent and ask it to talk about itself, and sit back and watch it atrophy.

Charlotte happily seems to have escaped that circuit. But we still await the second play. The success of the first, and the poison of all that natter, will have made it that much more difficult. If it appears, that'll be grand. If it doesn't, the wealth of pleasure, insight and support afforded by the first should be enough for anyone.

Barrie Keeffe

I've always wondered about the helpfulness of the list of actors and production team inserted at the beginning of a playtext. It's a kind nod to all involved, but it doesn't help conjure an idea of the first performance. Nor do critical quotes, since they're keener to give a gladiatorial thumb up or thumb down than to give an impression of a particular experience. Pictures are more helpful, but since they are often of figures or faces carved out of the darkness by light, they could be anywhere. What would really help is a picture of the set, and also of the theatre, a sense of the exact space where the play began.

The old Soho Poly space has gone the way of all theatres now, but it was extraordinary while it lasted. Tucked away in a side-street of Soho, through a featureless café, down some rickety stairs, and into a low-ceilinged cellar full of nooks and crannies and hidden passages, it was cramped, held up by visible pillars and dank with potential. It was claustrophobic but it could open up broad vistas; it was dark but it could loosen the imagination. It was a magic room. It was as if many of the stories of the city condensed themselves and sank under the earth into that cellar.

Barrie Keeffe is an exuberant and expansive writer. For Stratford East he wrote a proscenium-size pained comedy, *My Girl*, and a big full-throttle modern revenge play, *Wild Justice*. For Joint Stock he wrote an ebullient update of Middleton's play, *A Mad World My Masters*. He also wrote one of the finest ever British screenplays, *The Long Good Friday*.

He has a facility with language, taking the vernacular and new minting it into expressions of iconic force, which he shares with American greats like Chandler, Hammett and Runyon. How many still chant the climactic line from the film, 'Shut up you long stream of paralysed piss', in mock-Hoskins. Indeed much of that screenplay is locked into people's heads. Few others can turn out the phrase that summons up years of scars, bottles up a gallon of passion and still carries itself off with brutal style, like Keeffe can. There's no shortage of pale imitations, but few touch the original.

But for me his finest work is contained in the two trilogies of one-act plays he wrote for the Soho Poly in the 1970s, *Gimme Shelter* and *Barbarians*. He took all of his ebullience, exuberance and expansion and constringed it into six tightly packed little grenades. The theatre itself, its tension, its nucleal combustibility, the sense of energy packed into a small space, must have contributed to the event, but also to the creation. The sense of compacted force. Some of the treatment may look a little dated now, but the content – youthful alienation, racism, football violence, the need for a tribal identity, the failure of education – has proved itself evergreen. The language is a rich effusion of inarticulacy.

For anyone of the punk generation, these were the plays to suit the moment. They were the theatrical equivalent of The Clash. I can't think of much higher praise than that.

Franz Xavier Kroetz

For many, Kroetz was the guiding light of the 1980s. For others he was the most mind-bogglingly boring playwright history had ever thrown up. His fans always held him up as the realist's realist. The man who tested how far the theatre and realism could go in the search for completely truthful representation. For his detractors, he was a Bavarian loony who tested how far the audience could go before they started trying to kill the actors. His work was the *reductio ad absurdum* of realism.

The most pure example of his work, *Request Programme*, has the following lively plot. A middle-aged woman comes home from work, turns on the radio, does some darning, goes for a pee, cooks herself some dinner, eats it, listens to the radio, more darning, goes for a shit, finishes her darning, puts on her nightclothes, lines up a load of sleeping pills, consumes them, drifts off. Nothing else. That was it. Not a word was spoken. It's certainly a long way from *Das Rheingold*. But that's the Germans for you, nothing by half measures. It was the biggest hit in London. You couldn't move for people either at the Donmar or later at the Bush. They poured out afterwards, tears streaming down their faces. 'The most eloquent play in London', hymned the *Independent*.

A later play, *The Nest*, had a livelier plot, but included one extraordinary brain-busting episode. A waste-disposal man rolls a barrel of industrial effluent on to the stage, picks it up and empties it into a lake, then rolls it off again. That action takes about two minutes. He does it eight times. That's sixteen minutes of an evening watching a man roll a barrel on and off. Hmmm. Although the action was critically tied in to the story of the play (the man's child later bathes in the lake and is scarred by the residue of the effluent), it had an extraordinarily divisive effect on the audience. Some leant meaningfully forward and stared at the action as if it was saving their lives, some left, some fell asleep, some muttered 'Oh, for fuck's sake', some started whistling to pass the time.

The statuesque simple action turned the spotlight around from the play on to the audience. They were being examined; their tolerance, their curiosity, their patience. It probably turned a few off the theatre for life, and for some others it was a moment of pure delight. In an old *Goon Show*, Spike Milligan proudly announces, 'I knocked on the door one hundred times', and proceeds to do just that. After ten knocks, you giggle; after thirty, you laugh loud; after forty, you fall silent; by fifty, you're angry; by sixty, you're tearing your hair out with frustration; then round eighty it turns back to delight; and by the time you get to the hundred it sounds like the purest jazz. Literalism at its most deliberate can prove an unlikely gateway to the sublime.

Through the Leaves was Kroetz's best-known play, and in his terms it had a positively Homeric narrative about the relationship between a butcher and a spinster. In the first half alone there was an awesomely realistic blowjob, and a shag on the table. At the beginning of the second half, the actor playing the butcher came on and spent ten minutes meticulously washing his naked body. This incident finally proved too much for one theatregoer when I saw it (it must have been the hygiene that did it). He noisily dragged his wife out of the theatre, only to return, walk on the stage, and address the naked actor. 'You should have your grant removed,' he spurted, then strode out.

Looking back on it, these examples of ur-realism seem risible, and a sort of despairing fashion of the age. Anything so studiedly low-key is certainly rarely seen now in these buzzy, buzzed-up times. Kroetz himself went on to write richer, more mystical work, as if he had tired of the extremity of his earlier writing. But if I had to pick one writer who taught me why I loved the theatre, and why I felt it mattered, it would be Kroetz.

Tony Kushner

Kushner's first play, *A Bright Room Called Day*, was premièred at the Bush in the late eighties. A rich, dark, magical and political play about the moral thinning of the intelligentsia in 1930s Berlin, it was a disaster. The production was an unhappy one, the critics all came and said he couldn't write, the audiences didn't come at all. Sometimes with skill all around, and no shortage of good intentions, you can't prevent the seemingly inevitable car crash. Once the production had been and gone, the writer retreated back across the Atlantic, and that was presumed to be that from Mr Kushner.

Well, never trust first impressions. The next of Tony Kushner's works to appear over here was the full-throated roar of *Angels in America*, the play that defined the 1990s more than any other. It was rather as if Rembrandt had submitted a dark and precise still life of a couple of apples, had it laughed at, disappeared from view for a while and then returned with *The Nightwatch*. The fact that *Angels in America* came completely out of left-field made it all the more startling.

Angels was the play that everyone had been waiting for. It is ambitious, politically sharp, a good story that hops gleefully around the modern world, full of cheap jokes, magically imaginative, bold, silly and grave. Through the Aids prism it looks death in the eye, and in that reflector, and through that refractor, it understands afresh what it is to be human and what it is to be alive. It makes new sense of us.

There's an honourable line of plays through history that look squarely at death – *Oedipus at Colonus*, *Hamlet*, *Three Sisters*, *Waiting For Godot* – and each play brings back fresh news about how we live. *Oedipus* showed man straining away from his relationship with blood and nature; *Hamlet*, the Renaissance human giddy with the scary exuberance of his own mind; *Three Sisters*, a culture lost in its own culture, and feeble before the barbaric onslaught of modernism; and *Godot*, the frightened bleak souls drifting around post-Holocaust and post-Hiroshima. It's looking at death that reveals how we live. That's why *Angels* was so seriously refreshing. It burst through the glib and grey despair that has met death for so long, and revealed this dazzling peacock of colours – camp, cruel, tender, generous, vicious, vivid and delightful. It proved capable, and proved us capable, of the most enormous surprises. What could be better than that?

Tracy Letts

The venerated and venerable Michael Codron was looking distinctly surprised. He had just transferred *Killer Joe* from the Bush to the Vaudeville. It was opening night, fifteen minutes before curtain up, and he was doing his discreet walk-round of the dressing rooms. He had just emerged from an actress's room. He was pale. 'Are you all right?' I asked. 'Yes. Yes . . . I just found . . . er . . . the actress rogering . . . er . . . being rogered by the writer,' he said in some alarm. 'Oh. Oh dear,' I said, 'What did you do?' 'I said "Good luck",' he replied, a spasm of foolishness crossing his face. He walked away, throwing a light command over his shoulder, 'Make sure they're ready, Dominic.'

The actress, Holly Wantuch, is sadly no longer with us. She was one of those good, big souls that death clutches at as soon as it can. Her beloved, the writer Tracy Letts (as in *Thunderbirds* a man, to sort out confusion for the English) is still here. He wrote one of the landmark plays of the 1990s.

Killer Joe is a travelling firework, delighting, provoking, challenging and thrilling wherever it goes. It went off first in Chicago, then Off-Off-Broadway, then in Edinburgh, then at the Bush, then in the West End, then Off-Broadway and who knows where next. Following the London productions it was translated into a host of languages and has since popped up all over the world.

I first caught up with it at the Traverse during the festival in 1994. It was the end of a long day of conferences, lunches and drinking. As usual in Edinburgh, no one was going to see much, they were all listening to the rumour fantasy, trying to find out what was hot. *Killer Joe* was definitely the ticket. To keep spirits high, I joined two senators of British theatre for a modest toot of charlie before the show. The effect of that and the show itself, made for one of the most galvanizing evenings in the theatre I had ever enjoyed.

Set in a trailer in Texas, the play didn't take long to engage. Within seconds, a woman was on with no knickers on. Within a minute, a man had made a crude joke about it. For an uptight, PC theatre audience, this was like opening the door to Disneyland. More goodies followed – fat men with amusing underpants, guns, willies, a tender and erotic seduction, a complicated and enthralling plot, a violent murder, wonderful character-driven jokes, a tense stand-off, then a stunningly combustible violent denouement. This was a long way from David Edgar, and all of it delight. All of those denied goodies – plot, suspense, eroticism, black humour, darkness – were suddenly recklessly on display. The response was tumultuous.

We met up with the cast, director and author afterwards – the men all unfeasibly tall – and were as delighted by them as the show. They knew how to party, yet were serious about their company's style of work – a visceral, emphatic naturalism that set out to out-*Steppenwolf Steppenwolf* and succeeded. It became vital that we got the show to the Bush. It wasn't easy and we had to fight for it, but it proved immensely rewarding.

It would be no justice to Tracy if I made the play seem like simply an exercise in bad taste, trailer-trash exotica. A sort of dramatic Jim Thompson. There's much more to him. He has a Chekhovian control of theatrical mood, and an equal ability to switch or subvert mood with a single deft stroke. He can make the freakish and the strange look perfectly normal, and can crank the banal up into the mythical without showing the gear changes. He has an eye for the emblematic detail. In *Killer Joe* the violence inherent in mass consumerism was neatly shown by an act of forced fellatio with a chicken drumstick. And he writes seriously and deeply unsentimentally about love, and its hideous dereliction in the present day.

In both *Killer Joe*, and his later play *Bug*, love appears in a variety of guises. Love as power play; love as commercial commodity, as emotional blackmail, as displaced fantasy, as incestuous obsession, as grand hypocrisy, as almost anything but the conventional sentimental prettiness. He articulates it most clearly in *Bug*, where love appears as the disease that kills us, yet at the same time the disease we're all desperate to catch. The deadly germ we spend our lives searching for. Tracy's articulation of this peculiarly sour truth is unforgiving.

Doug Lucie

Doug Lucie wrote a series of brilliant bilious chronicles recording the texture of life under the shadow of Thatcher. He hit his stride at the beginning of the eighties and since then, through *Hard Feelings*, *Progress*, *Fashion*, *Grace*, *Gaucho* and *The Shallow End*, he has charted the consistent moral deterioration of England.

Doug has chosen his exemplary settings well. The first play is set in a student's shared flat in Brixton in 1981 as the riots flicker then rage outside; the second in a stripped pine front room of a politically correct Hampstead home in the mid-eighties; the third in various shadowy but well-appointed offices from the world of advertising; the fourth in the gardens of a decrepit stately home about to be bought up by an evangelical American organization; the fifth in the Greek villa of a drug-dealing Howard Marks figure who is entertaining his old university buddies as the forces of law and order close in; and the sixth in the gardens of a media magnate who is celebrating his daughter's wedding.

If anyone was looking for a perfect encapsulated record of the way we have lived in Britain for the last twenty years – what's been shining on the surface, and the sewage running through below ground – then I'd immediately point them to Doug's work. The breakdown of political certainties, the unstoppable growth of the media, the ditching of socialism, the discreet but deadly hand of the new world order, all of these percolate through his work.

But they percolate through people, not through speeches and debate, through people in life.

Lucie is a humane satirist. The characters he creates are true, but, lightly flavoured with a pinch of bile, they become exaggerated on to the borderline between the real and the grotesque. They have the clean lines of a Doonesbury, the mad eyes of a Steve Bell, and the neurotic reality of Rattigan. His plays, although replete with content of the moment, are fascinatingly old fashioned in their structure. Lucie is a covert purveyor of the well-made play. His models are Rattigan, Coward and Maugham, and his work is all the stronger for it. The set is often fixed, the characters generally bring a letter of introduction from the author as they come on, the narrative is gripping and full of well-oiled surprises, business is well thought through and the jokes emerge organically from character. The firebrand of the last twenty years is also one of the most skilled and conservative craftsmen.

The changing reaction to Doug's work has almost been as interesting as the work. In the eighties when the liberal media were all squarely aligned against the order of the day, they championed Doug as a hero. Yet in the nineties as the supposedly liberal press succumbed to Thatcher's theatre, and worked themselves into orgiastic frenzies over the meaningless, Doug's solidity of content, his sheer matter, was a rebuke to them, and they turned on him. Lucie's work has remained consistent and strong. The world has turned. It will turn back.

Roy MacGregor

(Much of this essay first appeared as an obituary for Roy MacGregor, a colleague whom I worked with on three occasions. Its tone, as I hope will be understood, is therefore distinct.)

The first time I met Roy was in a squalid little room at the Bush. He'd come up to talk about his first play *Our Own Kind*. We'd read the first half and were fired up about it. A play about council estate racism – traditional territory for bleeding-heart victim plays – it had a scope, a rhetoric and an attack that was truly original.

Roy was a surprise. The play's fire and flourish seemed to find no equivalent in the faintly lugubrious, gentle man we met. His preternatural calm and habitual hangdog expression always misled people. They underestimated the amount going on inside. Unlike the playwrights who noisily advertise demons they don't actually possess, Roy had real demons, and he dealt with them quietly.

But what became clear, even at a short meeting, was a quite extraordinary and very rarely met sweetness of spirit. Behind the stiff manner, the briefcase and the middle-management front there was a genuine and particular grace. It was the grace of a man who has been to the end of despair, seen most of the squalor and torpor on offer, and then turned the corner. The grace of a man who, knowing all the bad, allows himself to be continually surprised by the good.

Roy led a life split into two separate acts. The radical contrast between the first and second gives the largest insight into how he attained such an uncommon grace. Act One was a long aimless drift, the restless wandering of a talented man out of touch with himself. There was a period as a blues guitarist, jamming all over Europe from the King's Head to American air bases in Germany; there was a time as a graphic illustrator, using and developing his gift for sharp characterization; there was everything else from selling insurance door to door round Highbury to hiring out ski equipment in the German alps.

As with many whose sense of their potential fails to match their sense of achievement, something had to fill the gap. For Roy it was booze, largely, although he dabbled fairly far and wide elsewhere. But booze was No. 1. He never bragged of his ex-drinking, although the hints he dropped implied a fairly Herculean intake. Much of the eighties Roy spent in Germany. It was at the end of that tawdry decade, when his marriage had collapsed, that Roy returned to England, locked himself into a bedsit in Bristol with a crate of booze and almost drank himself to death. For him it was the end of the road. He had tried everything, seen everything, been everywhere and found no lasting answers. Rushed to hospital in a state of internal collapse, Roy looked up and saw a priest reading the last rites beside his bed.

The second act began with his miraculous escape from the embrace of his own angel of death. With his recovery, a clarity broke through into Roy's life, and a purpose. He wanted to write. He didn't know what, but he knew he wanted to write. So, encouraged by therapists and counsellors, he started. And having started, he couldn't stop.

Writing filled the gap in Roy's life. All of the talent that had been there before found its natural outlet; the musician released itself into cadence and phrasing; the illustrator into accuracy and detail; the self-destruct mechanism coin-flipped into the most prodigious and determined creativity. For a while he lived on cornflakes, and spent the rest of his pennies on writing materials. He read enthusiastically, picking up Ibsen and Priestley and Miller and Griffiths, and with the cheek of the auto-didact he took them on, on their own territory. He always liked big stories, weaving together private pain with public injustice.

The Bush eventually produced two of Roy's plays, *Our Own Kind* and *Phoenix*. The first was a fairytale; a wonderful cast, great reviews and a huge hit. The second – an extended parable about post-unification Germany – was a perfect consolidation. Both plays inspired many other writers to take on braver, bolder topics. They broke through the timidity that shrank new writing at the time. They said 'Look, you can do this'.

The plays themselves were picked up and performed all over the world. Roy was garlanded with a few awards, including the first Meyer-Whitworth Award, and was liberally commissioned by other theatres. But the waiting and the dithering and the capriciousness got him down, and it wasn't long before he was seduced away by television. For three or four years, Roy wrote a huge amount of popular television, stamping his hallmark truth, anger and grace on all he touched. But Roy was always looking and hoping to return to the theatre, his first love. He was beyond joy when we told him that we would be producing his last play *Snake in the Grass*, an Ibsenian study of class and corruption in an English market town, at the Old Vic.

But then life, which had given Roy such a magnificent second chance, decided to kick him in the teeth. Roy rang me in January of that year and told me he had cancer, and that it looked very bad. He hoped that he would make it to see the show, but he feared he wouldn't. Through all our subsequent conversations and correspondence, Roy never once complained about his fate. He described his upcoming death as 'natural', saying that all endings were natural, as natural as all beginnings. He retired into the care of his magnificent mother, who endured many of his darker moods, and provided him with the unquestioning environment we must all hope for at our end. Hours before his death, his eyes were still bright with his remarkable calm.

We presented *Snake in the Grass* shortly after Roy's death. It was a passionate and beautifully acted production, that seared its audience, and honoured its author. A cast of twelve brought it to fine life aided by thirty extras. To the amazement of all involved and much of the audience, many of the critics turned on it, the recent death of its author notwithstanding, and sneered with a profound contempt. The play fell foul of the London assumption that class has disappeared in England and we all live in some middle-class paradise. Occasionally the smallness and viciousness of that band of brothers can still take the breath away.

Roy wrote large, clumsy plays. He was never strong on finesse or polish, but his work was always redeemed by large-heartedness and magnanimity. Always in his work, there would be a moment, a spread of compassion, that would remind an audience of what they can so easily forget – that we should always remember how greatly we can surprise ourselves, and each other, by our warmth and our generosity and our courage. And that we are all capable of change, profound change, and change for the better.

I think I'll meet happier men than Roy, but I don't think I'll meet any better.

Frank MacGuinness

Directors would kill for more plays like *Someone to Watch Over Me*. It is a director's dream made manifest. You get to take three actors, you chain them each to a different radiator in a small room, and . . . that's it. No blocking, no discussions about why you go here or there, no major motivational problems, just work out where the radiators are to go, then leave the actors to it. Heaven.

For those that don't know the play, it's the classic of the 'stuck-in-a-lift' genre. It's a pot-boiler situation that's transmuted by compassion and imagination into art. An Englishman, an Irishman and an American are all held hostage in Beirut. The play observes their initial suspicions, their macro- and micro-geographical disputes, their fights, their thawing and their eventual love. We see how they support each other in the most dignified human endeavour, the endeavour of remaining human. Role play, wit, fantasy and memory are all corralled in to keep their minds alive, their spirits good and the play lively.

It's almost everything you'd want a chamber play to be – enthralling, funny, heartbreaking, truthful, tough and affirming. Every theatre in London wished they had got hold of it, Hampstead was the lucky one. An actress friend said to me after seeing it, 'Why don't you put on plays like that?' If only.

There are admittedly many delicate questions of tone for a director but one overriding decision can sort all that out. A young director I know worked on it at university. He worked himself up into an enormous lather over whether it was an Artaudian tragedy, a piece of Brechtian gestus, a mood piece, naturalistic or symbolic; he agonized over its hidden meanings, its Shakespearean echoes. He wrote a three-page closely typed letter, setting down all his dilemmas, to its original director, Robin Lefevre, an old colleague of mine. He got a postcard back: 'Dear Mark, It's a comedy, Yours, Robin'.

McGuinness is habitually not a chamber writer. He writes expansive, experimental, wild, imaginative, epics – the most notable of which *Observe the Sons of Ulster Marching Towards the Somme* is a beautiful meditation on the nature of Unionism, courage and love. His hallmarks are wit and pain. But *Watch Over Me* is remarkable because he catches all that spirit and wildness and life and traps it like a genie into a glass jar. The compression is as telling as the compassion.

Conor McPherson

When I started at the Bush in 1990, writers would have paid you to have their plays on. The outlets available to them were so few, and so rare. They would kill for any small opening through which they could be heard. Their faces were saturated with old hopes and old disappointments, and if you offered them a production, tears would well up in their eyes.

By 1995, it was a different story. Directors, literary managers and agents were now seeking out new talent like pigs on a truffle-hunt, and behaving with the same decency and decorum. The contest to acquire the good new play was as genteel as the contest for construction contracts in Palermo. By then, if you offered a writer a production, they would look inscrutable, and ask how much you were going to spend on marketing.

So when a battered and dog-eared copy of *This Lime Tree Bower*, by Conor McPherson, arrived through the mail we were ready to turn it round quickly. Once we'd read it, we wanted it.

In formal terms it was clever, theatrical and genuinely new. The storytelling device had been covered before (mainly in Friel's *Faith Healer*) but never with the same lack of rhetoric, and extraordinary immediacy. And this was a new Ireland being described. There was no twilight, no mysticism, no sentimentality, no white horses on cobbled streets. The world of the play was searingly modern, and presented its characters with hard modern moral choices. It was immediately clear that behind the vernacular ease, there was a powerful brain ticking away.

It was sent in first by someone who'd seen it at the Dublin Festival. This was good, since it meant few complications. Then it was sent in again a week later by an agent, which was less good. The agent was Nick Marston. This was bad. An excellent agent, but also a wily and devious cove (the two things often go together), Nick had previously robbed us of another play, just when we were on the point of signing. He gave me his solemn promise that he was offering *This Lime Tree Bower* to the Bush and the Bush only. This meant that we had to move very fast.

Fortunately I was just about to spend a week in Animaghcerriag – a grand country estate in Co. Monaghan – running a workshoppy thing for a group of young Irish writers. One of them was Conor McPherson.

Although I dreaded it, it turned out to be a delightful, drink-sodden week. My main talent was organizing the whip-round for the box of booze required each evening. In the afternoons I was supposed to give each writer a sort of tutorial. I felt hopelessly ill-equipped for something so pompous, so decided to go on a different adventure in the countryside every afternoon. This led to me almost drowning one playwright in a marsh, where we sank to our waists, and wondered who'd be the first to cry out for help, and almost scaring another to death whom I merrily led into a field of angry bullocks in the dark, armed only with a walking stick.

Conor was saved for the last afternoon. I'd said nothing to him all week about his play, and decided we should go on a boating trip. We took a leaky little boat out into the great lake at Animaghcerriag, just as a big storm was brewing. I rowed him out to the middle of the lake, shipped oars, then popped the question, 'So, can we do your play then?' The rain started to spit, the oars were in my hands. He was most definitely compromised.

This Lime Tree Bower was a tremendous success at the Bush, as fresh on the stage in Conor's bare production as it had been on the page. No one knew quite why, but they all knew something big was happening. There was the modernity of the Ireland it portrayed, there was the sense of ethical probing, and above all there was the entirely seductive modesty of the event – three guys, telling a story, that's it. It was the modesty of the truly self-possessed.

We commissioned a new piece from Conor, and he wrote *St Nicholas*, his brilliant solo turn about a dyspeptic and discontented theatre critic who falls in amongst a group of London vampires. This is the third in a line of modern adventure stories he's written as monologues. The earlier ones were *Rum and Vodka*, and *The Good Thief*. The pattern in each is not identical but similar. A man in an acute state of tension, stretched to breaking point by the lies of his life, happens on a chance to break free, takes it, goes wild for a while, gets lost in dissolution, then returns to the world able to deal with its, and his own, lies. It's the classic rite of passage, but each tale talks directly to its audience. There's no shortage of men, or for that matter women, sitting out there in the dark, living a lie and about to snap in half with tension. Conor takes them by the hand, conducts them into their fantasy, shows how that fantasy can quickly turn to nightmare, then leads them back to their own lives.

There was a fashionable saw about Conor at the time, amongst people who have to have something to say: 'Yes, he's good, but can he write dialogue?' Well, yes he could, he wrote *The Weir*, one of the most successful plays of the last twenty years. *The Weir* is the most fantastically clever confection of different traditions of drama, as well as being an entirely original piece in its own right. There's a bit of

Synge in there, some O'Casey, some Friel, some Murphy, some Billy Roche, so it sits four square in the Irish tradition of storytelling and naturalism. Yet there's also quite a few of the strands that developed through the nineties mixed in, a bit of horror, some child abuse, some spooks, some serious spritualism and a little of the redemption of human contact stirred in at the end. It's an extremely cleverly put-together blend. But Conor's own rhythms, his own humour and his own probing moral sense, make it distinct and all his own.

Also, as with the monologues, there is a deeply careful responsibility for the audience throughout. He takes them by the hand, settles them into the bar at the beginning with some chat, gives them a few laughs to lull them in, then gives them a minor fright, then a major one, then a major, major major one. Then he changes key brilliantly moving from reported to personal experience, and he terrifies the audience and drains them. Then having taken them out to the edge of where they want to go, he walks them home with the last story, a simple modest, but universal tale of lost love. Then he gently turns out the lights.

It's the most awesomely assured bit of storytelling, – controlling and manipulating the audience with a sure and kind touch. It also reveals a depth of understanding for the lost hopes of the old and the middle-aged and the young that is hard to source. Conor is a one-off.

David Mamet

The truism that an original creator's greatest enemies are his disciples is nowhere better manifested than in the theatre. Stanislavsky's complicated route to creative humility degenerated into the mannered self-indulgence of the method. Brecht's complex, delicate and humane fables were quickly vulgarized into the sloganizing of agit-prop. Beckett has spawned the most horrific breed of post-nuclear landscapes featuring lost figures spouting cod poetry of despair. And Mamet has led to a whole generation deciding that. The only way. To write. Is like that. Motherfucker.

The explosion of expletives in his writing has worked a necessary correction to the self-censoring prudishness that preceded his work. He has sent other writers off further into the vernacular. Young writers now compete to find the phrase or idiom that is comprehensively more filthy, terse, and compact than anyone has found before. They boldly go. They perform complex linguistic manoeuvres around fuck, cunt, shit and their many compounds, like duelling banjos or competitive ballerinas comparing *pas de chats*. Mamet is their zen master. The well of the vernacular is an endlessly fruitful one.

The style of writing, the stopped phrases, the abbreviations, the eruptive thoughts, the obliquities, that's more of a problem. Mamet knows how to make it work, most of his imitators don't. Mamet knows how to make each unit, be it a word, a phrase or a sentence, lean into each other. Underneath the staccato language, there is always a muddy river of intentions, desires and old frustrations, which connect the disordered fragments on the surface. A sewage system which makes the city work.

Unfortunately with many of his imitators, the sewage system doesn't work, and all of the detritus spills back up again. The poetry has become a mannerism. The imitators don't understand that it was a particular cultural and personal situation that originated it. The style is nothing without the source. Since the source is known only to the author himself, it cannot be imitated. Therefore any imitation of the style is bound to be empty and redundant.

Mamet has hardly deterred a following. All his writing, and the occasional bout of teaching reveals a heavy pedagogic strain in him. This is unfortunate, since as with Brecht, his theory is brilliant and persuasive, yet diminishes the strength of his work. Just as Brecht always claimed an intellectual distance and cool analysis for his work, while in fact it is seething with primal passions and emotional manipulation; so with Mamet, where he claims that all writing should be about motivations, intentions and hunger, in fact one of the chief pleasures of his writing is its observation and texture.

I wouldn't put anyone off Mamet's prose writings since he talks more sense than ten ton of academics, critics, drama teachers and dramaturgs squeezed into a box. His book, *True or False*, is the best book about acting in a long while, and exposes drama teachers for the charlatans they predominantly are. But even that lapses at the end into a dogma, which is so extreme that it makes one feel uneasy just to read it.

Mamet's idolatry of motivation, his belief that a story is only the sum of its characters' desires, is a strange negation of much of what is rich in his own work, and the history of dramatic writing. He shouts this at you all the time, if it doesn't carry the story, if it isn't directly related to the story then cut it, cut it, CUT IT. This is a nonsense. It denies texture, digression, colour, meditation, wit. It denies everything that makes a play particular. Take any great play and remove everything that doesn't carry the story, and you'd destroy it. *Godot* would be a sketch, *Timon of Athens* an episode of *Topsy and Tim*.

In his extremity, he barks that the only purpose of a joke is a punchline. Everything should be co-ordinated towards that end. If any part is not helping towards the punchline, then it's not funny. Well, I'd hate to get stuck in a Chicago joke session. A grim and determined drive through to the end of each joke. It may be that we come from a particularly *Tristram Shandy* culture (imagine that poor digressor landing in Chicago, 'Cut the crap Shandy, you motherfucker, and get to the point'), but surely everywhere appreciates that the telling is as important as the tale. What makes a true comedian funny is not just the punchline, but the persona, the attitude, the take, the particular world they conjure up.

It's almost as if Mamet is ashamed of his own talent, as if he's saying, 'Look, anyone can do this. It's just logic and science, there's nothing to it.' Could anyone write an *Oleanna*? Possibly. In this case the doctrine might have overcome the artist. It's a functional piece. Could anyone write a *Sexual Perversity in Chicago*, *Edmond*, *American Buffalo*, *Glengarry Glen Ross*? I don't think so. I don't think anyone else could get close.

Patrick Marber

Different theatres have different drugs of choice. There are alcohol theatres, of which the Bush was one, largely characterized by a progression through anger, joy, sentimentality and despair, according to a prescribed daily rhythm. There are dopey theatres (generally the worst), defined by a philosophical approach to their own poor box-office returns, and by the laid-back mutability of their shows. There are the occasional Ecstasy theatres, which hurtle from brightly coloured buoyancy to muted deflation with alarming rapidity.

And then, more than anything, there are cocaine theatres. This remains the principal drug of choice in theatreland. The drama it produces is hard with clarity, producing vivid cartoon shapes and immediate strong statements. Yet its clarity only really exists with reference to its own clarity. Look at me, I'm clear, I'm bright, I glisten, it says. Certainly, but what are you saying, you ask. There is a pause. Ermm, I don't know, but I'm clear and I'm bright and I glisten. Such drama is also deafeningly emphatic ('I'm right, I'm right'), while simultaneously resonating with paranoia ('aren't I?').

More than anything you get this with classical acting and Shakespeare. Actors, left high and dry by their fuckwit directors, often have a reassuring toot before they go on. Hence the *boom* school of acting. The 'I may not know what any of this means, but by God I can shove it up you' style, which usually owes its provenance to backstage cubicles.

You also often find it with some new plays. I hardly know Patrick Marber, and for all I know his only stimulant of choice is peppermint tea, but his plays are the quintessential cocaine plays. Their vivid emotional colours – power games, eroticism, chance – and the more muted ones – rejection, loneliness and hollowness – are the colours that tend to go with that exhilarating and dreary drug. And as with cocaine, the enormous importance given to a limited range of topics tends to block out the real pulse of life. Just as when you take coke, you find yourself being brilliantly articulate about a few tiny platitudes, so Marber manages to make some fairly thin truisms seem like great profundities.

Judged as entertainment, Marber's two plays, *Dealer's Choice* and *Closer*, probably rank as the sharpest and best work to have appeared over the last decade. They are acute, sophisticated, thrilling and funny. He constructs tight, focused and driven plots, and balances texture with forward momentum perfectly. His characters are etched with the economy of a brilliant caricaturist. The journeys they go on aren't big on surprises, but they offer the pleasures of a vivid cartoon strip.

And he writes simply fantastic lines. This is almost a lost art, the art of the individual line. This is the line that the audience can appropriate, hold in their heads until the interval, quote to each other, then put into storage for a couple of days and roll out on occasion to revive the delights of the first moment it was heard. This has always been one of the great pleasures of theatre. It's the adult equivalent of the sweets that are thrown to kids during a panto; it's a gift. Nobody does it better than Marber.

He also directs his own work beautifully. He casts the

best actors around, draws wonderfully natural performances from them, stages them with chic elegance and keeps them rolling along. None of this is easy, and no one does it better. His success has bound a whole new generation more tightly to the theatre. I hope he continues to do so for as long as he is able.

We wanted very much to do *Dealer's Choice* at the Bush, and met Patrick briefly about it, but he was so inundated with offers that our chance of getting it was tiny.

So why carp? Because at the end of the day if a brilliant boulevard entertainer is held up as a major artist it does nobody any favours. Our present obsession with success is so pandemic that we are driven to equate a hit with a work of art. It's not; it's a hit. *Titanic* is a hit, *Joseph and His Amazing Technicolor Dreamcoat* is a hit, *Teletubbies* is a hit. They're all great, but they're not works of art. Patrick Marber's work is great, but it's not art. And if we call it art, which many do, being intimidated by its success, then we devalue the verbal currency.

What finally lessens it in my view is a lack of a real wish for good. With a Chekhov, with a Brecht, with a Beckett, you see a brilliantly realized and brutally honest vision, behind which there hovers the ghost of a better, fairer, more beautiful world. Without the dream of the latter, the former would lose all its tragic fragility. With Marber, (*pace* the Dickensian *faux-naïf* in *Closer*), beyond the tough surface, he always seems to lean for dramatic excitement on the threat of a chthonic lost world. A fake Pandora's box lurks beneath the surface, glimpsed occasionally for titillation. Beyond what we see is a chaos filled with violence, sexual desire and sexual disgust, and endless mutual loathing. This strikes me as a cynically inverted fantasy world, a peepshow exaggeration of evil to scare the punters. It's essentially a brilliant manipulation of the middle-class fear of burglars.

It's not only Patrick Marber who indulges in this. It's principally a director sickness. It's good to be seen to have a dark side. It's an easy tune to play on a middle-class audience. A little polite violence here, some sanitized sex there. Everyone gets a thrill, and goes home happy. No matter that this stuff is as close to the dark side as *Oliver* is to social realism, what is really offensive about it is how easy it is.

Chekhov wrote volumes of work, built schools, opened hospitals, interviewed ten thousand prisoners on Sakhalin island, kept his family, kept his patients alive, held hundreds as they died, spent fifteen years coughing his own life away, and still managed to keep hope in balance with despair, still managed to love life and its mad optimism. So many glib pseudo-artists these days, and most much worse than Patrick Marber, substantiate their ease from pain with a facile and glib pessimism. So many directors, who have led lives of pampered ease, are so quick to show us how dark and dirty the world is. Since this invention of pain, this spiritual hypochondria, is the sickness of the age, it goes down a treat.

Theatre as a manipulation of the audience's self-loathing. That's really depressing.

Martin McDonagh

One of the first things to travel through the broken Berlin Wall was porn. The first commodities allowed through the hole punctured by a glorious peaceful revolution were on a rickety stall. Videos, mags, posters, objects. Shortly after it came Andrew Lloyd Webber musicals.

No matter where you went in Eastern Europe or the Soviet Union post 1989, you couldn't help crashing into an *Evita* or a *Jesus Christ Superstar*. They fell on them as if they'd suddenly been allowed to speak the words of the Bible again. 'I don't know how to love him' rose up with all the ancient force of 'A spectre is haunting Europe'. Smart, intensely serious young directors, the Katie Mitchells of the East, would produce high art, ritualistic productions of *Cats*. Critics would discuss them as if they were reviewing the latest *Ring Cycle*.

If you tried to explain that this looked a tad peculiar from a Western perspective, and that we viewed the ennobled one's work as commercial and derivative tat, they would throw up their arms as if you were pissing on a crucifix. To them, it was sacred. Why? Because they'd been denied it. Because it was elsewhere. Glitz, glamour, melody and mindlessness, had all been in rather short supply for eighty years. Now they were allowed it, they were going to defend it. The quality of pure hunger they brought to a performance, and huge satiety they felt afterwards, almost transmuted it into art. Almost.

It's easy to feel superior about all this. It would be easy to neglect the fact that a multitude of walls came tumbling down at the same time over here. And to neglect that we had been denying ourselves a fair amount of goodies. For the theatre, stuck in an ideological rut, created its own iron rules, its own NKVD, its own limited aesthetic. The obsession with victims, the further absurdities of political correctness, the dreary realism, the need for ideological declaration, the prevalence of journalism, the codified self-pity; there was an equivalent, although less severe, cate-chism over here. It was the wrong-headed inheritance of Brecht; Berthold without all the good bits.

The process by which this was broken down was a peculiar one. Since no one recognized there was a problem, no one recognized the solution when it happened. Primar-ily it was the achievement of a group of young writers who forged through the locked door into the grey room, and splashed a fuck of a lot of colour about. Everything we had previously been denied – devilry, wit, camp, plots, sus-pense, identification, thrills, mess and magic – all this psychedelia of crazy colours claimed its ground and refused to be budged.

This is the process by which Martin McDonagh, one of the most skilled and brilliant creators of theatrical pot-boilers I have ever come across, has come to be thought of as an artist. Like the Russians, we are delirious at being suddenly allowed theatrical delights we have been denied access to for a long time. These plays are naughty, they're wild, they're elaborate and beautiful pranks. The sheer wicked bliss of having writing like this in the mainstream is so great, such a surprise, that people frantically try and ensure that it doesn't go away. The ring-fence of art is drawn around it, and all is well.

Martin sent a lot of his early work to the Bush. The evidence of talent was clear, but he had nowhere to put it.

There was a Pinterish play, a piece of absurdism and early signs of the Galway voice. There was the occasional cracking line, there was a great desire to transfix with a story and there were moments of beautifully observed and organized hilarity. There was nothing remotely Irish about them, nor was there anything particular to say. There was just talent. Buckets of it.

We passed on Martin's work, but found him an agent, and helped organize a reading for him. It was shortly after that a couple of things happened to him. First, he saw *Killer Joe*, a play of such pure unapologetic narrative drive, and wild dark humour, that it set something free in his own imagination. Second, he started to pay respect to the land of his forefathers, or, to be precise, its dramatic output. Martin's work is drenched in the plays of other Irish authors, of Tom Murphy, Billy Roche, Beckett, Synge, O'Casey, even Wilde. Since his greatest talent is as a pasticheur, he is able to reproduce perfect forgeries of any of these writers at will. And with fair justification. As T.S. Eliot said, 'Good writers borrow, great writers steal.'

In spite of that great thief's maxim, this remains for me the flaw in *Beauty Queen of Leenane*, and the subsequent trilogy. There is too much quotation, it is too directly from other fiction. The rub and resistance of life is absent here. The slow comedy of the world is not reflected in its manic hysteria, nor is the deep pain reflected in its titillating sado-masochistic narrative structures. As pot-boilers they are masterful, but they are not yet a lot more.

Using his great narrative skill, and a strong imaginative grasp of theatrical plasticity, he has come up with a unique voice. It's a pastiche soup, a blend of Irish greats, with a pinch of sick punk humour thrown in. Its greatest achievement is that it is entertaining. It asks the audience to live on the edge of its wits, and at the ends of its nerves. Thrills, spills and laughs, served up giddily on the surface of a violent, cruel, chthonic world. This is increasingly what a late-twentieth-century audience wants. Delights spinning over hell. Martin gives them what they want. Like the Russians, they can't believe they're allowed to enjoy it.

However, Martin is young, driven and serious about his work. About his talent there is no question. If he can simply return to the well a little more often, he may yet prove great.

Arthur Miller

The cliché about Arthur Miller is that he looks like a figure off Mount Rushmore. A monolithic, totemic figure hewn out of American rock. The fact is that he's an astonishingly handsome man, and like Nelson Mandela, he seems to get more attractive the older he gets.

When he appears as a grand old man to see revivals of his work through their last stages, he sends erotic shockwaves pulsing through the companies. It's amazing the number of young actresses I've spoken to who've worked with him briefly, and developed incredibly strong and dirty infatuations. Part of it will be the living legend element, and part of it will be the vicarious thrill of the proxy contact with Monroe (it remains very hard for many of my generation to believe that she actually existed). Most of it though is the man himself – wise, mature, seen-it-all and damned good-looking.

Also like Mandela he has survived to be one of the few unimpeachable living saints of the age. He's suffered personally, he's been victimized politically; he's held passionate beliefs that landed him in trouble, and he has learnt to moderate them to accommodate the rough edges of the world and the human heart. What's more, he's remained young, forever young, funky without being a prat, and full of humour.

Unlike Mandela, his wilderness years (in terms of recognition) have come at the end of his life, rather than the middle. Try as hard as he can, he cannot revive the excitement of his purple patch between the late forties and the mid-sixties. His work still appears regularly, some of it with some success – *Broken Glass*; some of it without any – *The Last Yankee*; and some just float in the middle – *Ride Down Mount Morgan*. Nothing has achieved the old impact.

Various theories are advanced for this, conspiracy and otherwise. The American public cannot forgive his politics or his personal life; the commercial theatre cannot contain his moral authority; we live in a shallow age. I suspect the answer is much simpler. The plays aren't very good. They are enigmatic, intelligent, elusive and troubling, but there remains something fundamentally arid about them. Their progress is functional rather than organic, their rhythm deliberate not spontaneous. They are dough that doesn't rise.

It's hard to analyse the difference between the late and the great works. It's hard to say 'there, that's it, put that back and all will be well'. There is some incredible gravity throughout every instant of *All My Sons*, *Death of a Salesman*, *The Crucible*, *A View From the Bridge* and *After the Fall*; there is an immanent moral passion, a huge prophetic sense of the importance of each word, that just disappears thereafter. The work is loaded with the tension of that moment, the tension of lives under the Holocaust, under the bomb, under McCarthyism, under the Cold War, under the exquisite tensions of his own life. From the middle of that mess, he came up with some of the best sense of the century.

Something seems to have flown away after he wrote *After the Fall*, almost as if he made a perverse Faustian pact. In return for the sacrifice of his gift, his path to immortality, he chose happiness and a quiet, secular and mortal. Such happiness could not fund the scale of his work. But he deserved it, and his relationship with posterity was already on a secure footing.

Adrian Mitchell

A passionate exponent of children's drama, Adrian Mitchell, one of our foremost poets, has an extraordinary record in bringing wonder to the stage. He has long been at the forefront of experimental drama. In the sixties he put together *Marat/Sade*, and *US* for Peter Brook; he has a hugely accomplished record with lyrics for musicals, including *Animal Farm* for Peter Hall; and for a long time he was a one man band promoting the work of the Spanish Golden Age, before a younger generation arrived and decided it was all their idea. He produced beautiful, buoyant versions of *The Mayor of Zalamea*, *Life's a Dream*, *The Great Theatre of the World*, and most famously, *Fuente Ovejuna*. His abiding passion for the narrative energy, the lyrical expansion and the hunger for life of Calderón and Lope de Vega, has left a huge mark on contemporary theatre. That would be a sufficient legacy, even if he had not produced all the other adaptations and original work.

He strives for and frequently achieves a Blakeian simplicity. His plays are a wild miscegenation of ribald humour, fantasy, horror, romance. Whatever is to hand is chucked into the mix as long as it's written in capital letters. Nothing minor is allowed in. His poetry is fuelled by a wide-eyed look at the world, and a turning away in rage at what has been done to it. His theatre is a magic place where a capacity for full-lunged hope triumphs (just) over the grime of experience. To paraphrase one of his own pithy masterpieces,

He breathes in sorrow, he breathes out joy,
Adrian Mitchell – the grave, but sunlit boy.

Gary Mitchell

Big, thrusting, Protestant plots. Gary Mitchell has carved
out a particular niche for himself, with some wonderfully
adept, beautifully textured thrillers – *Trust*, *As the Beast
Sleeps*, *A Little World of Our Own*, *The Force of Change*. He
writes from a particular perspective, from within the
Protestant community of Northern Ireland, and from its
violently disaffected wing. He's written up as the first man
to bring the news from that sector, but that's more
journalistic amnesia than anything else. Stuart Parker,
Daniel Mornin and Ron Hutchinson all posted dispatches
before him. But no one has reported so consistently, or
with such an acute understanding of the murderous
niceties of Loyalist tribal etiquette.

What marks him out from his contemporaries more than
anything else are his plots. You can almost see him looking
at the Irish literary tradition, and saying, 'Right you wispy,
textured, gabby, static, Southern, Catholic poets, let's stick
some narrative up you, and see how that feels.' He
constructs highly efficient thrillers, with life-and-death
moral choices ratcheting up the tension. There's all the
well-stewed tension of a thirties Bogart movie. It may not
be life, but it's highly theatrically effective.

The plots are grand, but there's a deeper distinction – his
understanding of the destructive loyalties of family.
Whether it be a small familial relationship, a large brood, a
working family (like the RUC) or the tribe, Mitchell

observes how those groups twist up their young, how the separate loyalties clash, how the women hold the power and suffer the pain, and how hard it is to break free from their genetic, moral and emotional codes. He offers no easy solutions, but there won't be any, until everyone understands the difficulty of the problem. Mitchell makes that clear.

John Mortimer

Sir John Mortimer has the look of a Faust who has said yes to the devil so many times that he's got nothing left to trade with. Once a smooth, accomplished and generous hearted purveyor of the well-made play, his original writing seems now behind him. The virtues that distinguished Rumpole – a rueful, claret-soaked sadness, a lightness of touch, an understanding of the everyday juxtaposition of pettiness and courage – also distinguished his plays. His most remembered work will be *A Voyage Around My Father* – a truthful, affectionate, pre-lapsarian portrait of his father that summons up an England that no longer exists.

Gregory Motton

Much the most reviled figure amongst the establishment, Gregory has carved out a career in permanent opposition. He's the Dennis Skinner or the Tony Benn of the playwrighting fraternity. Many of the most ambitious, if they suspect you have a different agenda from their careerist one, will ask if you're 'a fan of Gregory Motton', as if they were from the House Un-American Activities Committee.

How has Gregory managed to get up most people's noses? First, because he believes that theatre is an art, that art is serious and that art is distinct from entertainment. This doesn't go down too well in this day and age. If adrenaline isn't constantly high, if jokes, sentiment and ideas aren't bombarding the audience like bullets at Omaha beach, then an audience bred on hit culture finds it hard to maintain attention.

Gregory's work is obscure, surreal, pointilliste. It lives in the absurd of the present day, gathering together the detritus of our lives to form shapes and patterns that are simultaneously recognizable and strange. He takes a story and a world, atomizes it, then reassembles the constituent parts in a completely new way. The shock of the old, radically reconfigured.

He also quotes from a wide range of texts, lyrics and voices, with a seriousness that acknowledges the importance of tradition. It is partly this literariness, together with a dash of absurdism and high style that makes him so popular in France. In Paris, where they approach art with the same sombre Academie seriousness with which they approach everything from biscuits to bombs, Gregory is a big noise. In London, where they approach art as if it was a disease, he is a squeak.

Gregory hasn't helped his own cause by writing essays about everything that's wrong. He writes about theatre with insight, intelligence and passion. He has analysed with acuity the insane overstaffing of most theatre companies, and the criminal long-term neglect of most writers. A lot of the solutions he presents are perfectly practical. But the theatre village is a small, paranoid and bullying culture that does not like to be criticized from without, let alone from within.

Personally, I'm not Gregory's greatest fan. He wrote an achingly beautiful romance – *The Life of St Fanny by Herself*; a wonderfully magical and theatrical meditation on charm – *The Terrible Voice of Satan*; and a desolating image of split identity – *Looking at You (Revived Again)*. All of which I enjoyed and appreciated, and have stuck fast in the mind. Others, I've had trouble with. But many of the people I respect most worship Gregory.

But he flies in the face of the glibness and shallowness of contemporary entertainment, without compromise. There aren't enough people doing that.

Jimmy Murphy

Only one notable play to his credit, *Brothers of the Brush*, Jimmy Murphy has already succeeded much and promises more. His first play was modest and well turned, a story of four house-painters completing a job, while tensions and rivalries bubble amongst them.

What was remarkable was the way he managed to synthesize various different traditions without showing signs of his inspirations. First there was the Irish character study, with the attendant lyricism, humour, slagging and grace. Second there was the English work-play tradition, which was always based at the Court and reached its apogee with David Storey. This is the attempt to make the process of work theatrically poetic, both real to itself, and symbolic. Third there is the American modern jungle play, where colleagues (more often than not salesmen) compete, fight and betray each other, for the ever-diminishing slice of cake on offer. All of these influences seem to have been consumed and digested thoroughly, yet they do not interfere with the wholly original imagination behind the work. This is the sign of a true writer – invisible theft.

Tom Murphy

Realism is not just being real, it's an articulation of being real. The Royal Court in its full flowering of realism, during the Lindsay Anderson regime, treated the representation of life as a science. 'There is a particular angle in the grip on a cup of tea, a particular way of holding it, that brings the act of drinking tea to life,' the more pedantic will tell you. And they're right. Most realism is sloppy, actors just shambling around, arrogant within their own honesty, denying that there is an aesthetic to truth.

Irish actors understand this instinctively. They love the naturalistic style, but they know in their bones how to twist life, turn it and lift it, so that it is elegant at the same time as honest. Druid Theatre Company under the tutelage of Garry Hynes exemplified this work. They have an extraordinary tradition of presenting Tom Murphy's work, and manifest one of the most successful examples in the world of a company of actors giving particular life to a writer.

Their mettle was nowhere more savagely tested than with *Conversations on a Homecoming*, one of the great barroom masterpieces. Here they had to remember their lines, act truth, represent it and sink about eight pints each in the course of an evening. That's what I call acting. Some people think acting is exposure of inner emotions, some that it's looking pretty, some that it's waving their arms about and being physical. I'd suggest they were all cast in *Conversations* just to see how long they survived.

Conversations on a Homecoming must be one of the most beguilingly modest titles ever dreamt up. And for one of the mightiest plays. It is literally a series of conversations, but as with the best realism, not just that. Conversation is the essence and the centre of most of Murphy's work. The tide, the drift, the flares and fireworks of chat form the smokescreen behind which Murphy works an enormously serious intent. He is a master of inconsequential rhythm, of catching the pace of speech which is just passing by, but within which whole lives are crushed or rise from the ashes. Whether in the violent crackle of *A Whistle in the Dark*, the threnody of *Bailegangaire* or the fantastical sparring of *The Gigli Concert*, Tom Murphy aims at and hits the articulate truth.

Phyllis Nagy

Some writers you just can't get. Your friends, colleagues, family, can praise them to the skies, but the flavour just won't appeal. Phyllis Nagy is one of them for me. She writes wittily, imaginatively and outrageously. I'm sure she's terrific, but for me it always sounds like someone being a writer, rather than someone writing about being.

Anthony Neilson

One of the healthiest aspects of the New Writing Boom when it was at its zenith, before the press noticed it was happening and spoilt it, was its democracy. There was no centre. No one knew where the next event was going to happen, or who was going to set the pace that others had to follow. The new voice could pop up at the Man in the Moon, the Old Red Lion, the Bush, the Court, the Hampstead, even the Royal Shakespeare Company. There was often a thin pretence that there was some sort of ladder, and that an opening in one place was a proof of some sort of quality threshold higher than another. But no one really believed that. You were as likely to get a real dramatic thrill anywhere. The garage bands were for a brief and happy moment in the ascendancy.

No independent outfit turned out more regularly interesting surprises than the Finborough Theatre, and no surprise was as genuine or as welcome as Anthony Neilson. His first play, *Normal*, transferred there from the Edinburgh Festival, and he premièred three further plays there, *Penetrator*, *Year of the Family* and *The Censor*. He will no doubt go on to bigger things, but it would be hard to imagine much better.

His work is scorchingly dark. A sense of threat, of potential violence, sexual and otherwise, hovers over all his work. Sex is a weapon constantly wielded, often by women against men. There is no end of shocking incidents –

defecation, anal rape, hand relief, the whole kit and kaboodle – but the word shock seems inappropriately trivial in the context of his work. Shock is a tool of manipulation, and Neilson is far too personal a writer to manipulate. Unlike with certain writers who yield shock tactics with an infantile glee, Neilson seems almost reluctant to describe the acts he does. You can hear behind his work the wish that the world was all roses, blue skies and the missionary position, but it isn't and it grieves him that it isn't. As well as the violence, the fragility and the anarchy, there's an overwhelming feeling of sorrow. This fuels *Year of the Family*, a heart-rendingly plangent deconstruction of the modern family. It's this sorrow that sets his work apart, and makes it beautiful.

The Censor is a truly great play, a lethal miniature. It was contorted at the time into a shock-horror brutalist work, when actually it's an astonishingly tender tale of the awakening of love. The tale of how a film director convinces a low-grade censor that her work isn't merely pornography, it's one of those extremely rare plays that doesn't only nail a present sickness, but also suggests the glimmer of a remedy. As Chekhov could dream of a better world in time to come, without providing some glib programme of improvement, so Neilson looks four-square into the heart of our sexual darkness, and allows himself a brief dream of a better world. It's the mark of a truly moral writer.

We had our period of being dissatisfied with artists who provide glib answers. Now we should be starting to get dissatisfied with artists who just ask glib questions. They're both finally as easy as each other. Questions should be asked but within the framework of a better possible world. As Teddy Kennedy said at his elder brother Robert's funeral, 'Some people look at the world and say, why?

Some people dream of a better world and say, why not?'
Some artists, the best, do both. Neilson is amongst them.

Tamsin Oglesby

Tamsin's first performed stage play, *Two Lips Indifferent Red*, was an elegant satire-cum-discourse about women, beauty and perception. She invented a plot clever enough to allow her to range freely through the worlds of models, cosmetic surgery, photography and modern romance. The spine, which pulled it together, was the quest of a mother and daughter to get over themselves and each other. It was a new subject, and she created an innovative new form to contain it. Each move of the plot was natural, yet offered a new prismatic angle on the main argument.

What raised it entirely above its own subject was the modernity of the dialogue. She created a thick confection of self-conscious tropes. The characters question themselves, question each other, qualify what they're saying, shift subjects then return, let inner thoughts slip out and burble generally. It was a beautiful attempt at the shiftiness of modern conversation.

John Osborne

I don't want to add much to the reams written about John Osborne. Indeed he falls outside the strict remit of this book. I just think it's important to remember how bad his plays were, and how central that badness is to his greatness.

He lived, of course and thank God, prior to the creation of the British dramaturgy industry. 'Of course and thank God' because his work probably wouldn't have survived it. A mad lie that exists behind this industry is the myth of the perfect play. There is, we are led to believe, a perfect play, lurking at the back of Plato's cave. Those who have glimpsed its blinding beauty – principally directors, literary managers, critics and some actors – return to the world able to help poor benighted writers in how to bring their sad sublunary work closer to perfection. Narrative structure, musical arrangement, three-dimensional characterization, economy, all are tools to help writers see the light.

Now if anyone had approached Osborne with any of this baloney, he would have cheerily torn off their heads with his sabre of a tongue. His plays are horribly clumsy; the stories lurch, stall and accelerate wildly; the central characters – Jimmy Porter, Archie Rice, Luther, whatsisname from *Inadmissible Evidence* – bang on and on, fabricating cathedrals of rhetoric that are rarely challenged; the women are often poorly written; the sense of place is often vague. You could criticize his work for ever, but you could never touch it. Nor could you improve it.

It has dark, troubling insights; big ugly truths that can only be achieved through mess. It has fire, a raging forest fire that has little sense of its own direction or power. And it has life, and there is no improving life. There is simply life. Like O'Neill before him – an equally wild indulger in overblown rhetorical flatulence and an equivalent nailer of the hardest truths – Osborne makes clear the distinction between talent and greatness.

The literary management industry has done a power of good for theatre where it has discovered, nurtured and liberated new voices. Where it has given shyness, confidence. And it has done a power of harm where tinpot Tynanic tyrants have dictated to writers what makes a play. Each play is as completely new as each new child, or each new carrot. There is no 'what it should be', just as with a child, or a carrot. There is only that which keeps it alive, and only the creator can understand that.

Joe Penhall

We all make mistakes. No one more often than artistic directors of new writing theatres. Since every choice they make when casting or choosing collaborators involves human beings, each one involves an infinite of variables. Similarly, each choice they make when choosing a new play embraces a leap into the unknown. A new play has to be new if it's going to be a worthwhile adventure. Whatever is manifestly derivative will only satisfy the limited and the exploitative. But if it is new then no one has any idea how it will go down. There's no prior testing ground. So you're going to make mistakes, whatever happens. Anybody who doesn't is almost certainly playing safe, or employing excellent PR.

Joe Penhall, while he was still a local newspaper reporter, brought his first play, *Some Voices*, to us at the Bush. Since it was set in Shepherds Bush he thought it was a certainty to us. We liked it, but not enough to produce it, and let it go. The Court snapped it up, and when I went along to see it, I had one of the best evenings of my life. So it goes . . .

Joe's background as a reporter still resonates through all his work. He is defiantly unliterary, he gives you swift, hard, uncompromised truth – reportage from emotionally complex situations. He takes entirely quotidian situations, normal people living normal lives normally, in a nondescript contemporary London. Then he idly reveals the savagery and madness that lurks within such normality. He has no taste for faked despair or prurient violence. He prefers the epic within the domestic. Relationships between brothers, families, old friends, lovers, almost soapy on their surface, suddenly take on a mythic edge. The ghosts of literary models lurk behind his work, but discreetly hidden.

Sometimes I wish that he would allow his literary strain to indulge itself a little more. In *Pale Horse* he creates some unapologetically symbolist moments, and lets himself off the leash of naturalism a little more. Since the fabric of his observed world is so secure, the freedom is riveting. But since then he has returned a little more to the safety of observation. He is capable within a fairly banal landscape of sudden lyrical swoops. Ray, the schizophrenic in *Some Voices*, Charles the heavy with a mid-life crisis in *Pale Horse*, Richie's declaration of love in *Love and Understanding*, show Penhall's capacity to write at a height. I wish that he'd sometimes stay up there for longer. But I'm sure he would contest that such flowers only startle in a barren landscape, and he may well be right.

If one figure hovers behind Joe, he's a very old one. Taking in the madness, the jittery reality, the soaring lyricism, the lacerating wit, the anger at the world, he's the Euripides of London naturalism.

Winsome Pinnock

Without a doubt the most graceful playwright around, Winsome's plays are delicate, calm and civilized. They steal up on an audience, gradually asserting their emotional grip.

She's a trickster. At first her work seems simple and plain. The set-up is obvious, the issues are laid out, and the people seem maybe a bit representational. Then slowly the characters morph an extra dimension. They become real and strangely familiar, like friends. The situations become impossible, complex and confusing, like the world. And the stories become fractured, incomplete and broken, like life.

It's the best trick, gulling an audience into underestimating a work, and then gently revealing extra layers to them, as if they were discovering them for themselves. It's the great and enduring trick of most of Somerset Maugham's work. This is not wham-bam surprises, suddenly inverting expectations with mad jumps of form or content. It's a gentler, subtler art.

I saw *Leave Taking,* in a rather unsure production at the Lyric, and had a fine and deepening evening. A considerable but quiet emotion welled up through the course of the play. Though at first I had felt on top of the play, by the close I was doing all the learning.

Winsome has had a hard time being picked as a representative of too many things against her will. She's been asked to represent black writers, and women writers, and black women writers. Her work is not propaganda, and it seems unnecessary to expect propaganda from her elsewhere. She is better than that.

Harold Pinter

Still the biggest ship in the fleet. Still the aircraft carrier, from which many planes take off on shorter, less majestic trips. The body of work is immense, and the consistency with which he has hit targets over forty years is extraordinary. There hasn't been a great play for a long time, but the later work is fascinating in its own right, and also serves as a collection of wonderful prisms through which the earlier work can be viewed.

Peter Hall's contribution to Pinter's oeuvre is always belittled, with conventional wisdom confined to being sniffy about his productions. But it can't be simple coincidence that all of the largest, most expansive, furthest reaching plays – *The Homecoming*, *Old Times*, *No Man's Land*, *Betrayal*, *A Kind of Alaska*, *Landscape* – came out of that relationship. Pinter wrote the plays, and the achievement is entirely his, but Hall's contribution as a patron, a provocateur, an exhorter and, probably, an occasional pain in the ass, shouldn't be underestimated. The plays that preceded their collaboration, including *The Birthday Party*, *The Caretaker* and *The Dumb Waiter*, are more linear, and more lethally precise – deadly cocktails of vaudeville and the absurd. But the purple patch of the Hall years goes beyond this virtuosity to explore darker, more silent territory.

Looking back over the works en masse, several principal qualities stand out. The first is the surprising absence of deaths, and simultaneously the overwhelming immanence of death. Given the fact that on-stage fatalities have been a staple of drama or art since who knows when, it's astonishing that there are so few in Pinter. Yet throughout his work you feel the presence of death everywhere. The knock on the door, the noise on the stairs, the unseen character, all betoken death. It is a cloud that always hovers and hardly ever strikes. It is the main contributor to Pinter's uniquely creepy atmosphere.

This is art from the bomb age, from the era of universal destruction. Dying is no longer an individual business, it hangs over the heads of everyone. No one dies, everyone waits. Beckett was of course the first and greatest poet of this age, but Pinter is the most eloquent analyst of how it impacted on everyday life.

The unfortunate concomitant of this atmosphere is an overall draining of vitality. Where there is a death, in any work of art there will always be a balancing life, an energy, a release. This is true of the overall tapestry of life, social and individual, and of history. But without any hard evidence of death, without any actual fatalities, with only the insidious fog sneaking in through the window, all life and all energy is bleached away.

Is such an oppressive lack of vitality true to the world? Will such work eventually be considered dated? Will the art that lives so conspicuously under the shadow of the great dehumanizing events of the last century – Hiroshima, the Holocaust, the Cold War – come to seem like too petrified a response to the madness of history? Does the Theatre of the Absurd provide an important window on the human condition, or was it principally post-traumatic therapy? Will the writers who managed to retain the human personality, and the human narrative through such dark times – Arden, Osborne, Miller, Rattigan, Whiting – will they be seen to have flunked their responsibility? Who knows . . .

What will never date, or never age, is Pinter's great formal achievement – his placing of metaphor at the heart of the theatrical experience. In a time when loose naturalism was in danger of dissolving all art in the theatre, Pinter's cool and precise metaphors reasserted the importance of sculpting shapes deliberately. Like a metaphysical poet, Pinter takes a conceit and works it through with utter rigour and a ruthless imagination. If occasionally these metaphors seem a little too cool, a little too deliberate in their universality, it's a small price to pay for their perfection. And beside Beckett and Ionesco, they're a party.

The other most fascinating, but also most troubling, aspect is how closed so much of the work is. This is Pinter's trademark, his inscrutability. He is the man who never discusses his work, who never wears his heart on his sleeve, who poses conundrums, but gives no solutions.

This is what he is endlessly admired for, his essential mystery, the cool forbidding *closedness* of his work. It may be that this is the reason he has survived so long. In an age which is swamped with criticism, commentary, study and reflection, to be closed may be the only way to keep going. It would take a brave man to write openly from his heart for forty years and endure the kicks and sneers and cynicism that engendered. Shakespeare managed it for twenty-four years, but he never had to put up with twenty reviews telling him his latest effort was a profound disappointment. Criticism cauterizes the spirit. It disables courage and discourages openness.

While unreservedly applauding Pinter for negotiating a course through such tricky waters for so long, it's hard not to mourn that we live in an age where to be closed is a virtue, and to be open is a weakness.

The founding of Pinterland is without doubt one of the most significant achievements in post-war theatre. It's a place we all visit at times in our life. We come upon it unexpectedly in what the world throws up or in what appears from within. It is not the world in the way that the work of Shakespeare or Ibsen or Molière or Chekhov or Beckett is the world. The metaphors and the dynamics within it do not send infinite lines outwards reaching into time and people: they rather serve to bolster the closed mathematical perfection of each work. Pinterland is an island. Made of rock. It will take a long time for the sea to wear it down.

Stephen Poliakoff

Our most dedicated recorder of the modern. There is a discreet prejudice in most theatre in favour of middle-class good taste, and middle-class good taste is resoundingly against the modern.

A sort of spare Muji chicness tends to pervade drama. A lot of the emotional impetus behind the Empty Space movement is a desire to hide from the world, its clutter and detritus, to run away to a tasteful fantasy zone. Probably ninety per cent of Shakespeare productions of the last thirty years have had bare wooden planking floors. Why? Radical theatre companies strip the plaster on their walls, and reveal the crumbly brickwork beneath. Why? Props are minimal and iconic. Why? It's a terror of the modern, a yearning for some sort of never-there-anyway Scandinavian simplicity, a breathless collapse into the pages of a Conran-inspired magazine. The rational intention is probably to provide a clear space for thought and the imagination, but if we have to reject the world to understand it, our insights are going to be small.

Poliakoff has no such taste problem. He stares into the modern in all its garish tackiness with an appalled relish. Right from the start with *Hitting Town* and *City Sugar*, his domain has been shopping centres, Wimpy bars, concrete, pop music, strip neon, cheap casinos and video tapes. It's a plastic world, and Poliakoff nails it. And each synthetic surface in this world has corrupted its inhabitants, and left them with half-synthetic, half-human hearts. His plays are full of the lost and alone, wandering around with inexpressible yearnings. It is a world where normal human relations are so collapsed that parents search for children, and brothers for sisters, hoping to rediscover some sort of lost truth.

Even when Poliakoff delves into the past, he still observes the modern. Most writers when they go back a hundred years will use it as an opportunity for picnics and churches and floral dresses. Not Poliakoff – in *Breaking the Silence* and *Century*, it's all new railways, telephone poles and photography. Rather than pandering to any nostalgic ideal of the past, Poliakoff writes about the glimpses of the future that the modern affords us in any present.

His finest hour for me was the television play, *Caught on a Train*. All taking place on a train journey across Europe, Poliakoff juxtaposes the modern in a variety of forms, but personified in an impatient, short-termist businessman, against the old, all fortressed up in one elderly middle-European *grande dame*. It is an exquisitely observed confrontation, constantly shifting sympathies, and channelling the tectonic shifts of history through two beautifully realized people.

David Rabe

Plays can travel curious journeys. There's an assumption that the transition from finished manuscript to full production is logical and orderly; that theatres judge work purely on its quality, weed out the bad, approve the best and move forward confidently into production. This is very rarely the case – chance, instinct and wild-guessing are often the most important factors.

Many of the finest and most important plays of the last few years – *My Night With Reg*, *Someone Who'll Watch Over Me*, *Beautiful Thing*, *A Handful of Stars*, *Death and the Maiden* – suffered rejection before they found acceptance elsewhere. No artistic director is without some blush-inducing story of how they missed a hit. Since finally they have to follow their own enthusiasms, rather than the public's, there is no shame attached. Life would be much duller if any one impresario did have a hundred-per-cent record, and theatres are often more interesting where they miss the public mood than where they catch it. The failures reveal their spirit more clearly.

But few plays had a more curious journey than David Rabe's *Hurlyburly*. It was launched into the world with the most enormous hullaballoo in 1984. Premièring at the Goodman Theatre in Chicago directed by Mike Nichols, it quickly transferred to New York. With a cast including William Hurt, Harvey Keitel, Christopher Walken and Sigourney Weaver, it was never going to be a discreet opening. The prodigious amounts of narcotic abuse and the sexual frankness in the play added to its publicity value. Naturally it was a substantial success, but possibly more for the event than for the play. Those who saw it knew they were in the presence of truly exciting writing and a great new American play. Those who didn't see it thought of it as the play with the stars in.

There was a subsequent production five years later in Los Angeles, starring Sean Penn and Danny Aiello, directed by the author himself. This showing reasserted the strength of the text, offered some now-legendary performances and secured the play's reputation in America. It is now regularly revived all over the States.

But its fortunes have been even stranger over on this side of the Atlantic. There was hardly a theatre in London that had not at some point over a period of about twelve years shown a substantial interest in the play. One theatre held the rights for three years, several well-known actors separately picked up options for shorter periods, there were readings, attempted productions, discussions about productions, everything but a proper showing itself. It was probably one of the best-known plays never to have been produced here. When we decided to do the play at the Old Vic, and came to cast it, it was astonishing how many actors already knew and loved it, and had dreamed of doing it. Many could quote whole chunks.

Thankfully, at the Old Vic, we were able to tighten the net and make sure that less good work fell through. *Hurlyburly* had to wait too long for a London opening. The intervening years in the theatre had seen so much cocaine going up nostrils, and so many blow jobs and knee-tremblers and worse, that what was shocking in 1984, by 1997 seemed perfectly natural – simply a truthful depiction of lives in a vortex. And away from the hullaballoo of its opening, *Hurlyburly* could be seen for what it was.

But then our opening was not without its own hullaballoo. On the press night in a packed Old Vic, as the last act hurtled towards its drug-crazed, rhetorical, super-charged, philosophical climax, two figures in evening dress appeared on the stage. They asked the audience to leave as swiftly as possible by the nearest exit. Some generous spirit had rung the theatre to issue a bomb scare. No doubt one of the many well-wishers who abound in the theatre.

The police arrived and said it would take forty-five minutes to go through the auditorium. But amazingly seven hundred of the audience had stayed, hungry for completion. So, leaning heavily on the magnificent courage of our actors, we resolved to do the last twenty minutes in the mini park across from the Old Vic. The audience formed an orderly circle, critics crouched on the ground at the front, drunks gathered from pubs, buses beeped their horns, and the play was concluded. To an enormous huzzah. After which the whole audience returned into the theatre for the first-night party.

That's what you get for choosing a quote from a certain Shakespeare play for your title.

Hurlyburly, beyond its capacity for creating events, is an enormously influential play. It's as popular with writers as it is with actors, and it's not difficult to trace its mark. The psychological brutality, the twisted romance, the linguistic richness and the slipped reality all resonate in the plays of the last few years.

But what nobody has matched is its full-lunged bellow. With only seven characters and a single set, it manages to be enormous. It takes on everything – life, modernity, the man/woman thing, the cosmos, meaning, and it charges after all of them, hurling around language as if it was trying to break it. It nails Hollywood spot on. But unlike *Speed the Plow*, which in its rather mean-spirited way sees that as an end in itself, it goes after a lot more. It stumbles, it rambles, it loses its way, but its excess is magnificent. As the director said at the beginning, to set it in the right context, it's the American *Hamlet*. He's not far wrong.

Mark Ravenhill

'I regard much current morality as to economic and sexual relations as disastrously wrong; and I regard certain doctrines of the Christian religion as understood in England today with abhorrence. I write plays with the deliberate object of converting the nation to my opinion in these matters.'

George Bernard Shaw

Well, good on GBS for being so honest about it. Surprisingly few people recognize how far the shadow of the eccentric vegetarian has extended across the century he lived so much of his life and died in. The fact that the long-awaited Holroyd biography turned out to be as readable as *Finnegans Wake* has made his influence harder to discuss. But it can be traced in the work of many, and most prominently in the latest generation, in the work of Mark Ravenhill.

There's a gamut of parallels between the writers – verbal wit, a resistance to the morality of the preceding generation, and a keen sense of sociology. But the central similarity is that they both write scenes that are about what they're about. For me, this is a fault-line. It gives their work a momentum, a punch and a direction. This makes for invigorating intellectual excitement. But I can't help feeling that a scene's superficial meaning should conceal several riptides. Riptides that run beneath it, in entirely separate directions. The political surface – a wonderfully provocative place to start – should work as a cover for all of the intellectual, philosophical, emotional, revelatory, sexual cross-currents that swirl beneath. Occasionally these pop up with Mr Shaw and Mr Ravenhill, and where they do the result is startling, but there is no impression of their immanence.

The insight with which Ravenhill diagnoses society and the individual, and the articulacy with which he presents it, masks the fact that it's not entirely coming to life. His characters look into themselves, and at their peak, find a way of describing themselves. This is compelling, but not alive. It's perilously close to soap, where everyone knows and describes what they are feeling. Similarly, they understand the world around them, its emptiness and its bleakness, and find different ways of articulating it. Their understanding is packed with insight, and imparts an intellectual thrill, but again it's perilously close to journalism. Too little is left for the imagination.

Ravenhill's wit is not only verbal, it's also visual. He's capable of summoning up stunning theatrical imagery, but again this suffers from its own literalness. An old drug dealer watching a video of his son playing the violin, in *Shopping and Fucking*, is of course clever and striking, but once you've got it, there's not much more to get. The juxtaposition of Victorian strictures with modern fragmentation in *Handbag* is wittily done and striking, but makes its point at incredible speed, and then leaves nowhere to go. The same device is given a much more effective slow-burn in Churchill's *Cloud Nine*. Similarly with all the shock-horror barrage, the rimming, the wanking and the household implements, there's an immediate visceral impact, and then not a lot afterwards. Each moment is about little more than itself.

As a battle-hardened veteran of long years of filth and

shock, and having thought myself way above it all, I was surprised to find myself coming over all Victorian at the end of *Handbag*. Various forms of neglect and torture are visited on a baby, which I found more repulsive than I can explain. Such cruelty is nothing new in the theatre of course. Edward Bond's *Saved* first walked the walk. But with the Bond, there was a definite sense of the cost, of the weight of what was being done. In *Handbag*, it just comes over as a trick, a way to upset and stir. With Bond you felt he was having to control his own horror, with Ravenhill you can hear the faintest sound of a snigger in the background.

Some Explicit Polaroids, as well as being wonderfully funny, had the advantage of being cheekily explicit about its own explicitness. The Russian lap-dancer chants maxims about the death of socialism as if he was a billboard. Sometimes, with his wild mix of political self-knowledge and provocation, he seems to have strayed in from a lurid dream of David Edgar's. This play in particular owes a huge debt to Ravenhill's mentor, Max Stafford Clark. It shows up his strengths – wit, clarity, unsentimentality, and his weaknesses – a taste for journalism rather than drama, and a prurient fascination with a netherworld that exists more garishly in the imagination of the middle class, than it does in life.

Ravenhill has been taken up with a mixture of unease and need by the generation of Shavians that preceded him. David Edgar, David Hare and the critical nexus that apes them, respond to Ravenhill's work, because they know what he's up to. For them, his sociology, his treatments of subjects, his wit, are a last line of defence. As the barbarians of imagination and life and *genuine* doubt (rather than pleased-with-itself Marxist scepticism) pound on the door of their civilization, a civilization founded on explanation and argument and pattern, they use Mark to keep the wild ones out.

With his excessive and lurid imagination, his ludic deftness, his panic sexuality and his sheer cheek, Mark deserves better than to end up writing about things forever. He has a compassion for those living lives at the edge of existence, at the ends of life, which is unique to him. When he writes in that zone, he writes with a lonely beauty that is remarkable. He shows that life at its most attenuated is a funny mixture of colours – peaceful, angry and full of warm and silly laughter. If he can be left to operate there, and not forced to discuss *things*, he will write more and more extraordinary work. We should hope he does.

Yasmina Reza

Yasmina Reza is very rich.
Yasmina Reza est très riche.

Philip Ridley

For twenty-three of the twenty-four performances of *Pitchfork Disney* we presented at the Bush, Philip sat in the same place. With his trademark beret pulled defiantly down to his ears, he squeezed into the front row. His eyes stared and gleamed, luminous with excitement at the fireworks display in front of him. If you didn't know he'd written the play, you'd think he was a rather demented fan. On the penultimate night, I had to tell him he couldn't go in since we wanted to sell the seat. His fit of rage was worthy of a child whose favourite toy had just been taken away.

I stole *Pitchfork Disney* in an entirely disgraceful manner off another theatre, the Old Red Lion. It was vital to me that we produced it. I didn't fully understand it (I still don't), but it did exactly what I wanted the theatre to do at that moment. It took the expectations of a normal evening in the theatre, rolled them around a little, jollied them along, tickled their tummy, and then fairly savagely, fucked them up the arse. Armed with a gobsmacking central performance by Rupert Graves, it took London by storm, bringing in the old crowd and a new one, and made all their hair stand on end.

Its premise was reasonably familiar. In a vaguely future/modern/could-be-now world, a brother and a sister, who have been tethered together since birth, live in splendid isolation. Their life is a cycle of storytelling, myth-making and dealing with the terrors of an outside world which they hardly ever enter. Into this hermetically sealed island, walks a flash bobby-dazzler of a stranger, who proceeds to unlock their pasts and let out their demons. The play takes a turn to the even more weird with the late entrance of a bemasked, singing henchman.

It is purely theatrical; two claustrophobic hours in real time, setting off on flights of surrealist fancy that are impossible in any other medium. Philip uses theatre as a vehicle for the imagination. His rooms are claustrophobic crucibles, in which the modern age disgorges its most hideous imagery. His settings are the launching pads for visions that are apocalyptic, perversely sexual, scarily Freudian and chillingly banal. These are children's nightmares writ large.

Performed right at the beginning of 1990, this was one of the first plays to signal the new direction for new writing. No politics, no naturalism, no journalism, no issues. In its place, character, imagination, wit, sexuality, skin and the soul. It's hard to write of Philip's spirituality, since he writes in a nether world, a world of the reverse-soul. He acknowledges an extra life in the human world, but it's full of rubbery demons and latex goblins. There's very little mountain tops or green grass round here.

Philip went on to write two plays for the Hampstead of equal excitement and authority – *The Fastest Clock in the Universe*, and *The Ghost From a Perfect Place* – which proved that he was very far from a one-hit wonder. The same claustrophobic setting, the same dark imagining, the same twisted relationships. They didn't create quite the same stir. The second and third helpings of a bizarre new flavour rarely do. But it's a flavour whose popularity should grow.

Billy Roche

One early January night, 1993, I stood alone in a thin scutty Wexford street, a terrace of grey stone houses. A low hanging mist had settled over the town, a fog so thick it seemed there was no one else in the world. The entrance to the opera house, disguised behind modest front doors, was in front of me. Our production of *The Wexford Trilogy* by Billy Roche was coming to play in the author's hometown. All was quiet, but nervous with anticipation.

I had hung around in the dressing rooms, until my uselessness had started to irritate even me. Someone politely recommended that I go outside and watched the people arriving. Better that than nothing, I thought, so stepped out and waited.

At about twenty-to-eight, a few desultory figures started to solidify out of the mist. A family here, a gang of kids there, a group of friends there, just a few at a time. A noise started to grow, and with it an excitement. The occasional brightening shadows turned into thick clusters of bodies. Then as curtain up approached, it became a solid wall. A wall of people marching with joy to the theatre. They filled the street. A couple of thousand had turned up, eight hundred to see the show and the other thousand-odd to savour it. The chat was high, the heads were up, the glint was in the eyes. They were excited and they were proud. My eyes were wet with tears. Wexford had come out to claim its own.

Almost six years before, in 1987, I'd sat in a toilet in the *Daily Telegraph* tower on the Isle of Dogs, frantically reading a script. I was very angry with it. It was good. If you're reading scripts in a hurry, you want them to be bad, so you can dismiss them. If they're good you have to be careful. This was very good. I was trying to combine a temporary job at the *Telegraph* with my script-reading duties for the Bush. That's why I was hiding in the toilet. The quality of the script, *The Boker Poker Club* (later entitled *A Handful of Stars*), meant that I had to spend a couple of hours closeted away.

I duly handed the script in to the then Bush management with a recommendation that they should produce it. They duly did. Two years later they produced Billy's second play, *Poor Beast in the Rain*. Two years later, by which time I had become artistic director of the Bush, we produced his third, *Belfry*. A year later we reprised all three as *The Wexford Trilogy*, performed them in repertoire at the Bush, took them to Wexford for one performance each, played them for a couple of months in Dublin, and then had all three televized by the BBC. Wherever it went it triumphed.

That is the bare bones of a much more colourful and interesting story, which would include, if anyone wanted to tell it, tales of some great parties, of some great fights and some enormous goodwill. The plays were peerlessly directed by Robin Lefevre. He assembled one of the three great post-war acting companies to perform them. The Billy Roche company was in the same rare class as Joan Littlewood's company at Stratford East and Bill Bryden's at the National. And each play was designed to perfection by Andrew Wood, who died shortly after the last, happy and proud in the knowledge that he had been involved with such high work.

As Jimmy Ellis, a highly respected Belfast actor, said to the company after the last performance at the Bush;

'There. You've done them. Now you can watch everyone else fuck them up.'

The plays afforded me probably my two best nights in the theatre – the first and second press nights of *Belfry*. The rarest pleasure that theatre can afford is when it provokes an action of the soul. Awareness is heightened, each individual and the group together feel their hearts and spirits growing. A bliss that is stretched to an airy thinness over despair spreads throughout the room. All that is played before the united congregation seems to live on the paper-thin, feather-light line between life and death. Each moment is beautiful because it is alive, each moment is beautiful because it must die and give way to another.

In a Shakespeare play, at a good production, on a good night, if you're lucky, you'll get about five minutes of this. At a Chekhov, if it's motoring, you might get about three. To enjoy just thirty seconds of it on a night out makes any ticket worthy of its price. On those two nights of *Belfry*, like rolling thunder, that feeling just went on and on. The audience sat stock still, their mouths open, their hearts squeezed up into their throats, praying that it would not stop. They could not credit that it could be so precise and so strong, so light and so deep, so trivial and so profound.

This is all a tremendous amount of wind around the plays themselves. All the wind serves as an excuse for me to say I do not really know why they are as great as they are. Smalltown Chekhovian drama is one way of looking at it, but does no justice to its huge effect. *A Handful of Stars* follows the rage and explosions of a young rebel as the society around him tries to destroy his originality. A perfect concise parable of how greyness loathes colour, and how good is turned to bad by fear of its own simplicity. *Poor Beast in the Rain* is the perfect well-made play. Set in a betting shop on the weekend of the All Ireland Hurling Finals, it chronicles the return of a mythic outsider and how he disturbs some delicate equilibriums. *Belfry* is a time play, dancing backwards and forwards around some incidents backstage in a church – an affair, a drink problem, a death. It is the most meditative and the most deceptive.

The plays defy analysis or description. They celebrate the mystery of life, as completely as they celebrate life. This has meant trouble for Billy with certain theatre managements and critics, who like to proscribe and categorize their work. If they can't find a box, they don't know how to cope with something.

It is enough to say that their creator Billy Roche is a man touched with genius, and that the plays are the best.

Peter Shaffer

The pot-boiler merchant *par caparison*. Peter Shaffer worked out the perfect stew for the middle-class that lapped him up. Rampant plots, a bit of high language, a surprising dollop of education, a swirl of intellectual difficulty, some Apollonian theatrical business, some Dionysiac theatrical business, and no-nonsense star parts. He is an astonishingly adept theatrical technician, which is displayed nowhere more clearly than in the scintillating ingenuity of *Black Comedy*.

Although Shaffer was educated in the well-made-play tradition, he was astute enough to realize that that form was past its sell-by date. His first play, *Five Finger Exercise*, offered a variation on that form; his later work achieved a brilliantly commercial combination of the well-made play and the epic. In *The Royal Hunt of the Sun*, *Equus*, *Amadeus* and *Yonadab*, he boldly merges Rattigan and Brecht, with his own poetic strain larded on top. It's a recipe that pleases everyone, the conservative audience get their story, and the seekers for some ill-defined 'more' (as in 'Yes, I liked it, but when I go to the theatre, I want something . . . more'), get their ill-defined 'more'. His later plays, *The Gift of the Gorgon* and *Lettice and Lovage*, have moved closer back to the old tradition, although with liberal splashes of ecstasy stirred in.

The most crucial commercial ingredient throughout his work, the one that plays largest with its middle-class audience and the critics, is that old ticket-seller, 'self-loathing'. Nothing shifts seats like the middle-class looking at their lives and finding them bereft. Shaffer was the master of his generation, Hare of the next, and it looks like Patrick Marber is going to pick up the mantle for this one. Shaffer found a particular source for this ongoing death of the self. For him it's located in a loss of belief, or faith, or magic in the West. In the *Royal Hunt*, we bemoan our smallness beside the savage clarity of Atahuallpa; in *Equus*, we are all belittled in comparison with Alan Strang's frenzied exultations; in *Amadeus*, we share Salieri's envy at the exuberant genius of Mozart. There is, of course, balance here. Shaffer clearly delineates the destructive effects of all this religious agitation, and the inability of civilization to accommodate it.

But it's not the balance that sells, it's the self-castigations and the attendant comfort. Theatre is full of this fake anagnorisis, this spiritual masochism dressed up as self-knowledge, and personally, I find it a bit distasteful. It's a cut-price form of tragedy. Most directors (especially those who 'bring out the inner darkness') build careers on it. Audiences love an evening where they can say, 'Oh aren't we terrible, aren't we small, faithless and secular? Isn't it awful?' then step lightly until the next bit of organized self-loathing. No one does it better than Shaffer. His plays are superlative entertainments, but we have to find a way round the success of this manipulation of self-loathing, if theatre is going to comprehensively regenerate itself.

Sam Shepard

What is a counter-cultural act these days? What is radical, anti-establishment or subversive in this happy shiny world? How can you stay consistently avant-garde, when the avant-garde is swallowed by the mainstream almost before it's given birth to itself? If, almost the moment anything new announces itself it's going to be surrounded by envoys from the mainstream waving banknotes of many denominations, how can it not surrender? Today's sensation is on tomorrow's beer bottle. Tonight's fringe première is next season's sitcom.

How can a theatre be innovative, when the very word has lost its meaning? When the theatres most praised for their daring and innovation – the 'powerhouses' we are regularly told – serve up a diet of star-driven middle-of-the-road classics, tasteful musicals, ten-year-old comedies about metropolitan adultery, and the occasional new play as a fig leaf to cover their naked opportunism, how are you supposed to reclaim the word? How do you counter such flab, such middle-class pseudo-danger, such mail-order-catalogue perversity, such third-hand derivative artiness?

I suppose there are two ways you can go at present. I'm about to produce a beautiful play by Somerset Maugham, *The Circle*. About five pages in, a dashing young chap appears in some french windows, and says, 'What about this tennis then?' In our present age of soft daring, such complete conservatism seems to me to be about as radical as you can get. Alternatively you can walk the Sarah Kane route and go anti-everything; anti-narrative, anti-character, anti-convention, anti-life. We need a few new giants to appear, to show us how to be daring and new and true, how to resist blandishments and live only for their work. We need a few new Sam Shepards.

Now, not knowing Sam Shepard, I might have him all wrong. He might sit at home all day, watching daytime telly, eating pizza, drinking Heineken and muttering about how Neil Simon earns more than him. We always like to live by fixed images of those we don't know. And there's no better image for Sam Shepard the playwright than the one served up by Sam Shepard the actor in the role of Chuck Yeager, the test pilot in *The Right Stuff*. Having pushed his new aeroplane to the outer brink of human and mechanical endeavour, having gone beyond the range of radar, crashed the plane, and with everyone believing him dead, a search party is sent after him. They scour the desert with their eyes and see nothing, until a speck slowly begins to grow in size. Zooming in on Yeager we see him wrecked, half-burnt, staggering purposefully forward, ragged, modest and wild, the spirit of all that is best about America.

This is nothing but a hopeless idealization, I'm aware, but it's a wonderful image for Shepard the playwright – going further, pushing the envelope, stretching the limits and returning each time half-alive.

It was Shepard's great good fortune that he did emerge from a counter-culture that had something to fight about. He emerged from the mulch of the beats and the rock'n'rollers and the flower-powers, from all the nay-sayers who had a viable yay to put in its place. They had an interest in creating new ideas of success, and new ideas of value that we seem to have lost since. They experimented to get closer to the nature of dreams, and truth. They didn't experiment in order to be different. A lot of this experimentation ends up as simple kookiness, and it's that that has dated fastest with Shepard. The language, its jazz and rock rhythms, is one of the great delights of encountering Shepard's work, but sometimes it is too tuned in to its own moment, and wallows too luxuriantly in its own hipness. Some of the dream/reality, reality/dream problem looks hopelessly dated, a seventies conundrum that can't have been unrelated to the amount of lysergic acid in the water system.

Shepard's quest for understanding drives through all the work. The humility of that quest, its wide-eyed searching, is what renders the occasional hipness forgivable. The range of the work is also formidable; from the Beckettian shards of life in the ten-minute and half-hour fragments; to the great fratricidal bellow of *True West*, to the deranged, unmanageable passions of *Fool for Love*; to the internecine tensions of *A Lie of the Mind*; to the elegant con-trickery of *Simpatico*, right through to the operatic magnificence of *Paris, Texas*. The range of the work is too desert-wide to enclose glibly, but through it all runs the lonely man, in the wide-open landscape, walking steadily, looking for the love he has known and lost. It is one of the defining images of the modern age.

Jack Shepherd

An unassuming, subtle, and quietly devastating actor, Jack Shepherd has written four plays that share the same qualities – *In Lambeth*, *Chasing the Moment*, *Comic Cuts* and *Half Moon*. Essentially they are plays for actors. They are conversation pieces. In the first play Blake and Tom Paine talk in a garden; in the second some jazz musicians shoot the breeze; in the third some tired old variety acts rehearse their patter; and in the fourth some Fitzrovian drunks babble into their liquor.

Shepherd is brilliant at catching a variety of flavours without ostentation; the naïve enthusiasm for ideas and language of Paine and Blake; the riffy chilled attitude of the musicians and the strained energy of the comics. Events happen, relationships are endangered or ruptured, lives are let go, but what matters most are the rooms and the talk. There's no overreaching ambition here, just observation, texture, talk. The points that are made are subordinate to the seamless amble of life.

The modesty of these plays is their courage and their ambition. Sometimes it's easier to set a play on the moon or in history or in a metaphor, than in a garden. Jack Shepherd aspires to simplicity. That's not easy.

Shelagh Stephenson

Shelagh Stephenson's first play, *The Memory of Water* was an accomplished and witty, nearly-dead-or-already-dead comedy. There is a whole sub-genre of such works, where two/three sisters, brothers or a combination of the two turn up to the hospital/deathbed/funeral of a father or a mother. Or if the agony is really being piled on, both father and mother. Initial cordiality quickly dissolves into tension, and tension spills over into aggro, skeletons come tumbling out of closets at an alarming rate, and all is eventually washed to the sea in tears of loss. Arthur Miller's under-rated *The Price* is the grandaddy of such works. Such genres grow of course out of common and current truths. Within our lives of comfort and pain exclusion, the death of a parent is for many the first confrontation with death, the loss of a certain sort of virginity. It leads to an examination of self and of family, and requires a necessary realignment. And hence the grand tradition of wake plays.

The Memory of Water is an honourable, though not entirely underivative addition to the genre. It offered three juicy acting roles for women, which don't exactly fall off trees, and hence, beautifully cast, it became a West End success. Her second play, *Experiment With an Air Pump*, was a far more ambitious undertaking, and altogether enthralling. Because it aspired so high, it wasn't treated as well as the first, which aspired less and got there, but that's the age. *Air Pump* runs two stories concurrently in the same house across two hundred years. The central motif is scientific experiment, the central question, how far should anyone go in search of scientific truth. But beyond that motif, Stephenson manages to explore families and love, zeal and betrayal with a warm compassion and a light wit. It also tells two cracking individual stories, which woven together become entrancing.

Air Pump is of course a distinguished member of another sub-genre, the parallel centuries play. This is where two or more stories separated by a distance of time run concurrently. They occasionally comment on each other, occasionally contrast. Most importantly they throw a new light and shade, a chiaroscuro of questions and insights, symmetries and asymmetries over each other. The genre includes *In Flame* by Charlotte Jones, the excellent *The Pool at Bethesda* by Allan Cubitt, and at its most civilized, *Arcadia* by Tom Stoppard. If there is a common parent for all of them, a genetic original, it's probably Brenton's *Romans in Britain*. It's gruffer, rougher and hugely less polished than all its offspring, yet that is exactly what any new invention has to be to force its way into life. It requires force, and strength, and clumsiness to forge the new. It is only time and the imitators who can add the polish.

What this all says about time and our present relationship with it is for larger brains than mine. Suffice it to say that we're in a very different place from Shakespeare who treated time as such a warrior enemy, a crusher of loves and dreams and poems and hopes, a fickle friend and a cruel deceiver. Plays which show time and history in a great steady onward march, now look naïve and silly. Time is more imminent now, more immanent; past, present and future are woven into a fragile threaded web of simultaneity. History will never be treated dramatically the same way again.

James Stock

One of the most painfully neglected talents around. James wrote three startling plays that burst onto the scene, as the eighties turned the corner into the nineties, and the world of monochrome gave way to psychedelia.

The most reductive description of James would be an egghead who lived on the edge of Madchester. The freedom and wildness of that town, at that moment, are reflected in the acrobatic energy of his writing. While its imposing Victorian architecture equally lends the writing a stern intellectual and moral authority.

The plays hop round history and geography like a philosophy PhD on acid. The first, *Prick Song for a New Leviathan*, dropped an occasionally naked Hobbes into the turbulence and turmoil of the English civil war. The language was authentic without being archaic, and the imagination was boldly Brechtian without being generalized. The salty language and microscopic physicality (there was intense focus on a bleeding wound and on a flaccid willy), rooted the free-form philosophizing elsewhere. This was a play, premièred by Plain Clothes Co. at the Old Red Lion in 1990, which had been rejected by all the established subsidized theatres as too bold. Its main crime for them was its aspiration. The manner in which it was put together – profit-share, cheaply and with great passion – and the fuss it caused, was one of the early warning signs of how new theatre was moving away from the centre towards the independent theatres.

Blue Night in the Heart of the West was premièred at the Bush in 1991. It blew everyone's heads off. A meditation on Americana, it opened in the Midwest with a mother and son having their annual Independence Day fuck, and got progressively weirder from there. It traversed America, including digressions on Scottish topiary, the Vietnam War and a memorable monologue on 'serving suggestions'. At its heart was a splendidly dystopic picture of small-town USA, and a wonderfully dysfunctional family, still held together by an animal desire to possess each other. It spiralled downwards into the weirdest finale imaginable, which seemed at the time strangely apposite. This was taking on Sam Shepard on his own ground and, for me, beating him. It was Shepard with a perspective on his own work, and without the macho tension.

The Shaming of Bright Millar opened at the Contact in 1992, and eventually transferred to the Court in 1995 under the title *Stargazy Pie*. When I saw it in Manchester, it was a revelation, showing how high and how far James' talent could reach. I sat in the large auditorium with only about twelve other people, and we all collectively had our minds bent and warped. The historical grasshopping continued here. It swooped between Hitler in Nazi Germany, an ancient Cornish bedlam where the mad had their heads drilled open, California with its modern body fascism and a modern Cornwall where an ancient German woman and her granddaughter tried to piece together the fragments of their life, after the daughter/mother between them has immolated herself. And it manages all that with a light touch.

Each zone that James travels too, he catches the smell of. You always feel you can taste the world he takes you to. His travelling is real; it is not dry or merely illustrative. *Bright*

Millar encompasses everything, but at its heart is the oldest paradox in tragedy – living is a sickness that cannot be borne, dying is a terror too great to face. This paradox and other equally elemental ones that swim in the depths beneath James' work, give substance and emotional strength to his work.

The subsequent production of this play at the Court did it few favours. The brick-batting he took for it, alongside the excessive praise for work that was appearing at the same time, seems to have driven James back into his shell for a while. This is a crime.

In the short term in the theatre, achievement is everything. The modest well-constructed little number about nothing at all will always win. In the long term, achievement is nothing. In the short term, aspiration is derided. Work that is ambitious like James' – that aims to break hearts open and expand minds at the same time – will always be up for the sneers and jibes of the envious. But in the long term, aspiration is everything. James' work should be remembered.

One of Melville's most unfortunate statements in *Moby Dick* runs; 'Only the smallest erections are achieved in their own lifetime.' There are a few laughs and some comfort in that.

Tom Stoppard

One of the greatest joys of working on new plays is having the writer in rehearsal. There are sometimes attendant pains as well – some writers have too fixed an idea of physical shapes, some can't understand the time it takes to get things right, some haven't majored in tact. (Although in almost all cases the writer will be more right than anyone else in the room, it is still the directors job to mediate a communal sense of right.) Yet whatever the pains, they are far outweighed by the amount that can be learnt from a writer.

The actors learn from looking and listening. The writer's bearing, the way he holds himself, his attitude to others, the way he dresses, the lines he cuts through space, his confidence or lack of it in the world, will tell an actor much about the spirit of the play. The way she talks, her cadence, her vocabulary, her ease or lack of it, her honesty, will tell an actor as much about its rhythm. And unlocking rhythm and spirit are the keys to entering the secret garden of a play's life.

The directors learn from talking to the writer. To some extent this is a matter of asking as many dumb questions as possible about the text. But to a larger extent this is a matter of trying to discover why a play was written. To my mind, plays emerge from gear changes in their creator's lives. At some point before a play's inception, there will have been a small or a major seismic event, a red shift, a realignment of the self and its view of the world. This might have occurred five weeks, five months, five or fifty years before. It might have been love, it might have been loss, it could be kicking junk, or the death of a friend, or learning to drink, or a mid-afternoon Maurice Chevalier movie.

In some way that event has changed the artist. If, as a director, you can find it out, you can start to understand the source of a play. If you can hear the unheard voice, the distant echo of the big bang, you can start to make sense of the writing. Every choice you make must then reflect that insight. As Kandinsky said, 'It is clear that the choice of object that is one of the elements in the harmony of form must be decided only by a corresponding vibration in the human soul.'

This is not a prescription for directors to sit writers down at the beginning of rehearsals and interrogate them. Nothing could be more counterproductive. These things emerge obliquely through filters of trust, or they should not emerge at all. But how much better off a director is in the knowledge that a writer has just recovered from a broken heart or piles, than indulging in spurious intellectual baloney about literature and tradition. Insight into a source, normally the result of intuition and common sense, will always take precedence over intellect.

One should also never fool oneself that discovering a source is discovering the whole story. One should respect privacy, respect the mystery of another's life, and also respect the endless truth of one's own ignorance. But a source is a place to start.

What if the writer is dead? Well, with a Chekhov, thankfully there's a wealth of detail, there's the letters, the biographies, the memoirs, the details, the living memorial of Melikhovo. If you root around for long enough, smelling, looking, obsessing over odd details (his father's mad shop was my first way in), you can start to feel some ripples from the life.

What of Shakespeare? What can a director do? Not what they habitually do, which is to look out old press clippings of previous productions, and read some angular academic nonsense. Guesswork, saturation in the plays, meditation and bringing something of your own is all I can tentatively recommend. Although I'm no fan of heritage productions, how much better to have lived in Shakespeare's day. Not because they all thrilled to the King James Bible, not because they were better people, but because they all knew him, the actors and the audience, they knew the source. What clarity and honesty and vigour they must have seen, without all the ludicrous accretions that have barnacled him since.

And what has all this to do with Tom Stoppard? Well aside from the fact that he treats the subject of biography directly in *Arcadia*, it is fascinating to watch how he conceals or reveals his life. Disclosure or lack of it is what makes his work interesting.

In his absurdist pure comedies there is all the gloss and the brilliance and the dazzling technique, and precious little personality. Bright lights of show, running from any mention of substance. The best of them, *After Magritte*, *Inspector Hound* and *Travesties* have a benign pottiness that keeps the remorseless cleverness enchanting. The worst of them, *Jumpers* and *Rosencrantz and Guildenstern* – that rather garish lean-to cheekily tacked on to the beautiful and austere monument that is *Waiting for Godot* – are just remorselessly clever.

Then there are the encrypted plays, the crossword puzzles written in a code that I hope gives pleasure to the author, because it doesn't spread a lot around. *Hapgood*? What was that about? Spying and quantum physics, with as much heart as a quark. *The Invention of Love*, encrypted within the elitist code of academe, had one enchanting scene juxtaposing youth and age, but elsewhere seemed to delight in its own fastidious opacity. Mystery is marvellous, if you feel secure in the knowledge that at some level it is mysterious to the author as well. But if you feel that he has a secret and is withholding it from you as a source of power, it's rather like dealing with a lunatic who keeps telling you he's got a map showing where he buried his underpants but he's eaten it.

Then there is the odd large-scale disclosure of *The Real Thing*. Suddenly everything comes tumbling out of the closet – stale marriages, sleeping with actresses, writer's envy, fear of age, conservative aesthetics and politics. Having retained a philosophic detachment for so long we suddenly get the whole smorgasbord. And what a strangely thin meal it is, tasty and tasteful nibbles of modest middle-class existential angst from leafy Richmond. Although it hedges its own bets with a wonderfully sustained attack on the evils of sincerity – the famous speech about the art of making a cricket bat – it seems all too clearly sincere itself. And although the reaffirmation of the power of love at the end is moving, the structure that creates it is suspiciously close to an Aga saga.

And then there is *Arcadia*, which strikes me as a masterpiece, the equal of anything written this century. Here disclosure, encryption, concealment and delight all dance hand in hand together. Its breadth, its wit, its imagination, its invention, its terrifyingly painful sense of fragility together with its strength of spirit, are breathtaking. It bowls you along with the excitement of a well-made play, yet forces into that structure more care and wisdom than you would have imagined possible.

I was always in awe of it, yet had no sense of where its emotional source or strength came from. Then I read a highly intrusive but very clever profile of Stoppard in the

Guardian. He himself gave nothing away, but the journalist dug and dug, and thought hard, and dug again, and found an absolutely compelling and frighteningly true reason to explain the emotional power of *Arcadia.* I won't rehearse it, out of respect for privacy, but the journalist had done the director's job. She had found a source. And a source which could inspire such a mighty play.

David Storey

At the Bush, we would never commit to doing a play until
we'd met the writer. It was an insurance policy. No matter
how wonderful the play, how witty, how original, how
clever, if the writer smelt of bad intentions, we'd let it go.
There was one play that three theatres including us were
chasing after. Ostensibly it was a shocking but thoughtful
play about the violence within and without children. We
met the writer – a thin, beady, ambitious soul. He talked to
us about box-office yields, and where he saw his career
going. We dropped it fast.

There's a story about one of the decade's great hits – a
dark, moral thriller. Neither the theatre nor the cast had
met the author until the third week of rehearsal. By this
time they had all excavated huge amounts of pain to do
justice to his script. They had met victims and perpetrators
of the most appalling cruelty. They had watched disturbing
videos, and read degrading books. They had wept, empa-
thized, grieved and come through to the other side. They
awaited the arrival of the author with some trepidation –
the man who had transcribed this dark passage of the soul.
Eventually he arrived, bursting through the rehearsal room
door, filofax in hand, with these words: 'I'm hot! I'm hot!
I'M HOT!'

Writers come in all shapes and sizes, of course. They can
have any sort of temperament, any sort of nature. They can
be dull or brilliant; shouters or shy-boots; wild messers or

prim tightarses. One of the most successful Irish playwrights of recent years has a compulsive Hoovering habit;
another is a terrible drunk. There's no proscription. But
there is something about the act of writing a play well, the
act of creating a *separate* world peopled with *separate*
characters, something about that act of spread imagination
that would make it very hard for a good writer to be a
complete asshole. Thin people will always write thin plays,
but there is something about creating moments of on-stage
reality that will always require something quick, alive and
generous in the soul of the creator.

I only say this as a prelude, an extended prelude, to
saying that David Storey is, to my mind, one of the greatest
playwrights in the world today, and also one of the most
impressive men I ever met. The magnificence of the plays
matches the man. He somehow manages to be curmudg-
eonly, stubborn, didactic, withdrawn, sour and charmless,
at the same time as being warm, generous, good-hum-
oured, kind and unstintingly loyal. His eyes can fill with the
most scary contempt, without letting go of the most
subversive twinkle. His judgements can be biblical in their
severity, yet without losing an extraordinarily human
empathy. He can leave you feeling like a worthless idiot, yet
entertaining the notion that he has a sneaking regard.

Each year for five years, one of my favourite rituals was
the judging of the George Devine Award. Convening for
four or five sessions at the home of Jocelyn Herbert, youth
(or comparative youth) would confront age (or comparative age), and each would play their role to the full. On one
side the regulars would be myself, Stephen Daldry and the
Court's literary manager of the time. On the other side
would be Jocelyn, David Storey and the playwright Donald
Howarth. We, the young, would hustle, bustle, itch and try
to get things moving, while the older generation would
mourn the world's decline, grieve over friends who'd

passed and murmur about death's approach. It was a largely white room, and as the light from outside slowly failed, and it turned a shady grey, a sense of history misted the room. Kindly ghosts shimmered.

We sometimes thought it should be renamed the David Storey Award, since he so completely dominated the proceedings. He would find the play he wanted to win quite early on, and then proceed to defend it as if it was Rorke's Drift. Any competition would be destroyed with withering ferocity. Few dared to challenge him. For three years running, I took him on. Twice I lost, retiring bloody and bruised. On the one occasion I won my case, he stomped off, saying he would never return. An argument about the merits of a play quickly became an argument about the essentials of life, and all the rest of us apart from David would turn out to be as crashingly WRONG about that as we were about everything else. Yet it was his exactingly high standards and his passion for quality that maintained the importance of the award. I learnt as much on those evenings about the necessary difficulties of great art, as I have in any other arena.

I came to reading David's plays late, since fashion has quite resoundingly turned against them, and read them with growing amazement. Has there been a greater play written since the war than *The Contractor*? Has there ever been more elegantly tripping musical dialogue than there is in *Home*? Has anyone achieved a realism as pure, truthful and yet still poetic as Storey achieves in *The Changing Room*? Has anyone mined the seam of class and family and come up with coal as black as he does in *In Celebration*? These are works of art, unique, temporary and enduring.

What distinguishes his work? A strong, plastic theatrical sense. He can create great moments, exceptionally vivid in their context. The dance in *The Contractor* and the appearance of the mother in *In Celebration* are beautifully crafted. Modest everyday incidents suddenly take on a totemic force. His dialogue is deceptively quotidian, gliding along with a seamless naturalism until you suddenly realize the sensibility that is shaping it. He has a wonderful way with silence, suddenly opening floodgates of emotion into relationships where language cannot stay afloat. He can tell a complex story through looks, glances and nudges, stimulating an audience's imagination to understand, rather than squaring up and staring them down. And his people are alive, alive from their dirty fingernails to their sweet souls.

Although David would probably think it complete cock, it strikes me that there is no more true inheritor of Chekhov's gift than him. He has taken the form, the structured, poetic naturalism with history trembling gently underneath, and transposed it to a new world and a new class. He has found within that a new language, more concrete than Chekhov, more reductive, more understated, yet the spirit remains the same.

A theatre director said to me recently that Chekhov ruined the twentieth century. He said that with *Three Sisters* and *The Cherry Orchard*, playwriting had reached such a peak of perfection that it had nowhere left to go. It was the end of history, as it were. Content, form and life could never again be achieved so completely. This reminded me of those who always claim that democracy reached its apogee in the Athens of Pericles. It was of course great for everyone, bar the small matter of women and slaves who comprised over two thirds of the population. A democracy that works for only a quarter of the people can't be that great a democracy. It was a great model, but models and the mess of life don't always correspond. The mess moves on and models have to be re-invented. Chekhov did reach something close to perfection with those two late plays. I directed *Three Sisters*, and will testify to its greatness until the cows come home. But for later generations these plays can only serve as models, not texts. And models have to be re-invented.

Some in this century have reacted to the cloud of Chekhov by being deliberately and hysterically different. Expressionism, alienation, absurdism, ur-realism, poetic drama, all have served as violent excursions from what has been seen as the hegemony of naturalism. And some have reacted by acknowledging Chekhov, acknowledging the tradition and taking it further. David Storey enfranchised a whole new world with his plays, just as Billy Roche has with his Wexford plays. This is as noble a task (if not more noble) than reacting angrily. They both take his peerless spirit and imbue it into new mulch.

It is not only in terms of form, and historical sense, that Storey corresponds to Chekhov. There is also a correspondence in content. Both share the same sense of the sickness of aspiration, the agony of wanting. The search for Moscow has always been a paradigm for man's desire for more, and the endless war between his desire for more and his desire for peace. In Storey's plays there is the acute sense of the need to escape class, the need to climb, to better, to change and how that wrestles with the need to belong. The battle between the two, fought mainly in silence, leaves very few unscarred. It is piercingly true to the world he writes of, and an elegant pattern for all.

He also deals in Chekhovian large theatrical metaphors. I can think of no better metaphor for contemporary life than the mantling and dismantling of the marquee in *The Contractor*. Just as the cherry orchard in Chekhov's play exemplifies the movement of history, the destruction of beauty and the fragility of nature, so Storey captures the essence of modern life. In our careers, in our relationships, in our art, in our identities, what are we all up to, if it's not raising tents to keep out the wind and rain, then taking them down and moving on. At least a cherry orchard lasted a while: our tents last only a season.

So, to put a simple question, if he is such a great writer, why do we hear so little of him? David Storey certainly had his hour in the sun. For about eight years between 1967 and 1975 he was the golden boy, with all his plays opening, transferring, winning awards and the whole shower of glitter. For everyone of course, there are different periods and different kinds of productivity. David has continued to write plays, novels and poetry with great success, but for my money without the respect that is his due. He lost the favour of the press corps in spectacular fashion, when he physically attacked the lot of them, after they'd murdered one of his plays at the Court. David is an ex-professional rugby footballer, and our national newspaper critics most certainly aren't. So it was a singularly one-sided contest. But what the critics lack in muscle they make up for in memory, and they haven't been particularly kind since.

How do some writers rise and some fall in fashion? The answer, sadly, is that, as in all walks of our contemporary life, it is the ones who want and seek that most often get. Amongst writers, as amongst others, it is the power hungry, the greedy, the paranoid, the manipulative and the ruthless who rise to the top. They work on theatres, on critics, on journalists, on panels, on conferences, on funding organizations. It's a wonder some of them find the time to write plays. And often, it is the large spirits who get swamped.

One sometimes wonders about the Greek age. We all know that Aeschylus, Sophocles and Euripides were artists of manifest greatness, but were they also the boys with the best PR, the best agents, the best lawyers, the best act. Have greater writers been buried under sand and stone, because they did not hustle enough? We can only hope not, and, if we are to remain sane, believe not. Posterity is our last resort of trust. And if posterity is true, it should reveal a giant in David Storey.

Judith Thompson

Judith Thompson was one of the crack troop of frontline dramatists who erupted out of Canada in the nineties, and who subverted everyone's ideas of drama, and more radically, Canada. She dealt in shock in a similar way to Brad Fraser, but her images of brutality were far more felt, and less aesthetic. Thompson reports from the underclass tales of the extremely poor, destitute in pocket and in spirit. She brings her characters completely to life, and without authorial comment. Yet she knows that the audience watching her dramas will not be the people in them, and she handles the distance between the audience and the characters with a wonderfully deft sensitivity. Something in the architecture of the work reminds us that what we are seeing is wrong, that people shouldn't live this way, without banging us over the head about it.

A strain of poetry infuses the work, yet it is the poetry of everyday life, not an imposed one. She wrote one play, *Crackwalker*, about two couples, of perfectly observed realism, and another, *The Lion in the Streets*, a hellish kaleidoscope of urban street life, into which the surreal frequently exploded, rather as it does in the Scorsese film, *Bringing Out the Dead*. There is a school of writers, predominantly female, who are beginning to find a way of marrying realism, poetry and the surreal within life, able to report truth, and at the same time raise it a few feet above the ground. It's a direction for the future.

Naomi Wallace

Strictly speaking, Naomi is a yank. But like many other Americans, she had to follow the strange route to success in New York, by starting out on the fringe of London. As one jaded Manhattan theatrico put it, 'You've got a better chance of getting to Broadway through Islington than you have through East Village.'

So Naomi's curious journey began with a production at the Finborough (*War Boys*), shortly followed by one at the Old Red Lion (*In the Fields of Aceldama*). She graduated to the Bush (*In the Heart of America*), after which a further play was commissioned which was produced a year later (*One Flea Spare*). The RSC, quick on the uptake, optioned and produced her next (*Slaughter City*) in the Pit. The Actors Theatre of Louisville then chose *One Flea Spare* for their Humana Festival of New Plays. The head honchos from the East and West coast fell in love with it there, and the king of all New York theatres, the Public, got to produce it. It won the Obie Award. From Earl's Court to Manhattan in five or six not-so-easy steps.

This is one of the most elegant examples of the rise up the ladder that I have known. Never staying too long on any particular step, each plateau that Naomi has reached has brought her work to the attention of a new audience, and made her talent attractive to more powerful players. She is continuing her determined ascent through the world of film at the moment. For someone of such hardheaded determination, climbing is as necessary as breathing, but I hope she realizes that there's nowhere to rest or settle on a ladder. Her work will prosper further when she settles in one place.

Naomi, in both her writing and herself, is a curious mixture of the old and the new America. At the new end, she has a ferocious intellect, trained to diamantine brilliance and focus by long years in academia. Together with this intellect goes a very modern, very self-aware sense of right and wrong. You can call this political correctness, you can sneer at it, you can even get hysterically defensive about it as Mamet does in *Oleanna*. But any of those reactions demean what is simply an attempt by a new generation of thinkers to set up moral rules for their generation in a new world. American radicals are at the forefront of this, and if their humourlessness is sometimes a tad tiresome, you have to admire the fact that they are trying to work something out.

The old America is something more natural and more easy in Naomi, and comes out of her childhood. She was brought up in Kentucky in a world of tractors and beers and horses and guns. The farm she grew up on backs on to the Ohio river, a great trading route for tobacco and whisky, and a great muddy brown thread running through American history. It's a blue-collar culture, tough and unforgiving. Its rhythms, its anger and its wildness, all course through Naomi's veins.

The coincidence of these two deeply contrary cultures in Naomi is what makes her writing fly. If you wanted to be romantic, you could call it an admixture of fire and ice; if you wanted to be direct, you'd call it shit with angles. Whatever it is, it makes for some of the most truly remarkable writing around at the moment. The voice is poetic; earthy while light, sensual while cold. The stories are lightly fractured myths, erotic fairytales broken up into instructive episodes, like Brecht's Lehrstucken, with magic sprinkled over them.

And the subject matter is often fiercely political. This sets Naomi apart from so many of her contemporaries. Unlike many others who have eschewed political anger, with Naomi it is still raw and fresh. And unlike many others who look at complex and tragic situations and echo Stephen's 'It's aw a muddle' from *Hard Times*, Naomi hasn't lost her proper conviction that, wherever there is tragedy, somewhere there will be a villain triumphant and somewhere else there'll be goodness squashed.

There is also, crucially, a sly and dancing wit beneath the rhetoric. Without it, the work would be overwhelmingly earnest and impossible to digest. A delicate, wry poise marks it out. The formal elegance this provides raises it above simple passion. The RSC comprehensively fucked up *Slaughter City* by completely ignoring its wit. They mistook it for the witless puritanical victim-obsessed seriousness of much seventies drama, and completely missed its modern edge. Naomi's great experiment is that she takes a Pandora's Box of volatile material and spreads a Jane Austen/ Michelle Shocked veneer over it. That is her art.

Naomi has covered a huge range of territory already: the Mexican border in *War Boys*; familial sexual dynamics in *Aceldama*; the Gulf War and racism in *In the Heart of America*; the meatpacking industry in *Slaughter City*; and the plague of 1665 in *One Flea Spare*. The last play is her masterpiece, and one of the truly great plays of the last ten years. We can only pray that, for all our sakes, she writes a couple more.

Nick Ward

Nick is a modern Dostoevskian innocent. He even has the eyes. Bold and direct. Not an innocent in the sense of being ignorant or missing what's going on, more in the antique sense of heightened sensitivity. The innocence that feels everything too acutely, sees everything too clearly. The innocence that knows about all the world's evil and wickedness, knows it both externally and internally, and still can't believe it goes on winning.

Like an Epicurean, Nick has always stared long and hard into the nature of things. He stares for minutes, days, sometimes months. He returns from these stares with an awareness of the charged poetry of all objects and the curious quest for goodness in people. His work, which deals in contemporary surfaces, is thus given a religious sheen. A charge.

Though he was an award-winning student and a big noise on the Edinburgh Fringe from his infancy, he made his first real splash with *Apart From George*. One of the first real events to emanate from the National Theatre Studio, this proved a big hit at the Traverse, on tour and at the Royal Court. A study of the bone-crushing nihilism of modern agricultural life, it moved silently and grimly between a tale of child abuse on a personal level and an examination of how a whole class (agricultural labour) has been made redundant and dispensable by history on a more public level. It did all this without speeches, without statistics, without debate. Just by minutely observing the appropriate moments in the lives of the characters. The subject matter was nothing new, the presentation was. It was spare, minimal and beautifully precise.

Like so many of the best modern writers and artists, Nick observed the dictum that the largest part of an atom is space.

He followed up with a commission for the National, *The Comfort of Strangers*, which observed the same loneliness, the same poetry, the same exploitation in the context of the modern city. Again he was able to cut out a very particular moment of history, and display it in the context of individual lives. Again he was as pitilessly spare. The play aimed for a Dickensian reach, which it didn't quite hit, and the effect was less surprising than with his first play, but it confirmed his status as a real talent.

A lot of success came very early to Nick. He always enjoyed the role of the outsider, which is a grand place to be, and in the twentieth century, an honourable one. But having set himself apart from the herd, he had less people with which to contextualize his highs, and later the unerringly consequent lows. There was no one to pull him down as he floated up, or hold on when he sank. After the comparative lack of success of *The Comfort of Strangers*, he disappeared off to make a couple of movies, and kept his head low.

But, with his third play, *The Present*, he resoundingly bounced back. Set in his native Australia, this was a far more lush, juicy and sensuous experience than his previous work. Two men, an English innocent youth, and a scarily dark sixties-casualty Aussie revolve around two beautiful and strangely similar women, one unapproachably cool, the other deranged with sexual greed. The circles they wheel around each other provoke laughter, fear and a consistent sexual pulse. It's a brew that's unique to Nick, a collision of modern neurosis and the expanse of the Australian sky, a mix of sex comedy and existential poetry. It was wonderful.

Nick's been quiet for a while since, but he's no doubt been staring, and no doubt he'll return soon and tell us what he saw.

Keith Waterhouse

The right way to live a life. It's questionable that Keith Waterhouse has had too beady an eye on posterity, but what a wonderfully open eye he's had on the here and now. He's written a shitload of plays, many of them with his regular collaborator Willis Hall, enjoyed many a West End success; he's written volumes of columns, novels, screenplays, consumed swimming pools of booze, and spread a broad table of pleasure for thousands of others. No gaunt-cheeked suffering artist here, and all the better for it.

His plays are the classic low-boulevard entertainments – warm jokes, vivid characters, twisty-turny plots, seedy milieus, a vivid sense of the loneliness of lives lived in hope and a broad smattering of pathos. He's written too many to number, and the prolific nature of his work has mitigated against its perfection of form. Actually that's not completely true. They often achieve a tightness of construction that is close to the Platonic ideal of the well-made play. But they are sometimes over-constructed, and that stifles their individual life.

However, if the base of the pyramid is broad the top will be high, and from his profusion, two of the mythic figures of the age have emerged, Billy Liar and Jeffrey Bernard. (The second was of course real, but so was Hamlet, after a fashion.) The English exemplars of the great dreamer and the great coper have both been wrought from his playwright's skill. He has worked, hacked and enjoyed his way into posterity.

Irvine Welsh

'We've got to get the kids in,' was the patronizing mantra that used to ring around theatreland. 'We've got to get them out of the clubs and the raves and the flicks and the internet cafés and get them back in the theatre. Harness all that energy and creativity.' We generally agreed until the first night of *Trainspotting*.

At the Bush, we'd always had a happily mixed bag. Young sat next to old, *Daily Telegraph* squeezed *City Limits* between its legs, American students sat on the feet of Romanian scholars, black and Irish and Japanese and Icelander and whatever. To be honest we never cared that much who they were as long as they were there. Number was what mattered. We would nod and smile when the Arts Council or local authority would babble on about demographics and serving the community, then get on with putting on the plays.

At one point we were asked to carry out a survey to establish the character of our audience. We produced a questionnaire, handed it out with zeal to the punters and dutifully collected it at the end. Once we had gathered a sufficient representative sample, we threw them all in the dustbin and made up a set of figures that looked good. Everyone continued nodding and smiling.

A theatre company has two essential jobs. First and foremost, to produce work to the highest standards of excellence, that it has a passion for producing. Second, to attract sufficient people over the course of a year so that it can stay open. That's it. Nothing overly complicated about that, you would have thought. But you would be wrong. Over the last twenty years, an energy-sapping deluge, a shitstorm of bureaucratic twaddle, marketing directives, outreach schemes, education plans, strategies, ploys, bursaries and awards have sapped much of the joy and most of the audiences out of theatre.

Theatre, by a mysterious alchemy known best by actors, less by writers, even less by directors and designers, less than that by marketing managers and hardly at all by Arts Council officers, theatre works or it doesn't. If it works, people come. If it doesn't, they don't. If audiences are dwindling now, it is largely because we have forgotten that simple truth. If we could redirect our money, resources and energy towards the stage, if we could return the authority to actors that they deserve, we would start to solve the problem.

Yet you still see actors and artists constantly patronized by marketing people and administrators, as if designing and mailing leaflets was equivalent to brain surgery, and bringing off the first act of *Three Sisters* was as difficult as pushing a pram. I remember late on a rather stoned and boozed night, before we brought *Three Sisters* into the West End, a young actor finding himself surrounded by marketing and admin folk. He decided to try and join in. 'We need a stunt for the opening,' they were saying. 'What about . . . what about . . . wait I think I've got it,' the actor titillated, 'what about if Dominic turns up dressed as a giraffe!!' 'Ho, ho, ho,' they all tittered, but dope lent him seriousness and he continued in earnest. 'No, think about it, the director turns up as a giraffe. It's an event. People write about it in the papers. People read about it in the papers. It's a sensation. Someone who's just read about it in the *Evening Standard* turns to someone else in a bar and says, "Hey, have you read about that Chekhov show. The director turned up as a giraffe. Maybe we should check it out. Sounds cool.'" Unfortunately, dope then lent everyone seriousness. A rather absurdly passionate argument ensued about whether or not I should turn up to a press night as a giraffe. Eventually the actor was forced to concede: 'Okay, okay, okay, a bad idea, okay, okay . . . How about a zebra!!'

Anyway, Irvine Welsh and getting the kids in. I vividly remember the night we did get the kids in. It was the first preview of *Trainspotting* at the Bush, and they all trooped in. They were a fucking nightmare. They smoked cigarettes, joints, even heroin (something of a theatrical first that), they talked amongst themselves, picked fights, spilt drinks and created whatever mayhem they could. About three-quarters of the way through the first half, an old theatre nightmare was made manifest, when first one, then another two, then four, then eventually about forty, simply got up and walked out, passing right across the stage. The depression this induced was quickly alleviated when they all en masse walked back in. They'd just nipped out for a piss.

By the interval, the person on front of house looked like a Polish cavalry officer a week into the Second World War. By the end, a group of us were in earnest discussion: 'The kids, how can we get them out. How can we get them back in to the clubs, raves, etc. Where are all those nice people in sweaters?' Needless to say, no one could be kept out, and the show was a storm wherever it went, in Scotland, at the Bush, on tour, even in the West End.

Irvine Welsh is, of course, not strictly a playwright. He's written one play, *You'll Have Had Your Hole*, which the critics took great delight in murdering. But the adaptations of his books, most particularly *Trainspotting*, have had a greater impact on theatre culture over the last six or seven years than most playwrights. But then again that's probably true of most areas of popular culture. In theatre terms, it's not just the content. There was a large school of New Brutalists arising at the same time, though his extremes – of vomiting, of digging in shit, of bloody tampons in tomato soup, of sex at funeral receptions – added some new colours.

What was more influential was the language, its richness, its wit, its violent vibrancy. The language manages to be simultaneously street real and fantasia artificial. This makes it properly theatrical rhetoric, of a type we haven't heard for a long time. Shakespeare's violent conjunctions of prose and poetry, of the gutter and the stars, the vernacular and the patrician, find some echo here. Yet what was most influential about Welsh's work was the celebration of the whole thing. Here was grime and old grease and sordidness and despair, and all presented with this festival, carnival edge. Life.

Anyway, Irvine Welsh. Good writer.

Arnold Wesker

It may be the hardest truth to say about any artist, but it still remains a truth. Many are only good for a while. We so desire our artists to be great forever, to be born great and to continue in that state uninterrupted until death, that we turn a blind eye to the more frequent truth. Many only hit it for a while. No one knows how artists earn their walk in the sunshine, the time of their life when they make, and when what they make is touched. If anyone knew how it worked, they'd write the cookbook and we'd all be doing it all the time. But the fact is, and it is one of God's cruellest facts, that it comes and it goes. When it's there, artists aren't conscious of it, they are just lost in making. When it's gone, they spend every waking moment trying to work out how to get it back.

The list of those whose purple patches have mysteriously appeared and disappeared, is amongst the most distinguished in history. Wordsworth, whose youth's fire fizzled into a revisionist old age; Chaplin, whose Biblical simplicity became mired in complexity; Orson Welles, who soused the conjuror's flair that scared its own creator in sherry; Preston Sturges, who hit screwball perfection for eight years in the forties then disappeared from sight; Roman Polanski, whose paranoid fantasies gave way to sophisticated perviness. And that's before you get on to the rock musicians . . . For a privileged few, the moment of genuine creation comes; for an extremely privileged very few, it lasts. All those early deaths for artists, especially the ones with the romantic revolutionary tag around their big toes, don't occur just because they're accident-prone. Many see the long future ahead, not being as able as they once were, and they head straight for the self-destruct button.

I have no desire to upset an extremely generous, thoughtful and wise man. But this strikes me as a truth for Arnold Wesker. I'm not sure he completely deserves the company I've mentioned above, but for a while during the late fifties and early sixties, he wrote a searing and wonderful collection of plays – *Roots*, *Chicken Soup With Barley*, *I'm Talking About Jerusalem*, *The Kitchen* and *Chips With Everything*. He enfranchised a new generation and a new class with these plays. He brought entirely new experiences on to the stage. He wrote balletic sequences of working life, and wonderfully imagined non-verbal set pieces, that for theatrical eloquence stuff almost everything achieved by physical theatre since. The strain of didacticism is ever a little too present, but his understanding of the darker recesses of the working-class mind was unique, and his articulation of it unsurpassed.

And then it stopped. He had a truly apocalyptically appalling time trying to get his play *The Merchant* on Broadway. He has written an entertaining book about the experience. But all the time, as you read the book, you hear an extra voice. It's God saying, 'Stop Arnold. Time's up. Time to rest.' No one wants that to happen to an artist, but it happens. Directors, who aren't artists anyway, can hack along exploiting the talents of others. Actors can repeat a few of their recent performances, and a bag of tricks they've accumulated, and go home and pray that it will all come back. But for writers, if it goes, it goes. Wesker hasn't rested of course. Who could? He regularly writes, and sends his plays around. They are thoughtful, and wise, and all right. But they don't cut it.

What Arnold Wesker did changed much, and changed theatre for the better. The texts that survive are still thrilling to see performed. They will never disappear. He was good. For a while.

Peter Whelan

Peter Whelan dives into history, swims deep, and comes up with small stories, pearls fashioned by the grit of life, that illuminate then and now.

In a series of plays – *Captain Swing*, *The Accrington Pals*, *The Bright and Bold Design*, *The School of Night* and *The Herbal Bed* – he has steered clear of kings and queens (although not neglecting great playwrights), and concentrated on the mechanisms of life through the centuries. Most writers, when they delve into the past, use it as a shortcut to myth. Everything is suddenly battles, romance, large-scale oppression or revolution. Whelan's characters are more likely to go shopping. This is not to say that the forces of history are not felt, just that they're not displayed. The most important quality is a truthful representation of life as lived. It's anti-rhetorical writing and entirely refreshing for it.

His other remarkable quality is his treatment of human kindness. He has a wonderful ability at showing how mankind under stress can behave well. Given the prevailing cynicism about human nature, this comes as a gentle and warm surprise. There is no happy clappy sense of good triumphant, just a strong sense that good is there. There is no exaggeration of ethical and moral contests, just a strong, vivid and true impression that good and bad co-exist forever in the world, in large moments and in small, in everything from ideology to the choice of design on a pot, to the preparation of sixteenth-century medicine. The small, personal and domestic moments of progress that Whelan charts, and the skill with which he evokes life as lived are immensely reassuring. In the most searching sense, comfort writing.

August Wilson

August Wilson has embarked on a noble undertaking – to record the experience of Black Americans through the twentieth century. His best-known works over here – *Ma Rainey's Black Bottom*, *The Piano Lesson*, *Joe Turner's Come and Gone* and *Fences*, all attempt to catch moments from a different decade through the century to exemplify the black experience.

The plays are rich in history. The sense of the past, the present and the future is as immanent as in any play of Chekhov's. It informs each moment, giving it the weight and the evanescence of life. But it is an entirely different type of history to our common Western understanding. It is the difference between written and unwritten history. Where we think of large historical and economic forces, big political events and the destinies of nations, Wilson's characters think in stories from the past, family myths, anecdotes and song. That oversimplifies it somewhat – since there is an acute understanding of historical migration throughout – but it is history written and understood in an entirely different syntax.

The texture of the plays is as different as its sense of history. Although often placed in single sets, there is a strong divergence from the rules of Western naturalism. Ghosts and spirits walk the stage in Wilson's plays – not as fey or arch symbols of this or that – but as real dynamic presences to be wrestled with and conquered. Songs and dances erupt from the conversations, not to decorate, but as a fundamental means of communication. And the language. The language is a thick molasses treacle of pain and hurt and hope. It is rich, erotic, absurd, passionate, dense and beautiful. The contrary rhythms of blues, jazz and gospel course through it. As textured and alive as William Faulkner or Toni Morrison.

The plays often follow a community or a family's path from hidden anguish through catharsis towards the light. The Oedipal model, in terms of an undisclosed pain, a blight on the land and a need to confront demons, seems to hover in the background. But if there is a quest that gathers them together, it is the need to find a place to stand. A place, moral and spiritual, to call one's own. Or, as expressed in *Joe Turner*, to find one's song.

We often pother and bother about how to promote black drama in this country. The solution is not that mysterious. Find a theatre and put on an uninterrupted diet of Wilson's work for a couple of years. He is a bright shining example to all others, black and white.

Snoo Wilson

Someone leant over to me recently at a fairly crowded party, and said, 'Who's that?' 'Who?' I asked, looking through the crowd. 'That one, the overgrown public schoolboy, the one who looks like someone just electrocuted his testicles.' 'Oh, that'll be Snoo.' 'Snoo who?' 'Snoo Wilson.' 'No! Snoo Wilson, it can't be. Is it really? Snoo Wilson. I love Snoo Wilson.' 'I'll introduce you if you want.' 'No, no, no, no, no, that'd spoil it. No. Wow. Snoo Wilson.' It made her night. She'd spotted the Lord of Theatrical Misrule himself.

It has remained to Snoo's huge credit, and probably his endless despair, that he has remained a guilty pleasure for so long. Like the beat poets, like Hermann Hesse, like Nick Drake, like Munch, like Reykjavik, he has remained a secret joy that people discover, then want to keep to themselves. Snoo probably wants nothing less than this. He probably dreams of all four theatres on Shaftesbury Avenue turning away punters, fist-fighting to get in to see his shows. But Ken Livingstone probably dreams of being a Viking warrior, and Viking warriors probably dreamt of being Ken Livingstone.

For those who haven't yet had the guilty pleasure, I'll try and give a cogent introduction to a couple of his works. Or at least a taste. In *More Light*, Snoo spotlights the sixteenth-century Italian philosopher, Giordano Bruno. Bruno invented a system of philosophy known as the Theatre of

Memory, an early meditational tool whereby he ascended to spectral planes. His work was deemed heresy by a vengeful Pope of the age, who in Snoo's play sat on a miniature Rome in the corner, and determined to punish him. To evade his pursuer, Bruno goes to heaven, or at least an intermediary stage. There he meets a female Shakespeare, is succoured by a barmaid, who turns out to be the daughter of a Greek god ('My dad's Bacchus. He's the god of wine') and encounters the English necromancer John Dee and his carnal assistant Kelly. Just to keep the conversation lively, he chucks in Elizabeth I, who keeps telling a nervous Shakespeare, 'I'd kill for a new play.' It is a witsome, wild, Rabelaisian grab-bag of all things Renaissance, and profoundly scintillating.

In another, *Darwin's Flood*, we meet, unsurprisingly, Charles Darwin, his wife, and more surprisingly Nietzsche, Mary Magdalene, Jesus, Nietzsche's sister and brother-in-law and a manservant with two faces. Nietzsche has a taste for being whipped, a job which Mary Magdalene, a leather-clad prostitute, is delighted to perform, having descended from a helicopter. Jesus is an Ulster competition cyclist, ever keen to hymn the joys of the open road and the Ulster fry. Neitzsche's sister and profoundly offensive brother-in-law are on the way to South America to found a racially pure community. For a reason I can't fully remember a flood of biblical proportions swamps Darwin's house, revealing the ancient Ark beneath it, on which they sail. After that it all becomes a bit cloudy. Here we have evolutionism, eugenics, religion and apocalypse. How it hangs together I can't remember, even though I produced it at the Bush. All I remember is a religious awe and big giggles.

These are but two in a long succession of barmy gallimaufries stretching back almost thirty years. The recipe has remained similar for that long; historical icons, a smattering of philosophy, a soupçon of heresy, a sprinkling of sex, a liberal dash of excellent jokes, and in each act three or four spectacular stunts that stretch directors and designers to their limits, and delight and amaze audiences. Tying each play together is a different and appropriate sensibility, a unique and undeniable mood emanating from the recesses of the author's cortex, which somehow co-ordinates the otherwise unco-ordinatable.

It is late sixties or early seventies wildness, unmediated by the flatness of subsequent time and circumstance. Snoo has his many critics. (And he has written plays where the extravagance of the invention has preceded the germ of sensibility. The result is empty theatrics.) All the 'But-what's-it-about?' school loathe him. One television critic once proudly told me that he'd spoken to an actress in *Darwin's Flood* who told him that the actors themselves didn't understand the play. As if that was the final word on the matter. As if no priest can deliver the liturgy without a collection of pat reasons for doing so. As if no actress can play Cleopatra without a copy of *Passnotes* stuffed down her cleavage.

The stage is at its best a mysterious habitat, beyond understanding. Snoo recognizes that and celebrates it. He has done so without compromise all his working life. He deserves to be celebrated himself. Perhaps those for whom he is a secret passion should be a little less discreet.

Charles Wood

When I was about eight, in the glory days of the television single play, an exocet missile landed in the middle of our family life one Sunday evening. Our great old friend Charles Wood had written a teleplay. From the blurb in the *TV Times* it looked vaguely familiar. It was about a television executive called Patrick O'Hoole (my father's job and first name), his wife Jennifer (my mother's name) and their three children Sean, Jessica and Dominic (my siblings and me). They all lived on a farm in Somerset (our home), they were half-hearted hippies (our lifestyle), and the play was to cover a weekend when they were visited by a writer and his wife.

Now I'm fairly sure that even at an early age we were all well enough aware of the various self-deceptions, hypocrisies and tensions involved in trying to balance a cosmopolitan and a rustic life. We ploughed on anyway, since as a unit we all enjoyed it. Yet our meagre self-knowledge wasn't enough for our old friend, who, to help us on the path to enlightenment, wrote a lacerating portrait of a family farced with sixties neurosis, grand deceptions and large pomposity. The O'Hooles were frightful, riven and silly. The writer and his wife were saintly and wise.

Everyone should of course rise above such things, but it's not easy. A shroud of gloom descended over our home for a few months. It wasn't just a small matter of everyone we knew watching. It was also the six or seven million others who would unwittingly be hooting at this gleeful exposure.

Whether the portrait was true or not could never be resolved. It was, of course both true and not true. It was his truth, but not ours. A situation seen through a glass of bile will never be the same as one seen through a glass of love. The situation will be the same, the perception will differ.

What was so profoundly naff and tacky was that it was so bluntly a portrait. There was no disguise, no shrouding in metaphor, it was just sniggery insult. Charles Wood belonged to a gang of writers – including Peter Nichols and Tom Stoppard – who merrily cannibalized each other's lives, affairs, achievements and failures in a variety of projects. Little was sacred. It was a profoundly sixties and seventies trait. The recent biography of Pinter by Michael Billington has revealed the almost journalistic proximity between his life and his work – although Pinter is better than any at raising personal experience into impersonal parable.

The playwrights of that period were rather like the confessional journalists of today – constantly disgorging how they're dying, or their marriage is failing, or they're depressed, or how their children give them hard-ons. Some of this stuff is beautifully, exquisitely written, so why is it that it always leaves me feeling dirty? I had a good sob just yesterday over a piece of wonderful prose by Maggie O'Kane in the *Guardian* about how dearly she treasures her child, having met bereaved mothers in Kosovo. But I wasn't sure I had any right to know. Is it Victorian to feel that some things are best saved for quiet conversation over a kitchen table, and that intimate secrets and newspapers don't go together? Why should discretion always be attacked as neurosis?

In a similar way I feel uncomfortable with *A Day in the Death of Joe Egg*, with *The Real Thing*, with *Betrayal*, with

Roots, and with any number of other dishes of life served up warm. Just as I feel uncomfortable with anyone skimping on my family with bad art. Some material should be transformed by the imagination, or saved for the third whisky.

The phrase 'Playwriting is all journalism or autobiography' has been ascribed, probably wrongly, to Max Stafford-Clark, the guru of new writing through the seventies and eighties. It probably stands as a monument to what was wrong with much writing through that time. Thankfully the recent surge in writing has seen the return of the story, the separate world, the imagination, the metaphor, the centrality of poetry – all that keeps art separate from the chunks of life that create it.

That childhood experience has led me to feeling very wary of signs of autobiography in plays. It also led me to believe that Charles Wood must be a prize cunt. However, rereading his work it quickly becomes clear that he is a very fine writer, and a hugely underrated one. He is largely lost to the theatre now, but the loss is film's gain, since he has written three of the best British films of the last forty years, *Help*, *The Charge of the Light Brigade* and *Tumbledown*. No one in film or television has a better understanding of the military mind, or the madness of men's love of violence.

He sings of arms and the man, but also of the voice that sings it. He is as fascinated by the presentation of war as by its own madness. Two of his plays, *Veterans* and *Has Washington Legs*, deal with the relationship between films and war, the conjunction of the two insanities throwing up fascinating insights covering wider fields. Another play, *Dingo*, treats the squalor and cruelty of world war, but also the way in which that squalor was spun and parlayed into something more gracious than it was. He lends the same hard-eyed lack of sentimentality to his portrayal of the tatty world of provincial rep in *Fill the Stage With Happy Hours*, one of the cruellest plays yet written about the theatre.

When Charles Wood is describing the dance of various different forms of madness, military, film or theatrical, he demands to be watched. When he's elevating gossip to entertainment, less so.

Nick Wright

Like many born and bred South Africans, Nicholas Wright has that natural hauteur that always makes me feel as if I should apologize. Though I'm never quite sure what for. He's always well turned-out, always calm and always has the lucid godlike view.

Nick has created a certain critical tone – objective, omniscient, technical and self-aware. It is witty, but dry, drained of much personality or passion. He strains for objectivity, for old-fashioned academic authority, though the desire for authority is disguised by the surface lightness. He has developed this through a series of masterclass articles for the *Independent*, and a book on ninety-nine great plays. It has made him, in the absence of much competition, the dominant critical voice within the business.

The maintenance of such tone through thick and thin has also made him the theatre world's principal fixer. He is the Mandelson of theatreland, the well-connected discreet presence. He was the literary manager at the National Theatre and later an associate, ever an important voice in programme decisions. He briefly ran the Royal Court, and has remained a highly influential board member. He has written for and directed at the RSC. He has always been one of the main decision-makers at the National's Studio; the country's best forcing ground for young talent. In the small village that is British theatre, this makes him a very powerful player.

To a great extent, Wright has used all this influence to the greater good. He spots talent and backs it. He introduces it to useful outlets, and to other talents, which might make interesting combinations. Through his own efforts, he has helped to bring many young writers and directors into the light. He works at this tirelessly and, in the process, has given away a lot of the energy and resources he could have spent on his own gift. A fine, sharp and wise playwright, he produced little theatrical work for a long time after his biggest hit, *Mrs Klein*.

Yet, there is a wafer-thin line between generous networking and exclusive croneyism. Nicholas Wright respects a variety, but nothing like as wide a variety as there is on offer. His preference for technical accomplishment, for style, for middle-class subject matter, may have meant the exclusion of many from the areas over which he has influence. His own preference for cool despair over a torn heart, and for a light titter over a filthy laugh, has prevailed in the theatres that have followed his lead.

This is far from the result of conscious villainy on his part. He doesn't sit at home plotting the rise and fall of theatre-folk, like a thespian Talleyrand. It's simply the result of too much influence being centred in one individual. Unless that individual has quite staggeringly pluralistic taste, unless he is a veritable Proteus, he is always going to end up an excluder as well as an includer.

Happily the wait for one of his own plays concluded with the delightful *Cressida*. The summation of much of his knowledge of the theatre – its history, politics, bitching, passion, kindness and its endless circular renewable fascination – this play proved one of theatre's great love letters to itself. Although that makes it sound self-indulgent, it managed to prove tough and astringent at the same time as adoring. It was hampered by a squeaky clean production that was about as Jacobean as a Prada handbag, but greatly heartened by a turn amongst turns from Michael Gambon in the centre. It would be wonderful to see more.

Richard Zajdlic

'How much have you earnt this month, you jammy fucker?' would be the refrain that greeted Richard Zajdlic whenever he entered the office. We had recently produced his play *Rage*, and his income had gone into orbit. Surrounded by the dank poverty of the mushroom box we all worked in, he would mumble some extraordinary figure, and look furtively ecstatic.

Funnily enough, the press had fairly sourly dumped on *Rage*. But the calibre of the cast he had attracted (Sue Johnson, Nicky Henson, Helen Baxendale, Sasha Hails) and the evidence of their eyes alerted TV and film sharks to the talent on display. An embarrassment of commissions followed and he went on to become the driving force behind *This Life*. There's a presumption that people leave theatre because of the money elsewhere. That they all go ga-ga when some besuited exec waves some banknotes in their face. It's true up to a point, but not the whole story. The prospect of being mugged by the snap judgements and cabal mentality of the press doesn't exactly have them hurrying home to their first love.

It would be a shame if Richard were lost to the theatre. He has a rare talent for creating atmospheres charged with a high level of erotic and aggressive tension. In both *Rage* and *Infidelities*, he dips into extreme emotional territory and watches how modern humans, at the edge of grief or anger, manage (just) to stay human. It's no mean feat. Happily he returned to the Bush with *Dogs Barking*, a savage depiction of the collapse of a domestic relationship, which showed that he has lost none of his fire.

Afterword to the 2002 edition

The introduction to this book – a flailing attempt to cobble together the incoherence of all the arguments within – contains one rather staggering understatement. That is that the book would soon be out of date. I intended this in a purely theatrical way. And it has of course proved to be true in that limited sense. Many of the writers within have written new works, twisting the reach of their work into new valleys, thus re-configuring the shape of what went before. Several have had their work successfully revived, thus ending the neglect that I bemoan here (although many are still left in the cold). And of course several new writers have forced their way into the light, bringing new voices, new ideas and new forms although the new writing boom does seem to be hobbling a little.

But the book is now dated in a more profound sense. The great shudder that wobbled the world on 11 September 2001 as I was shunting my way slowly from Oxford to Leicester on Virgin trains, has re-configured the landscape completely. Much of the thinking in this book seems almost quaint, pre-lapsarian, in this timid new world. There was a booming complacency that preceded 11 September, an End-Of-History self-delusion that believed that competent administrators would manage bull economies into a never ending future and we would all be left to settle the grander issues of ethics and aesthetics, untroubled by pain or blood. True, the signs of strain were showing at Seattle and Genoa, and true, Sharon and Bush did seem to rise out of nowhere, looking more Fu-Manchu than Fukuyama. But no-one could have predicted how far this single event would sling us backwards nor how fast.

The Full Room was written in part out of my experience of

Europe, Western and Eastern, before, during and after the end of the Cold War. That was the great defining historical action of my life. After a while I felt that I had come to an understanding, however limited or facile, of its movements, grand and small. I had a sense of how it reached into everything I experienced – the colour of maps, the psychology of friends, the lurches of fashion. And I used that sense in my working life which revolves around reading and uderstanding plays. So it informed this book – not entirely, but significantly. That knowledge didn't disappear when the twin towers fell, but it suddenly became hugely less relevant. History had jumped forward, leaving my fragile grip on its workings even less secure, and leaving me, and I imagine others, once more overwhelmed by the sheer scale of our ignorance.

One of the greatest scares provoked by that disaster and the subsequent rather lop-sided war in Afghanistan, was how quickly it drove people back into their Cold War fancy dress. The left lurched for their boiler suits as swiftly as the right grabbed at their uniforms and all the old lazy, patterned, simplified thinking returned. Each side were evil to each other, everyone was an enemy again. After a decade in which we had all learnt to remind ourselves that the human is a many shaded, multi-coloured, infinitely variable beast, it was back to the old black and white. The sounds of doors being closed and locked shut within previously open minds was as scary as the images on the box. It was also of course just what the perpetrators of either side desired. These people live to create gangs, tribes, movements, nations, folk, peoples, whatever – their terror at the absence of their own personalities drives them forward – and they love the sight of people forgoing themselves for the joy of the throng. I hope that we do not lose sight of the primacy of ourselves for too long and we remember that being a difficult arse is just as important in a time of crisis as it is in a time of calm.

It may seem grotesquely presumptuous to segue from a global calamity to my book, but I am a theatre director, so fuck it. We all love to aggrandize our problems to an excessive degree. My favourite reaction to the global crisis was from my friend

Catherine Johnson. *Mamma Mia,* the show she had written the book for, was about to open on Broadway when disaster struck, and there was talk of delaying or pulling her show. Her Bristol accent snapped, 'Fucking Osama Bin Laden. Cunt. He's ruined my musical'. There is nothing like a bit of ironic self-interest to trump acres of broadsheet angst.

When this book first come out in hardback, it caused something of a furore. It sneaked into public during a soft news period between Christmas and the New Year when editors are leaning on arts editors for any old piffle to fill pages. This book proved the ideal piffle. There duly appeared big features, shocked reactions, essays and profiles. Within a month I travelled from being held up as an anarchist rebel, out to destroy all that was dear to the theatre Establishment, to being berated for not being rude enough and for the mildness of my insults. Soon after, of course, nobody was writing about it at all, once they had all returned to their favourite sport of clubbing the RSC to death.

The gist of the media brouhaha was that the book was a relentless attack on the theatre Establishment. This failed to mention the fact that 95% of the book is overwhelmingly, overweeningly positive and that the negative comments are balanced with the positive. The intention of the book is obviously not to wreck the house but to start a party in it. But it would be disingenuous to claim that I was not scared by the reception.

The way it went down in the business was peculiar. Broadly speaking there has been support, but all *sotto voce*. I received three anonymous letters, which always presses the alarm button, but in fact they all turned out to be generous and supportive. Several people took me away from groups, walked down corridors, slipped into private rooms, winked conspiratorially, and then whispered 'I love the book'. Others have passed on congratulations through colleagues or friends, but all with a rather weirdly clandestine aura.

Of course there was also a certain amount of rage. But again it was muted. One playwright tried to start an internet site, entitled 'Playwrights Who Hate Dominic Dromgoole'. It did not take off. Senior directors informed me obliquely via colleagues that I had blotted my copybook, and that I had made my career difficult for myself in the future. One elderly actor at the Garrick Club, in an infantile display of playground Establishment bullying, asked my uncle over the mock turtle soup to tell me that they all had 'long memories'.

The timidity of all this, both the support and the attacks, did make me wonder about the profession I am in. What sort of creative business is it that lives in such fear? Why does theatre enforce these ludicrous laws of *omertà*? Why does it follow the 'we-look-after-our-own' code of every bent police station? Aside from the fact that the book is not an attack on theatre but a celebration of it, you have to wonder what sort of institution it is that is so terrified of assessment or analysis whether from without or within. True, we do spend our lives being berated by middle-aged male pundits who savage the theatre with all the ferocity of their own self-loathing, but is that any reason to build the city walls thicker and higher? I would have thought it was all the more reason to go out and give them a good whupping. But to go out as an army of loose but enthusiastic individuals, not goose-stepping in tight-lipped obeisance to the rules of the game.

There were other reactions of varying degrees of complexity. Some said it was grudge book, an attack on well-known writers because the writers I had championed had been neglected. That does not quite square with the fulsome praise the book sauccs over Pinter, Ayckbourn, Stoppard, Storey, Churchill, Griffiths, Mamet and all the other big guns. Nor does it square with the success rate of the writers I had championed, most of whom could not have wished for better fortunes thus far. Another complaint was that it was a puff for my friends. Well, they only comprise about a tenth of the book, and frankly, most of them do not need any puffing.

My favourite reaction was the one that diagnosed the book as a peculiarly clever bit of self-promotion, a sort of extended career double bluff. People have rung up admiring this form of attack-defence, or defence-attack, as if it was a manoeuvre pinched out of Sun Tzu's *The Art Of War*. 'Canny', they have said, 'I see what you are up to'. For which I am extremely grateful, since I myself have no idea what I am up to. There is an element in my profession that is so steeped, saturated and stained with politics that they cannot conceive of an action devoid of it.

No, the truth is banal and mundane and is transparently available in the introduction. The book simply sets down what I think of a number of writers. In the process, I try to communicate the fact that we are living in an age when more people than ever before have written plays.

If there is a more serious intention for the book it is as a blast on behalf of the personal aesthetic. Theatre is riven with little clubs and cliques all following their party line. The physical theatre mob, the empty spacers, the hard-headed politicoes, the acolytes of naturalism, the shock troops, the pure technicians, the lovers of charm; they all operate in their seperate corners, muttering and mumbling at each other. The book was a simple attempt to say that there should be no rules beyond the deepest and quietest ones, to stop anyone from enjoying anything. The saddest sight is to see someone not laughing because they have been told something is coarse when every bone in their body is tickled. Or someone sitting grim-faced, determined not to be upset by something shattering because they have been told it has insufficient historical context.

There are of course important laws to be obeyed and vital lines to be drawn in the sand. But they are the important ones about respect for dignity, and genuine freedom, and imagination, and life. They are not laws about dramatic structure, or which -ism is the best -ism, or whether something is sufficiently theatrical. If something is funny or sad or joyous, let it be, and work out why; do not work out why things are funny, sad or joyous, then try and find something to fit the formula.

There are certain critics who feel they have to have a line on things, so they can double underline their own fragile personality, 'Look at me, I dress in chic black, I admire Sarah Kane, I spit on Alan Ayckbourn, it all works', or 'Consider me, I wear a tweed jacket, drink claret, snooze off in the first act. That Caryl Churchill's a bit strident. Bit of a character, aren't I?'. These are the self-same critics who accuse some plays of being two-dimensional. If they ever come up with a thought or an emotion or an insight that escaped their own caricature, that attack might have a little more force. But it is not just some of the critics, it is a sizeable amount of the profession and a large quantity of the audience as well. It is the imprisonment that many prefer, the immersion in a collective point of view that does not accord naturally with the kaleidoscopic chaos of one's heart.

My favourite theatrical moment of last year – 2001 – was not during a new play but in *Hamlet* at the National. Everything Simon Russell Beale did was touched and graced and all the rest but one line snapped my head into a new shape. 'And therefore as a stranger give it welcome', Hamlet retorts to Horatio, who is troubled by the appearance of the ghost. Beale impacted a life-time of rage into the first two words, then stopped himself, drew breath and with infinite sweetness and patience walked Horatio gently through the rest of the sentence. His life and sanity seemed to depend on Horatio's acceptance of the thought, but his spirit was too delicate to belabour it. Let be. It was a beautiful definition of goodness, of openness, of being alive to all of the world and of the difficulties of enacting it.

There is no greater pleasure than the theatre, no more broad attack on the senses, the intellect, the imagination, the heart and the soul. It is too precious a resource to be spoiled by opinions, especially those of others. The whole thesis of this book is simply this: See what you see, and if you love it, love it and if you don't, don't big time. Bring all that you have to the occasion, whatever clumps of elegance or sewage that have stuck to you along the way but let it be your elegance and your sewage, no-one else's.

Our aesthetic is almost our last way of understanding ourselves. We used to define ourselves through our relation to the church, later through our relation to politics. Which church we joined, which party, how fervently, how wisely, how responsibly, all these questions helped us to colour ourselves and each other in. Both now seem to have gone the way of the dinosaurs though maybe now due a revival. We now work out who we are and let the world know, through our aesthetic, whether expressed through shopping, or eating, or drinking, or movies, or theatre, or opera. Any aesthetic, just as with any self, is far too precious to be sacrificed to a party line. Our cultural choices are far too valuable a means of bolstering the self to be lost on a sense of needing the security of the crowd.

And at this particular moment, when we are all being asked to club together yet again and commit murder in the name of some gang we do not subscribe to and detest, to weaken the strength of another gang we loathe just as heartily, now seems as good a moment as any to re-attest the importance of the individual aesthetic. Do not give it a pattern, do not give it a design. It may acquire one for a while then lose it, then regain it. But there is no need for a particular shape – an aesthetic can be smooth and consistent, or lumpy and clumpy – the only important factor is that it is chosen truly, and that it is personal.

So the next time you are sitting there dying of boredom, surrounded by people pole-axed with indifference, but all pre-programmed by reviews and publicity and opinion to look with reverence on a load of inept dreck (Peter Brook's *Hamlet* comes to mind), then blow a silent raspberry. And the next time you are tickled, or stirred, or moved by anything that you are told must be cheap or gaudy or fey, go with it. It may save the world.